Critical Essays on

H. G. WELLS

CRITICAL ESSAYS
ON
BRITISH LITERATURE

Zack Bowen, General Editor
University of Miami

Critical Essays on

H. G. WELLS

edited by

JOHN HUNTINGTON

G. K. Hall & Co.
BOSTON, MASSACHUSETTS

Published 1991.
10 9 8 7 6 5 4 3 2 1

Library of Congress Cataloging-in-Publication Data

Critical essays on H.G. Wells / edited by John Huntington.
     p.   cm.—(Critical essays on British literature)
  Includes bibliographical references and index.
  ISBN 0-8161-8856-4 (alk. paper)
    1. Wells, H. G. (Herbert George), 1866–1946—Criticism and
interpretation. I. Huntington, John. II. Series.
PR5777.C67   1991
823'.912—dc20   90-25743
                                             CIP

The paper used in this publication meets the minimum requirements
of American National Standard for Information Sciences—Permanence
of Paper for Printed Library Materials, ANSI Z39.48-1984. ∞™

Printed and bound in the United States of America

To my mother

Contents

◆

General Editor's Note

♦

The Critical Essays on British Literature series provides a variety of approaches to both classical and contemporary writers of Britain and Ireland. The format of the volumes in the series varies according to the thematic designs of individual editors and the amount and nature of existing reviews; criticism is augmented, where appropriate, by original essays by recognized authorities. It is hoped that each volume will be unique in developing a new overall perspective on its particular subject.

John Huntington's introduction traces the life of H. G. Wells and its relationship to his work and critical reception. Huntington surveys the history of Wells's reception by major critics over a fifty-year span, acknowledging the harsh criticism as well as the defenses of Wells as a major literary figure. Huntington avoids essays that have been reprinted in other collections and concentrates instead on the three major areas of Wells criticism that most affect the present position of Wells's work in the canon: Wells's debate with Henry James about the purpose and value of the novel, Wells's late fiction, and his autobiography.

ZACK BOWEN

University of Miami

Publisher's Note

◆

Producing a volume that contains both newly commissioned and reprinted material presents the publisher with the challenge of balancing the desire to achieve stylistic consistency with the need to preserve the integrity of works first published elsewhere. In the Critical Essays series, essays commissioned especially for a particular volume are edited to be consistent with G. K. Hall's house style; reprinted essays appear in the style in which they were first published, with only typographical errors corrected. Consequently, shifts in style from one essay to another are the result of our efforts to be faithful to each text as it was originally published.

Introduction

◆

JOHN HUNTINGTON

I

H. G. Wells poses many difficulties for modern criticism. He is important in a number of areas but, at least to current tastes, he is supreme in none. Unlike James Joyce, whose every thought and gesture the age finds admirable, Wells's accomplishment is always in question. However, he cannot be simply relegated to minority status. Unlike John Galsworthy, for instance, Wells does not rest comfortably in a neat little niche in a corner of literary history. A disruptive presence in his own time, he remains to this day an enigmatic and provocative figure who forces us constantly to rethink our categories and to reconsider our values.

Much of the commentary written on Wells has assumed that the points he makes are clear and has spent its primary energies summarizing and defending him. Moreover, since Wells engaged in a wide variety of literary pursuits, critical attention to his work has been dissipated by being spread thinly. He has been discussed as the originator of the scientific romance, the father of anticipation and futurology, a comic social novelist, an autobiographer, an international activist, a journalist, an educator, and finally, not commonly held up for admiration but nevertheless relevant to any understanding of what he meant to his age, a notorious philanderer. If Wells's literary stature were to be evaluated on the basis of sheer abundance, on the sustained outpouring of energy, he would doubtless be ranked as one of our greatest novelists. Of course, abundance itself is not a literary value, and in Wells's case, since he lacks a masterpiece to anchor his other productions, it may even distract from an accurate understanding of his accomplishment. This collection attempts to orient critical discussion by focusing on close interpretive analysis of particular works. Wells's obvious successes are acknowledged, but the essays here concentrate on areas that are generally ignored or are debated. These perspectives present Wells as a more complex and difficult writer than is often assumed.

II

As Lionel Stevenson notes, of all the major English novelists, only Wells and Dickens come from the lower middle class.[1] Wells's upbringing—escape from his upbringing might be a better term—places him in a special relation to the traditions of literature. Wells himself thought of his life as exemplary. His last really successful work was the *Experiment in Autobiography* (1934), and many of his novels recount his own experiences growing up (e.g., *Love and Mr. Lewisham, Kipps, The History of Mr. Polly,* and *Tono-Bungay*) or are written in response to events in his life (e.g., *The New Machiavelli, Boon,* and *Apropos of Dolores*). Wells also used his art to explain and defend his participation in national and even world affairs as a journalist, an activist, and a subject of controversy and scandal. We need to know about Wells's life, but we also need to exercise some caution when we use the facts of it to interpret his work, for his response to events is anything but simple: his triumphs are not free from anger, his escapes entail regret.

It is generally agreed by his biographers, his critics, and even by Wells himself that Wells's ascent from the precarious bottom rung of the lower middle class defined his life.[2] What we may call his heroic childhood consisted of a rebellion against class expectations and the achievement, almost entirely on his own, of an academic success that allowed him finally to define his own relation to class. Wells's father, Joseph, was a genial man who supplemented his income from a small and not very successful shop in Bromley by working as a professional cricket player. Wells's mother, Sara, a stern, religious woman against whose influence he would react all his life, was "in service." In his early teens, Wells lived with her while she was head housekeeper at Up Park, the house that would become the model for Bladesover in *Tono-Bungay*. While such quarters granted the young Wells access to libraries and a glimpse of a life of privilege, they also afforded him an uncomplimentary perspective on the British class system, not to mention the anxious knowledge that any further decline in fortunes meant a catastrophic collapse into the abyss of the working class.

A cautious and realistic woman, Sara Wells decided that her son's success and security lay in yard goods. If part of Wells's heroic childhood involved escaping the trap of his class, an equally heroic aspect of it was his escaping his mother's ambitions for him. With considerable effort and by spending a good part of her savings, Sara Wells obtained for her son, at two separate times, assistantships in drapery emporiums. The first position collapsed within a month because Wells was inattentive on the job. The second lasted two years; Wells deliberately ended it first by walking out and trekking the seventeen miles back to Up Park, and later by convincing his mother and father, in person and by repeated and insistent letters, that were he to remain a draper's assistant, his life would be over. He wanted to take advantage of an arrangement he had worked out on his own to be an assistant teacher at the Midhurst School, run by Horace Byatt.

Wells's contract with Byatt required him to teach younger boys while he "mugged up" subjects for national examinations. The school could then claim that these subjects were being taught; there was an award of four pounds for every advanced first, with corresponding awards for lesser accomplishments. Wells spent his evenings learning textbooks. As he later tells it, "the immediate result, so far as my mind was concerned, was to make me read practically the whole outline of physical and biological science, with as much care and precision as the check of a written examination poses" (*Autobiography*, 137). Wells recouped more than his salary in grants for the school. During this extraordinary year Wells finally proved to his mother and to himself that one could succeed by learning—a truth not at all self-evident at the time—and he was awarded a "free studentship" at the Normal School of Science, South Kensington. There Wells spent three severely impoverished years. His first year, studying under T. H. Huxley, the great champion of Darwinism, Wells would call "the most educational year of my life" (*Autobiography*, 161). The next two years, under professors Guthrie (physics) and Judd (geology) saw Wells begin to burn out. He completed the curriculum, but he failed the final examination in geology. He received the B. Sc. from the University of London in 1890, but there was clearly no future for him in scientific research as such.

For the next few years, Wells patched together a livelihood by teaching. In 1891 he began to publish some articles on science, the first being "The Rediscovery of the Unique"; over the next years he mastered the art of the verbal "sketch" and managed to earn some money by such journalism. In 1891 he also married Isabel, a distant cousin. In May of 1893, he had a nearly fatal bout with consumption, and in December of that year he ran off with Amy Catherine Robbins, whom he had taught in a night class a year earlier. When his divorce from Isabel became final, he married Miss Robbins; throughout their life together, for reasons no one has satisfactorily explained, he called her Jane. It was a confused, tumultuous time for Wells; he lived with comic desperation and, despite very poor health, great energy.

In 1895 Wells achieved literary success: *The Time Machine* was serialized in W. E. Henley's *The New Review* and received enthusiastic notice. Later that year Wells published *The Wonderful Visit,* and over the next three years he published *The Wheels of Chance, The Island of Dr. Moreau, The Invisible Man, The War of the Worlds,* and two collections of short stories. This five-year period marked a creative burst that few serious writers can approach, much less match. Wells both invented the genre of the "scientific romance," as he called it, and established its canon. Had he never written anything else, Wells would certainly have been famous as the originator of science fiction—as the "Realist of the Fantastic," as Conrad called him in an enthusiastic letter.[3]

Wells was not content to be confined to the ghetto of the scientific romance. In 1900 he began to publish fiction based on his own experience (*Love and Mr. Lewisham*). In 1901, with *Anticipations of the Reaction of Mechanical and Scientific Progress upon Human Life and Thought,* a forecast of the technology, social structure, demography, and philosophy of the world in the year 2000, he defined yet another genre for which he would become famous. This last book was a great success; it attracted the favorable notice of Beatrice and Sidney Webb, and led finally to Wells's becoming a member of the Fabian Society. From now on he was not just a literary man, but a seer, a socialist, and a man of the future. For the rest of his life, in addition to the many major literary and intellectual projects he undertook, he proselytized for his vision of the sane, unified, rational world to come.

In the next few years, after he and Jane had had two sons, Wells became a public proponent of enlightened relations between the sexes. In 1906 he began a serious affair with Amber Reeves, a member of the "Fabian Nursery." By the affair's convoluted end in 1909, Reeves had borne his child and agreed to marry another man. Many friends worked hard to salvage the social respectability for Wells that he seemed determined to abandon. In 1911 he met Rebecca West and began a relationship that would last a decade and produce another child.[4] While he spent enormous energy on these extramarital affairs—at one point he fled to France with Amber Reeves with at least the thought of remaining in "exile," and he established numerous households with Rebecca West—he never stopped writing and publishing at a feverish pace. He also remained married to Jane until her death in 1928 and, with her cooperation, maintained his family and a rather elaborate home that often hosted visitors and weekend gatherings. In the late 1920s and early 1930s he had a strangely difficult and apparently unpleasant affair with Odette Keun, and in the later 1930s he renewed a relationship with Moura Budberg, Gorky's former companion, whom he had first met in Moscow in 1920. Wells's fiction often reflects the ideals and stresses of these amours to an extent that Beatrice Webb could explain his attempt at maintaining his relationship with Amber Reeves after she had married by calling it "a sort of *Days of the Comet* affair."[5] The women in Wells's fiction, from Ethel in *Love and Mr. Lewisham* and Isabel Rivers in *The New Machiavelli* to Dolores in *Apropos of Dolores* and Brynhild Palace in *Brynhild,* tend to be modeled on women in his life.

Just before Wells disturbed the moral equanimity of the Fabians with his affair with Amber Reeves, he had sought to reform the society by involving it in active politics. He was resisted by its founders, especially Beatrice and Sidney Webb, who saw the group's main purpose as informational and educational. G. B. Shaw tried to mediate the struggle, which quickly became bitter. At a meeting in December 1906, Wells was forced to retract an amendment he had proposed that would have replaced the society's executive committee, and he soon withdrew from the society. From then on Wells was a maverick reformer advocating an "open conspiracy" of enlightened people working toward a vision of industrial international socialism that would be governed by a self-selected and self-sacrificing elite, "the Samurai" (in the *Autobiography* Wells compared them to Lenin's party members). Late in his life he became president of P.E.N. International and was one of the drafters of the declaration which became the basis of the United Nation's statement on human rights. Through this busy forty-year period, he kept up a steady stream of journalism.

In the first decades of this century, Wells was a declared feminist; he defended women's sufferage and, in *A Modern Utopia,* advocated wages for mothers and housewives. Yet his feminist sentiments were seen by feminists as compromised. In her review of *Marriage,*[6] Rebecca West scathingly mocked the feminism the novel claimed to advance. It is typical of Wells's mixture of enlightenment and egoism that this attack caused him to want to meet West. Later, when they were a couple, Wells would encourage West to work at her writing while he also expected her to maintain the household and take care of their child.

Throughout his adult life, Wells maintained friendships with many important male writers. He first met Arnold Bennett when they were school-mates together. He was George Gissing's close friend; in 1903 he rushed to France to be at Gissing's side as he was dying. At the turn of the century Wells lived in Kent, within bicycling range of Joseph Conrad, Henry James, John Galsworthy, Ford Maddox Heuffer (Ford), and for his brief stay before he died, Stephen Crane. With the exception of Bennett and Gissing, how-ever, Wells's friendships all had their difficulties. He and Conrad drifted apart,[7] and he ended up satirizing Ford in *The Bulpington of Blup.*

The most famous breakup and the one with the greatest significance for understanding Wells's work and for the history of the novel in general was that between Wells and Henry James. James was the established "master" when they became acquainted. For the first decade of this century, Wells was humbly admiring, and James encouraging but always annoyingly unsatisfied with Wells's work. James would praise Wells's fiction but would want to rewrite it, and at one point in 1902 he even proposed collaborating with Wells on a novel. By 1911 Wells had begun to define himself in print as belonging to a school of the novel opposed to that James ascribed to, and in 1915, in *Boon,* Wells satirized James's style very unsympathetically. In re-sponse James wrote some dignified letters to Wells, and their friendship was over. The debate, given new life in 1955 by the publication of the James-Wells letters, has continued. It would not be an exaggeration to claim that Wells's single most influential literary act was his attack on James.[8]

One further undertaking that bears mention in this brief survey of Wells's life and accomplishment is his plan to produce an encyclopedia of the knowledge necessary for an informed citizen of the world state. To this end Wells published *The Outline of History* (1920), which in 1966, writing on the one-hundredth anniversary of Wells's birth, A. J. P. Taylor described as still the best short history of the human race;[9] *The Science of Life* (1930), an introduction to biology and its implications for society that Wells wrote in collaboration with his son, G. P. Wells, and Julian Huxley, the grandson of Wells's great teacher, T. H. Huxley; and *The Work, Wealth, and Happiness of Mankind* (1932), a survey of economics. This effort of synthesis was in its way a recapitulation, near the end of Wells's career, of the great year of cramming at Byatt's Midhurst School.

Throughout the last two decades of his life, Wells continued to write novels and commentaries on the state of the world. His last complete book, *Mind at the End of Its Tether* (1945), marks a sharp change of direction: from the general optimism and bravado that characterize much of his work since *Anticipations,* this work swerves into deep pessimism and an apocalyptic intuition of the "end of things." Wells's son, Anthony West, wrote years later that this pessimism was always a part of his father's attitude;[10] Lionel Trilling found the book significant as a historical marker, a sign of the way the postwar world would look.[11]

III

In the first decade of this century, Wells was generally acknowledged as a major English novelist. Along with Arnold Bennett and John Galsworthy (Joseph Conrad would have to wait until later to be generally recognized), he stood for the generation that followed the still living giants, George Meredith, Thomas Hardy, and Henry James. By his death in 1946, Wells was almost neglected as a novelist. Addressing a gathering of scholars in 1960, Gordon Ray assumed the stance that his audience would be surprised to learn that Wells was a novelist.[12] From J. D. Beresford's 1915 book on Wells through Geoffrey West's *H. G. Wells* (1930), whose jacket blurb exclaims, "This man is more interesting than any of his books!" to Antonina Vallentin's *H. G. Wells: Prophet of Our Day* (1950), enthusiastic Wellsians have found him important not as a writer, certainly not as a novelist, but as a political activist and a seer.[13] In the early 1960s Warren Wagar published two books commemorating Wells's political ideals.[14] It is this vision of Wells that David Smith's recent biography emphasizes, and if this aspect of his life is fading from view, it has not fully disappeared. As recently as the international conference "Wells Under Revision," held in London in July 1986, a number of men and women who had worked with Wells in the 1930s and 1940s testified to his importance as a progressive force at that time. But inevitably this aspect of Wells has become "historical." He is a famous figure, more important than Oswald Mosley, less important than Winston Churchill. His political positions, which his contemporaries—not just his enemies—often found utopian, sound even more so as they lose connection with specific historical situations.

In one subculture, however, Wells's literary reputation has never declined. For the science-fiction world, which was being born in the middle third of this century, Wells was the patriarch. Hugo Gernsbach wanted to reprint him in his pulp magazines.[15] Robert Heinlein built a story around the moving roads in *When the Sleeper Wakes* and "A Story of the Days to Come." That Damon Knight could play a pointed variation on Wells's "The Country of the Blind" theme without ever mentioning Wells himself is a sign of how thoroughly the Wellsian corpus was taken for granted.[16] Wells's early scientific romances and his *Collected Short Stories* stayed in print, although sometimes in the form of children's books. Other scattered sources occasionally held the scientific romances apart from the general decay of Wells's literary reputation. T. S. Eliot and C. S. Lewis, despite their profound objections to what Wells stood for politically, could admire *The First Men in the Moon.*[17] V. S. Pritchett wrote an appreciative, though cautious, essay on the scientific romances in the late 1940s.[18] In 1946, in a short essay on Wells, Jorge Luis Borges found Wells's first novels "symbolic of processes that are somehow inherent in all human destines."[19] In 1961, Bernard Bergonzi published an important scholarly book that, if it did not singlehandedly rescue Wells's literary reputation, certainly made discussion of his literary merits reasonable.[20] In the secondary burst of interest that occurred in the early 1980s with the publication of critical books by McConnell, Huntington, Kemp, and Reed,[21] there is some attention to his later work, but the emphasis remains on the scientific romances.

Today the scientific romances hardly need a defense. It will generally be granted that with these works of the late 1890s Wells established the genre that thrives today as science fiction. Jules Verne and many others had used science and the future in fiction,[22] but Wells gave the devices a distinctive thematic coherence. Wells himself, in the introduction he wrote for *The Atlantic Edition of the Works of H. G. Wells,* treated the scientific romances as the product of a fairly simple formula—change one thing and see what follows—but recent criticism has shown that they are much more complex and of more serious interest than that reductive formula can explain. Critics have approached these works in complementary ways: by thematic and allegorical readings, by studies of image patterns, by various kinds of structural analysis, by sketches of autobiographical implications. Layer by layer, a picture has developed of a deeply resonant, profoundly coherent body of work that remains the great achievement of the genre.

The Time Machine, the first of the scientific romances, marks for most readers and critics the quintessence of the ironic imaginative mode that defines the genre for Wells. The novella is built on clear and powerful images that Wells uses to inquire into the central values and structures of industrial capitalism. The cozy bougeois study in the present contrasts both with the Elois' garden world of the surface in the year 802,701, and with the Morlocks' dark machine world underground. The Time Traveller moves through stages of understanding of these future spaces. He first envisions a pastoral utopia in which the "hateful grindstone" of "pain and necessity" has been "broken at last." Later, he restructures his understanding and sees the future as an inevitable degeneration from the present. Finally, he realizes that the Eloi are the Morlock's "cattle" and that, by the dialectical logic of domination, the supremacy of the aristocracy has led to its enfeeblement and the enslavement of the laboring class has led to its empowerment. The elementary, mythic simplicity of the tale allows for subtle meditations on the implications of the social structure and the leisure of the industrial civilization Wells knew. The social fantasy is then given an ironic perspective when the Time Traveller travels further into the future and witnesses the cooling of the sun, the stopping of the Earth's rotation, and the end of life on the planet.

One way to measure the precision and delicacy of Wells's achievement in such a work is to observe how easily they can go wrong even in his own hands. Wells himself agreed that *When the Sleeper Wakes* (1899) was not an artistic success. Paradoxically, its plot, itself derivative,[23] has influenced a number of important later dystopias (for example, Yevgeny Zamiatin's *We,* George Orwell's *1984,* and Ray Bradbury's *Fahrenheit 451*). It is not frivolous to conjecture that the very unsatisfactory quality of Wells's solution to a promising situation inspired other writers to try to tell it better; a more successful work might not have generated such rewritings. In any case, *When the Sleeper Wakes* misses the mark and becomes confusedly didactic. Part of the problem, as Bergonzi observed,[24] derives from the fact that Ostrog, the villain of the novel, stands for managerial policies not unlike those Wells himself would soon be publicly advocating. Such confusion is a sign of how seriously Wells was thinking in such a fantasy. It also heralds the arrogant rationalism in Wells's thought that was not above believing that if something makes sense for him, it must be right for everybody. The sensitivity and intricacy of the great scientific romances derives in part from Wells's resisting the temptations to such arrogance. A pervasive irony keeps them thoughtful and self-critical.

IV

The scientific romances, as Borges promises, will survive, to "be incorporated, like the fables of Theseus and Ahasuerus, into the general memory of the species and even transcend the fame of their creator or the extinction of the language in which they were written."[25] The novels, it seems, will suffer a different fate. Since his death, despite occasional praise from important writers such as Vladimir Nabokov,[26] critics have found Wells's novels unsatisfactory. In the 1950s and 1960s, Henry James's reputation reached its zenith, and it was generally understood that in their argument James had been right and Wells had been wrong. The tone had been set and the argument apparently ended by Mark Schorer's influential essay of 1948, "Technique as Discovery," that is excerpted here.[27] In Schorer's version, Wells is the self-defined enemy of "technique," and *Tono-Bungay* becomes meaningless because experience, however rich as a subject matter, has not been understood by means of technique. Schorer's essentially Jamesian aesthetic values have dominated the modern evaluation of Wells's novels so much that even Wells's advocates often appeal to them.

The difficulty of doing critical justice to Wells's novels has led critics to focus on *Tono-Bungay,* the novel that Wells himself acknowledged he had worked hardest on in an attempt to avoid the signs of haste and incompleteness that had been often pointed to in his earlier work. There is a negative paradox here: we seek to salvage Wells by resting his case on a novel that is in some respects atypical, that tried to meet the very aesthetic standards that he also, in works written at almost the same time, abjured. But given the social realities of aesthetic debate and evaluation, how better to begin the rehabilitation of Wells's artistic reputation than by examining a mediating work? Since Schorer has based his attack on Wells's lack of technique on this particular novel, it makes tactical sense to begin to make the Wellsian defense here.

Most subsequent treatments of *Tono-Bungay* are, in one way or another, dialogues with David Lodge's "*Tono-Bungay* and 'The Condition of England,' " which may well be the most important single defense of Wells we have. It places Wells's novel in a tradition different from that of Jamesian subjectivity. This important generic reorientation then allows Lodge to make the point that the focus of the novel is not on character—neither that of the narrator George nor his entrepreneurial Uncle Teddy—but on social insight, especially as conveyed by the passages describing physical spaces, buildings, and cities. While at a deep level Lodge may still be defending Wells in the Jamesian terms of coherence and completeness, his essay, lavish in examples and, after some conventional disclaimers, unambiguous in its advocacy, creates a critical space in which the novel can be discussed without apology or the distraction of defense.[28]

The alternative to the defense that praises Wells for succeeding as a Jamesian in spite of himself subscribes to Wells's advocacy of "ideas" and "content" over "technique" and "form." No one has mounted a full-scale, reasoned case along these lines, but the general tack has been sketched by Raymond Williams in his pages on Wells in *The English Novel*. Wells, as Williams sees him, is wrongly lumped with Bennett and Galsworthy. If he never quite catches what he is after, he nevertheless senses the crisis in English society and the need for new forms adequate to the impending change. His "bumptious" comic energy and his scan of the whole social horizon intuit a direction and a line that the Jamesian novel rejects. Wells does not see literature as an end in itself the way James does; for Wells it is always part of, or in the service of, some larger social goal.[29]

In his argument with James—the basic terms of which Wells had begun to develop as early as 1900 and had directed at Conrad as much as at James—Wells set up provocative contrasts that, after their initial defining use, could become distortions. He called himself a journalist as opposed to an artist, but we need to take this term loosely. *Journalist* covers, in this case, a wide variety of literary pursuits of differing seriousness and timeliness. Clearly, as a novelist he was not doing what he did as a polemical essayist. What warrants the term is the sense of immediacy: Wells wrote from a position involved in the debates of the moment. If he happened to strike off something that was "timeless," it was fine, so long as he did not miss the present moment's issue.[30]

Wells's realistic and autobiographical novels have experienced a rather different reception from the scientific romances and present quite a different set of interpretative and evaluative problems to critics. While the scientific romances fit a set of (self-established) generic guidelines, Wells's novels range over a wide generic space and are constantly exerting pressure on the generic categories. Autobiography can drift toward utopia (*In the Days of the Comet*), toward the "condition-of-England novel" (*Tono-Bungay*), or toward social comedy (*Kipps*). Romance and satire blend (*The New Machiavelli*). The conscious timeliness of much of his work—the advocacy of feminism in *Ann Veronica,* for instance, or the depiction of the home-front experience of the Great War in *Mr. Britling Sees It Through*—may, especially for later readers, distract from the novel's "art." Wells's own claim that he was after something new—"I was feeling my way toward something outside any established formula for the novel altogether" (*Autobiography,* 418), while it was to some extent clearly self-serving, was also an intuitive attempt to reshape the aesthetic value system to bring it back toward a negotiation of immediate issues, "to have all life within the scope of the novel" (*Autobiography,* 417). Wells's claim to be a journalist was not self-denigrating; it was part of a large project of aesthetic and political reorientation.

Wells was a writer who thought in terms of genres: for certain subjects, such as autobiography or utopia, he had a conception of an appropriate tone, style, pace, and detail. He could "do" the genres. This insight lies behind Schorer's hostile observation that in *Tono-Bungay* Wells "founders . . . through a series of literary imitations—from an early Dickensian episode, through a kind of Shavian interlude, through a Conradian episode, to a Jules Verne vision at the end."[31] Although he worked with a generic palate, Wells did not conceive of the novel as a generic whole. *In the Days of the Comet* begins with a masterful rendering of the aspirations and frustrations of Leadford, the lower-middle–class protagonist who is somewhat like H. G. Wells himself. After the comet passes and renders the world "sane," however, the very language of the novel changes. From ironically accurate detail and close inspection of conflicting and difficult emotions, the narrative moves into soaring, abstract, periodic, "utopian" prose. In these novels generic boundaries do not hold; closure occurs, not by a rounding that integrates the end with the beginning, but by an opening away from the beginning into new problems and promises.

The practical critical strategies most in vogue over the last half century have not found "art" in such shapes and movements. Critics have sought whole units that will stand on their own and categories that can be clearly defined, even if they have also been aware that such categories are not quite sufficient. But to try to organize Wells this way is to deprive him of an essential aspect of his imaginative energy. I do not mean to argue the paradox that our inability to appreciate him adequately bears witness to Wells's success as a novelist, but those critics who do appreciate Wells almost invariably find themselves having to invent languages and categories that will give voice to their insight.

V

The essays collected here speak eloquently for themselves, but a word about the rationale of the whole collection is in order. I have tried to represent the full range of criticism on Wells to the extent allowed by space limitations, and I regret having to omit much fine criticism.[32] I have been conscious of two previous anthologies of essays, both of which appeared in 1977—*H. G. Wells: A Collection of Critical Essays,* edited by Bernard Bergonzi, and *H. G. Wells and Modern Science Fiction,* edited by Darko Suvin with Robert M. Philmus[33]—and I have tried to make this collection not a second edition of either of these works but a new statement. After much consideration, I have decided not to reprint anything from these collections. I most miss David Lodge's "*Tono-Bungay* and 'The Condition of England,' " a landmark in the interpretation and resurrection of Wells, but it is readily available, both in Bergonzi and in collections of Lodge's work.

In general I have sought out essays that in some way change our usual understanding of Wells. The three areas that have benefited from new thinking are, first, the debate with James about the purpose and value of the novel; second, Wells's late fiction; and third, Wells's life itself. The collection focuses on these areas. The scientific romances remain popular and a field of rich critical production, but the very security of their place in Wells's opus and in the larger system of literature has given me the confidence to slight them in this collection. In general, the important advances in the reading of this part of Wells's work have not entailed revisions so much as deepenings of already understood values and understandings. Darko Suvin's essay is distinctive in that it appreciates the accomplishment of the scientific romances, but it also has a sharp sense of their ideological strategies and compromises.

Mark Schorer's pages on *Tono-Bungay* remain the definitive criticism of Wells's "art." They offer an important reading of the novel, and they give the Jamesian perspective a specificity that the discussion James and Wells themselves engaged in lacks. Schorer's pages serve as an introduction to the issue of Wells as novelist and artist. Patrick Parrinder's "*Tono-Bungay* and *Mr. Polly*" approaches *Tono-Bungay* by seeing it in the context of other Wells fictions and understanding it as a complement to Wells's comic and utopian dimensions. Linda Anderson, in "Self and Society in H. G. Wells's *Tono-Bungay*," draws attention back to character; she sees character not in the traditional terms of self-creation common to the bildungsroman but as a construct of society. For Anderson, George Ponderevo renders in himself the problems of the society that created him. Though "the novel" is at the center of the Wells-James argument, for us to understand Wells's position we need to recognize the full range of his fictional interests. David Hughes's essay on *A Modern Utopia* begins to demonstrate how Wells's art gave shape to his thought, and points out how much technique mattered for him, even in fiction that is not strictly novelistic.

After 1910 Wells continued to publish novels steadily; though these works receive occasional brief mention, the work of the next decade has not received much concentrated study. Curiously, a comparatively strong revival of interest in work after 1920 has taken place and is represented here by excerpts from Robert Bloom's *Anatomies of Egotism* (1977) and William Scheick's *The Splintering Frame* (1984). Scheick attempts to rekindle interest in Wells's later work by proving that it evidences more "technique" than is generally supposed. He draws attention to the devices of self-conscious narrative that the old picture of Wells as an innocent, utopian propagandist obscures. Bloom's work, less intent on integrating Wells into recent aesthetic fashions, analyses a few late novels very closely to discover their thematic complexity. Robert Philmus's essay on the *Anatomy of Frustration* is also included for its careful analysis of the relation of Wells's technique to his social thought.

The collection concludes with four quite different approaches to Wells's life and influence. The historian A. J. P. Taylor's "The Man Who Tried to Work Miracles" is a vigorous—I am tempted to say "Wellsian"—polemic against Wells's utopian mission. My own "Problems of an Amorous Utopian" finds value in Wells's struggle to treat, even as he represses them, central conflicts in his life and thought. Nancy Steffen-Fluhr's essay on "Women and H. G. Wells" finds defensiveness and even desperation behind Wells's promiscuity. Such abrasive readings of matters in which Wells himself took much pride may seem to some admirers of Wells simply hostile, but there is no longer any point in holding on to idealizations of Wells. These essays pay Wells the compliment of trying to see him wholly and realistically. Finally, to fill out the portrait of Wells, the collection ends with Robert Crossley's eloquent rendering of Wells's inspirational presence in his own time. Wells was an extraordinary force for enlightenment, and these essays lead us toward an understanding of the sources of his energy. They also help us to see that he must be taken seriously, not necessarily on the terms of his own self-estimation, but as a complex human figure whose achievement is in part his ability to make constructive use of what he would call in his *Autobiography* his "ordinary brain."

Notes

1. Lionel Stevenson, "Wells, the Voice of an Epoch," in *The History of the English Novel, vol. 11, Yesterday and After* (Towota, N.J.: Barnes & Noble, 1967), 11.

2. The following brief sketch is drawn from many sources. Wells's *An Experiment in Autobiography* set the pattern for talking about his life. Norman and Jeanne Mackenzie's *H. G. Wells: A Biography* (New York: Simon & Schuster, 1973), published under the title *The Time Traveller* in the United Kingdom, remains the basic biography, though David Smith's *H. G. Wells: Desperately Mortal* (New Haven: Yale University Press, 1986) is an important complement.

3. Patrick Parrinder, ed., *H. G. Wells: The Critical Heritage* (London: Routledge & Kegan Paul, 1972), 60.

4. Gordon Ray was widely accused of taking West's side in his depiction of the affair in *H. G. Wells and Rebecca West* (New Haven: Yale University Press, 1974); his book has been answered by their son, Anthony West, in his memoir *H. G. Wells: Aspects of a Life* (New York: Random House, 1984).

5. Mackenzie and Mackenzie, *Biography*, 253.

6. Rebecca West's 1912 review in *Freewoman* is reprinted in Parrinder, *Heritage*, 203–8.

7. Fredrick R. Karl, "Conrad, Wells, and the Two Voices," *PMLA* 88 (1973): 1049–65.

8. In addition to the usual biographical sources, one can find a reading sympathetic to James in Nicholas Delbanco's *Group Portrait: Joseph Conrad, Stephen Crane, Ford Madox Ford, Henry James, and H. G. Wells* (New York: William Morrow, 1982).

9. A. J. P. Taylor, "The Man Who Tried to Work Miracles," *The Listener* 76 (1966): 83.

10. Anthony West, "H. G. Wells," in *Principles and Persuasions* (London: Eyre Spottis-woode, 1958), reprinted in *H. G. Wells: A Collection of Critical Essays*, ed. Bernard Bergonzi (Englewood Cliffs, N.J.: Prentice-Hall, 1976), 8–24.

11. Lionel Trilling, "Mind in the Modern World," *TLS* (17 November 1972): 1381–85.

12. Gordon Ray, "H. G. Wells Tries to Be a Novelist," in *Edwardians and Late Victorians: English Institute Essays, 1959*, ed. Richard Ellmann (New York: Columbia University Press, 1960), 106–59.

13. J. D. Beresford, *H. G. Wells* (New York: Henry Holt, 1913); Geoffrey West, *H. G. Wells* (New York: W. W. Norton, 1930); Antonina Vallentin, *H. G. Wells: Prophet of Our Day*, trans. Daphne Woodward (New York: John Day Co., 1950).

14. W. Warren Wagar, *H. G. Wells and the World State* (New Haven: Yale University Press, 1961); W. Warren Wagar, ed., *H. G. Wells: Journalism and Prophecy, 1893–1946* (Boston: Houghton Mifflin, 1964).

15. In an exhibit of Wellsiana curated by Patrick Parrinder from material in the Urbana Wells Archive was a marvelous letter from Gernsback to Wells whiningly asking why he charged Gernsback permissions fees while he gave his work to others for free. Wells thor-

oughly and angrily annotated the many misstatements in Gernsback's letter and at the top made a note that he should watch out for this scoundrel.

16. Both Heinlein's "The Roads Must Roll" and Knight's "The Country of the Kind" appear in *The Science Fiction Hall of Fame,* ed. Robert Silverberg (New York: Avon, 1970).

17. Parrinder, *Heritage,* 320.

18. V. S. Pritchett, "The Scientific Romances," *The Living Novel* (London: Chatto & Windus, 1946), reprinted in Bergonzi, *Critical Essays,* 32–38.

19. Parrinder, *Heritage,* 331.

20. Bernard Bergonzi, *The Early H. G. Wells* (Manchester: Manchester University Press, 1961).

21. Frank McConnell, *The Science Fiction of H. G. Wells* (Oxford: Oxford University Press, 1981); John Huntington, *The Logic of Fantasy: H. G. Wells and Science Fiction* (New York: Columbia University Press, 1982); Peter Kemp, *H. G. Wells and the Culminating Ape* (New York: St. Martin's Press, 1982); John R. Reed, *The Natural History of H. G. Wells* (Athens: Ohio University Press, 1982).

22. See Paul Alkon, *Origins of Futuristic Fiction* (Athens: University of Georgia Press, 1987); Robert M. Philmus, *Into the Unknown: The Evolution of Science Fiction from Francis Godwin to H. G. Wells* (Berkeley: University of California Press, 1970); and Darko Suvin, *Victorian Science Fiction* (Boston: G. K. Hall, 1983), published in the United Kingdom as *The Discourses of Knowledge and Power.*

23. See R[ichard] D[ale] Mullen, "H. G. Wells and Victor Rousseau Emanuel: *When the Sleeper Wakes* and *The Messiah of the Cylinder,*" *Extrapolation* 8 (1967): 31–63.

24. Bergonzi, *Early H. G. Wells,* 152.

25. Parrinder, *Heritage,* 332.

26. Vladimir Nabokov, "An Interview," *Paris Review* 41 (1966): 92–111.

27. Mark Schorer, "Technique as Discovery," *Hudson Review* 1, no. 1 (Spring 1948): 67–87, reprinted in *The World We Imagine: Selected Essays* (New York: Farrar, Straus & Giroux, 1968).

28. David Lodge, *Tono-Bungay* and 'The Condition of England,' " *The Language of Fiction* (London: Routledge & Kegan Paul, 1966), reprinted in Bergonzi, *Critical Essays.* Lucille Herbert, in *"Tono-Bungay:* Tradition and Experiment," *Modern Language Quarterly* 33 (1972): 140–55, reprinted in Bergonzi, *Critical Essays,* argues that the conclusion of the novel is neither ironic, as Lodge would have it, nor a contradiction, as Schorer had argued, but, dismayingly for Herbert, unambiguously clear in its commitment to an antihumanist faith in science. The destroyer in which George Ponderevo steams past London at the end of the novel is intended to appear just as brutal as it seems, and Wells admires it. Herbert bases her argument on evidence from other Wells writings, *First and Last Things* in particular, and on the appearance of related ideas in the work of D. H. Lawrence.

29. Raymond Williams, *The English Novel: From Dickens to Lawrence* (London: Chatto & Windus, 1970), 101–5.

30. In her dissertation, "Narrative Theory: Henry James and H. G. Wells," *DAI* 45 (1984): 1760A, Paula Hooper Mayhew argues that the debate was not conducted in terms that contribute to narrative theory. The best concise defense of Wells's position in the Wells-James debate is to be found in Patrick Parrinder and Robert M. Philmus's Introduction to their *H. G. Wells's Literary Criticism* (Towota, N.J.: Barnes & Noble, 1980), 178–88.

31. Schorer, "Technique," 74.

32. William Scheick and J Randolph Cox, eds., *H. G. Wells: A Reference Guide* (Boston: G. K. Hall, 1988) is an invaluable annotated bibliography of all that has been written on Wells through 1986.

33. Bergonzi, *Critical Essays,* and Darko Suvin with Robert M. Philmus, eds., *H. G. Wells and Modern Science Fiction* (Lewisburg, Pa.: Bucknell University Press, 1977).

Major Writings of H. G. Wells

◆

There is no modern scholarly edition of Wells's writings. The standard edition for citation remains *The Atlantic Edition of the Works of H. G. Wells*, 28 vols. (London: Unwin, 1924–27), the publication of which Wells oversaw: he revised many of the texts and wrote prefaces for each volume. But in clarifying his own works he often changed them significantly, and in individual cases there can be strong arguments for using other editions. For the fiction Wells wrote after the publication of the Atlantic edition there is less of a textual problem, thanks to the sad fact that most of this work has not been republished and thus only one version exists in print. Given this state of textual uncertainty, I see no reason to try to make the primary citations in the essays of this collection uniform. By the same argument, any concise bibliography of Wells's works will necessarily be arbitrary and of little use.

Nevertheless, as a testament to Wells's prolificness and to the variety of his interests, and as a concise guide to readers wishing to date and relate the books referred to in the following essays, it is important that a list of Wells's major writings accompany the critical essays. The following list of Wells's book-length works is based on *H. G. Wells: A Comprehensive Bibliography*, 4th ed., rev. (London: H. G. Wells Society, 1986). I have also consulted J. R. Hammond, *Herbert George Wells: An Annotated Bibliography of His Works* (New York: Garland, 1977).

CHRONOLOGY OF BOOKS PUBLISHED BY WELLS DURING HIS LIFETIME

Textbook of Biology (1893)

Honours Physiography (with R. A. Gregory) (1893)

Select Conversations with an Uncle, Now Extinct, and Two Other Reminiscences (1895)

The Time Machine: An Invention (1895)

The Wonderful Visit (1895)

The Stolen Bacillus, and Other Incidents (1895)

The Island of Doctor Moreau (1896)

The Wheels of Chance: A Holiday Adventure (1896)

The Plattner Story, and Others (1897)

The Invisible Man: A Grotesque Romance (1897)

Certain Personal Matters: A Collection of Material, Mainly Autobiographical (1897)

Thirty Strange Stories (1897)

The War of the Worlds (1898)

When the Sleeper Wakes (1899)

Tales of Space and Time (1899)

Love and Mr. Lewisham (1900)

Anticipations of the Reaction of Mechanical and Scientific Progress upon Human Life and Thought (1900)

The First Men in the Moon (1901)

The Discovery of the Future: A Discourse Delivered to the Royal Institution on January 24th, 1902 (1902)

The Sea Lady: A Tissue of Moonshine (1902)

Mankind in the Making (1903)

Twelve Stories and a Dream (1903)

The Food of the Gods and How It Came to Earth (1904)

A Modern Utopia (1905)

Kipps: The Story of a Simple Soul (1905)

In the Days of the Comet (1906)

The Future in America: A Search after Realities (1906)

Socialism and the Family (1906)

The Misery of Boots (1907)

New Worlds for Old (1908)

The War in the Air, and Particularly How Mr. Bert Smallways Fared While It Lasted (1908)

First and Last Things: A Confession of Faith and Rule of Life (1908)

Tono-Bungay (1909)

Ann Veronica: A Modern Love Story (1909)

The History of Mr. Polly (1910)

The New Machiavelli (1911)

The Country of the Blind, and Other Stories (1911)

Floor Games (1911)

The Door in the Wall, and Other Stories (1911)

Marriage (1912)

Little Wars: A Game for Boys from Twelve Years of Age to One Hundred and Fifty and for That More Intelligent Sort of Girls Who Like Boys' Games and Books (1913)

The Passionate Friends (1913)

An Englishman Looks at the World, Being a Series of Unrestrained Remarks upon Contemporary Matters (1914)

The World Set Free; A Story of Mankind (1914)

The Wife of Sir Isaac Harman (1914)

The War That Will End War (1914)

The Peace of the World (1915)

Boon, the Mind of the Race, the Wild Asses of the Devil, and the Last Trump, Being a First Selection from the Literary Remains of George Boon, Appropriate to the Times (1915)

Bealby: A Holiday (1915)

The Research Magnificent (1915)

What Is Coming: A Forecast of Things after the War (1916)

Mr. Britling Sees It Through (1916)

The Elements of Reconstruction (1916)

War and the Future: Italy, France and Britain at War (1917)

God the Invisible King (1917)

The Soul of a Bishop: A Novel (with Just a Little Love in It) about Conscience and Religion and the Real Troubles of Life (1917)

In the Fourth Year: Anticipations of a World Peace (1918)

Joan and Peter: The Story of an Education (1918)

The Undying Fire (1919)

The Idea of a League of Nations (1919)

The Outline of History, Being a Plain History of Life and Mankind (1920)

Russia in the Shadows (1920)

The Salvaging of Civilization (1921)

Washington and the Hope of Peace (1922)

The Secret Places of the Heart (1922)

A Short History of the World (1922)

Men Like Gods (1923)

The Story of a Great Schoolmaster, Being a Plain Account of the Life and Ideas of Sanderson of Oundle (1924)

The Dream: A Novel (1924)

A Year of Prophesying (1924)

Christina Alberta's Father (1925)

The World of William Clissold: A Novel at a New Angle (1926)

Meanwhile: The Picture of a Lady (1927)

The Way the World Is Going: Guesses and Forecasts of the Years Ahead (1928)

The Open Conspiracy: Blue Prints for a World Revolution (1928)

Mr. Blettsworthy on Rampole Island (1928)

The King Who Was a King: The Book of a Film (1929)

The Common Sense of World Peace; An Address Delivered to the Reichstag (1929)

The Autocracy of Mr. Parham: His Remarkable Adventures in This Changing World (1930)

The Science of Life: A Summary of Contemporary Knowledge about Life and Its Possibilities (1930)

The Work, Wealth, and Happiness of Mankind (1931)

After Democracy: Addresses and Papers on the Present World Situation (1932)

The Bulpington of Blup (1932)

The Shape of Things to Come: The Ultimate Revolution (1933)

Experiment in Autobiography: Discoveries and Conclusions of A Very Ordinary Brain—Since 1866 (1934)

The New America: The New World (1935)

Things to Come: A Film Story Based on the Material Contained in His History of the Future 'The Shape of Things to Come' (1935)

The Anatomy of Frustration: A Modern Synthesis (1936)

The Croquet Player: A Story (1936)

Man Who Could Work Miracles: A Film Story Based on the Material Contained in His Short Story (1936)

Star Begotten: A Biological Fantasia (1937)

Brynhild (1937)

The Camford Visitation (1937)

The Brothers: A Story (1938)

World Brain (1938)

Apropos of Dolores (1938)

The Holy Terror (1939)

Travels of a Republican Radical in Search of Hot Water (1939)

The Fate of Homo Sapiens: An Unemotional Statement of the Things That Are Happening to Him Now and of the Immediate Possibilities Confronting Him (1939)

The New World Order, Whether It Is Obtainable, How It Can Be Attained, and What Sort of World a World at Peace Will Have to Be (1939)

The Rights of Man, Or What Are We Fighting For? (1940)

Babes in the Darkling Wood (1940)

The Common Sense of War and Peace: World Revolution or War Unending? (1940)

All Aboard for Ararat (1940)

Guide to the New World: A Handbook of Constructive World Revolution (1941)

You Can't Be Too Careful: A Sample of Life (1941)

Science and the World-Mind (1942)

Phoenix: A Summary of the Inescapable Conditions of World Reorganization (1942)

Crux Ansata: An Indictment of the Roman Catholic Church (1943)

'42 to '44: A Contemporary Memoir upon Human Behaviour during the Crisis of the World Revolution (1944)

The Happy Turning: A Dream of Life (1945)

Mind at the End of Its Tether (1945)

POSTHUMOUS PUBLICATIONS AND IMPORTANT COLLECTIONS OF WELLS'S UNPUBLISHED WORK

Henry James and H. G. Wells: A Record of Their Friendship, Their Debate on the Art of Fiction, and Their Quarrel, ed. Leon Edel and Gordon N. Ray (Urbana: University of Illinois Press, 1958)

Arnold Bennett and H. G. Wells: A Record of a Personal and Literary Friendship, ed. Harris Wilson (Urbana: University of Illinois Press, 1960)

George Gissing and H. G. Wells: Their Friendship and Correspondence, ed. Royal A. Gettmann (Urbana: University of Illinois Press, 1961)

The Wealth of Mr. Waddy: A Novel (written 1898–99) (Carbondale: Southern Illinois University Press, 1969)

H. G. Wells: Early Writing in Science and Science Fiction, ed. Robert M. Philmus and David Y. Hughes (Berkeley: University of California Press, 1975)

H. G. Wells's Literary Criticism, ed. Patrick Parrinder and Robert M. Philmus (Totowa, N.J.: Barnes & Noble, 1980)

The Man with a Nose, and Other Uncollected Short Stories of H. G. Wells, ed. J. R. Hammond (London: Athlone Press, 1984)

H. G. Wells in Love: Postscript to an Experiment in Autobiography (written 1935–42), ed. G. P. Wells (Boston: Little, Brown, 1984)

ESSAYS

♦

Wells as the Turning Point
of the SF Tradition

DARKO SUVIN

H. G. Wells's first and most significant SF cycle (roughly to 1904) is based on the vision of a horrible novum as the evolutionary sociobiological prospect for mankind. His basic situation is that of a destructive newness encroaching upon the tranquillity of the Victorian environment. Often this is managed as a contrast between an outer framework and a story within the story. The framework is set in surroundings as staid and familiarly Dickensian as possible, such as the cozy study of *The Time Machine,* the old antiquity shop of "The Crystal Egg," or the small towns and villages of southern England in *The War of the Worlds* and *The First Men in the Moon.* With the exception of the protagonist, who also participates in the inner story, the characters in the outer frame, representing the almost invincible inertia and banality of prosperous bourgeois England, are reluctant to credit the strange newness. By contrast, the inner story details the observation of the gradual, hesitant coming to grips with an alien superindividual force that menaces such life and its certainties by behaving exactly as the bourgeois progress did in world history—as a quite ruthless but technologically superior mode of life. This Wellsian inversion exploits the uneasy conscience of an imperial civilization that did not wipe out only the bison and the dodo: "The Tasmanians, in spite of their human likeness, were entirely swept out of existence in a war of extermination waged by European immigrants. Are we such apostles of mercy as to complain if the Martians warred in the same spirit?" (*The War of the Worlds,* book 1, chap. 1).

As Wells observed, the "fantastic element" or novum is "the strange property or the strange world."[1] The strange property can be the invention that renders Griffin invisible, or, obversely, a new way of seeing—literally, as in "The Crystal Egg," "The Remarkable Case of Davidson's Eyes," and "The New Accelerator," or indirectly, as the Time Machine or the Cavorite sphere. It is always cloaked in a pseudo-scientific explanation, the possibility of which turns out, upon closer inspection, to be no more than a conjuring trick by the deft writer, with "precision in the unessential and vagueness in

From Darko Suvin, *The Metamorphosis of Science Fiction* (New Haven: Yale University Press, 1979). Reprinted by permission of Yale University Press.

23

the essential"[2]—the best example being the Time Machine itself. The strange world is elsewhen or elsewhere. It is reached by means of a strange invention or it irrupts directly into the Victorian world in the guise of the invading Martians or the Invisible Man. But even when Wells's own bourgeois world is not so explicitly assaulted, the strange novelty always reflects back on its illusions; an SF story by Wells is intended to be "the valid realization of some disregarded possibility in such a way as to comment on the false securities and fatuous self-satisfaction of everyday life."[3]

The strange is menacing because it looms in the future of man. Wells masterfully translates some of man's oldest terrors—the fear of darkness, monstrous beasts, giants and ogres, creepy crawly insects, and Things outside the light of his campfire, outside tamed nature—into an evolutionary perspective that is supposed to be validated by Darwinian biology, evolutionary cosmology, and the fin-de-siècle sense of a historical epoch ending. Wells, a student of T. H. Huxley, eagerly used alien and powerful biological species as a rod to chastize Victorian man, thus setting up the model for all the Bug-Eyed Monsters of later chauvinistic SF. But the most memorable of those aliens, the octopuslike Martians and the antlike Selenites, are identical to "The Man of the Year Million" in one of Wells's early articles (alluded to in *The War of the Worlds*): they are emotionless higher products of evolution judging us as we would judge insects. In the final analysis, since the aliens are a scary, alternative human future, Wellsian space travel is an optical illusion, a variation on his seminal model of *The Time Machine.* The function of his interplanetary contacts is quite different from Verne's liberal interest in the mechanics of locomotion within a safely homogeneous space. Wells is interested exclusively in the opposition between the bourgeois reader's expectations and the strange relationships found at the other end: that is why his men do land on the Moon and his Martians on Earth.

Science is the true, demonic master of all the sorcerer's apprentices in Wells, who have—like Frankenstein or certain folktale characters—revealed and brought about destructive powers and monsters. From the Time Traveller through Moreau and Griffin to Cavor, the prime character of his SF is the scientist-adventurer as searcher for the New, disregarding common sense and received opinion. Though powerful, since it brings about the future, science is a hard master. Like Moreau, it is indifferent to human suffering; like the Martians, it explodes the nineteenth-century optimistic pretentions, liberal or socialist, of lording it over the universe.

> Science is a match that man has just got alight. He thought he was in a room—in moments of devotion, a temple—and that his light would be reflected from and display walls inscribed with wonderful secrets and pillars carved with philosophical systems wrought into harmony. It is a curious sensation, now that the preliminary splutter is over and the flame burns up clear, to see his hands and just a glimpse of himself and the patch he stands on

visible, and around him, in place of all that human comfort and beauty he anticipated—darkness still.[4]

This science is no longer, as it was for Verne, the bright noonday certainty of Newtonian physics. Verne protested after *The First Men in the Moon:* "I make use of physics. He invents . . . he constructs . . . a metal which does away with the law of gravitation . . . but show me this metal." For Wells human evolution is an open question with two possible answers, bright and dark; and in his first cycle darkness is the basic tonality. The cognitive "match" by whose small light he determines his stance is Darwinian evolution, a flame which fitfully illumines man, his hands (by interaction of which with the brain and the eye he evolved from ape), and the "patch he stands on." Therefore Wells could much later even the score by talking about "the anticipatory inventions of the great Frenchman" who "told that this and that thing could be done, which was not at that time done"—in fact, by defining Verne as a short-term technological popularizer.[5] From the point of view of a votary of physics, Wells "invents" in the sense of inventing objective un- truths. From the point of view of the evolutionist, who does not believe in objects but in processes—which we have only begun to elucidate—Verne is the one who "invents" in the sense of inventing banal gadgets. For the evolutionist, Nemo's submarine is in itself of no importance; what matters is whether intelligent life exists on the ocean floor (as in "In the Abyss" and "The Sea Raiders"). Accordingly, Wells's physical and technical motivations can and do remain quite superficial where not faked. Reacting against a mechanical view of the world, he is ready to approach again the imaginative, analogic veracity of Lucian's and Swift's story-telling centered on strange creatures, and to call his works "romances." Cavorite or the Invisible Man partake more of the flying carpet and the magic invisibility hood than of metallurgy or optics. The various aliens represent a vigorous refashioning of the talking and symbolic animals of folktale, bestiary, and fable lore into Swiftian grotesque mirrors to man, but with the crowning collocation within an evolutionary prospect. Since this prospect is temporal rather than spatial, it is also much more urgent and immediate than Swift's controlled disgust, and a note of fairly malicious hysteria is not absent from the ever-present violence—fires, explosions, fights, killings, and large-scale devastations— in Wells's SF.

The Time Machine (1895), Wells's programmatic and (but for the mawk- ish character of Weena) most consistent work, shows his way of proceeding and his ultimate horizon. The horizon of sociobiological regression leading to cosmic extinction, simplified from Darwinism into a series of vivid pictures in the Eloi, the giant crabs, and the eclipse episodes, is established by the Time Traveller's narration as a stark contrast to the Victorian after-dinner discussions in his comfortable residence. The Time Machine itself is vali- dated by an efficient forestalling of possible objections, put into the mouth of schematic, none too bright, and reluctantly persuaded listeners, rather than by the bogus theory of the fourth dimension or any explanation of the gleaming bars glimpsed in the machine. Similarly, the sequence of narrated episodes gains much of its impact from the careful foreshortening of ever larger perspectives in an ever more breathless rhythm. Also, the narrator-observer's gradually deepening involvement in the Eloi episode is marked by cognitive hypotheses that run the whole logical gamut of sociological SF. From a parodied Morrisite model ("Communism," says the Time Traveller at first sight) through the discovery of degeneration and of persistence of class divisions, he arrives at the anti-utopian form most horrifying to the Victorians—a run-down class society ruled by a grotesque equivalent of the nineteenth-century industrial proletariat. Characteristically, the sociological perspective then blends into biology. The laboring and upper classes are envisioned as having developed into different races or indeed species, with the Morlocks raising the Eloi as cattle to be eaten. In spite of a certain contempt for their effeteness, the Time Traveller quickly identifies with the butterfly-like upper-class Eloi and so far forsakes his position as neutral observer as to engage in bloody and fiery carnage of the repugnant spider-monkey-like Morlocks, on the model of the most sensationalist exotic adventure stories. His commitment is never logically argued, and there is a strong suggestion that it flows from the social consciousness of Wells himself, who came from the lower middle class, which lives on the edge of the "proletarian abyss" and thus "looks upon the proletariat as being something disgusting and evil and dangerous."[6] Instead, the Time Traveller's attitude is powerfully supported by the prevailing imagery—both by animal parallels, and by the pervasive open-air green and bright colors of the almost Edenic garden (associated with the Eloi) opposed to the subterranean blackness and the dim reddish glow (associated with the Morlocks and the struggle against them). Later in the story these menacing, untamed colors lead to the reddish-black eclipse, symbolizing the end of the Earth and of the solar system. The bright pastoral of the Eloi is gradually submerged by the encroaching night of the Morlocks, and the Time Traveller's matches sputter out in their oppressive abyss. At the end, the unforgettable picture of the dead world is validated by the disappearance of the Time Traveller in the opaque depths of time.

Many of these devices reappear in Wells's other major works. The technique of domesticating the improbable by previews on a smaller scale, employed in the vivid vanishing of the model machine, is repeated in the introduction to the Grand Lunar through a series of other Selenites up to Phi-oo, or to Moreau's bestial people through the brutal struggles in the boat and through the ship captain, or to the Cavorite sphere's flight through the experimental explosion raising the roof. The loss of the narrator's vehicle and the ensuing panic of being a castaway under alien rule (in *The War of the Worlds* this is inverted as hiding in a trap with dwindling supplies) recurs time and again as an effective cliff-hanger. Above all, Wells's whole first cycle is a reversal of the popular concept by which the lower social and biological classes were considered as "natural" prey in the struggle for survival. In their turn they become the predators: as laborers turn into Morlocks, so insects, arthropods, or colonial peoples turn into Martians, Selenites, and the like. This exalting of the humble into horrible masters supplies a subversive shock to the bourgeois believer in Social Darwinism; at the same time, Wells vividly testifies that a predatory state of affairs is the only even fantastically imaginable alternative. The world upside-down— where strange animals hunt Man, and the subterranean lower class devours the upper class—recurs in Wells, as in Thomas More. But whereas More's sheep were rendered unnatural by political economics, Wells's Morlocks, Beast People, and so forth, are the result of a "natural" evolution from the author's present. Nature has become not only malleable—it was already becoming such in More and particularly in Swift—but also a practically value-free category, as in bourgeois scientism. At the end, the bourgeois framework is shaken, but neither destroyed nor replaced by any livable alternative. What remains is a very ambiguous attack on liberalism from the position of "the petty bourgeois which will either turn towards socialism or towards fascism."[7]

The human/animal inversion comes openly to the fore in *The Island of Dr. Moreau* (1896) with admirable Swiftian stringency. Dr. Moreau's fashioning of humans out of beasts is clearly analogous to the pitiless procedures of Nature and its evolutionary creation. He is not only a latter-day Dr. Frankenstein but also a demonically inverted God of Genesis, and his surgically humanized Beast Folk are a counterpart of ourselves, semibestial humans. Wells's calling their attempts to mimic the Decalogue in the litanies of "The Saying of the Law" and their collapse back into bestiality a "theological grotesque" indicates that this view of mankind's future reversed Christian as well as socialist millennialism into the bleak vistas of an evolution liable to regression. *The Island of Dr. Moreau* turns the imperial order of Kipling's *Jungle Book* into a degenerative slaughterhouse, where the law loses out to bestiality.

Wells's next two famous SF novels, though full of vivid local color, seem today less felicitous. Both have problems of focusing. In *The Invisible Man* (1897) the delineation of Griffin hesitates between a man in advance of his time within an indifferent society and the symbol of a humanity that does not know how to use science. This makes of him almost an old-fashioned "mad scientist," and yet he is too important and too sinned against to be comic relief. The vigor of the narration, which unfolds in the form of a hunt, and the strengths of an inverted fairy tale cannot compensate for the failure of the supposedly omniscient author to explain why Griffin had got into the position of being his own Frankenstein and Monster at the same time. In this context, the dubious scientific premises (an invisible eye cannot see, and so forth) become distressing and tend to deprive the story of the needed suspension of disbelief. *The War of the Worlds* (1898), which extrapolates into xenobiology the catastrophic stories of the "future wars" subgenre, descends in places to a gleeful sensationalism difficult to stomach, especially in its horror-fantasy portraiture of the Martians. The immediate serialization in the US yellow press, which simply suppressed the parts without action, made this portraiture the most influential model for countless later Things from Outer Space, extendable to any foreign group that the public was at that moment supposed to hate, and a prototype of mass-media use of SF for mindless scare-mongering (inaugurated by Orson Welles's famous 1938 broadcast). The novel's composition is marred by the clumsy system of two eyewitness narrators, improvised in order to reconcile the sensational immediacy and the necessary overview. Of course, *The War of the Worlds* also contains striking and indeed prophetic insights such as the picture of modern total warfare, with its panics, refugees, quislings, underground hidings, and an envisaged Resistance movement, as well as race-theory justifications, poison gas, and a "spontaneous" bacteriological weapon. (In other tales, Wells—a lifelong lover of war games—added air warfare, tanks, atom bombing of a major city, and other bellicose devices.)

Except for the superb late parable "The Country of the Blind" ([book publication] 1911), Wells's sociobiological and cosmological SF cycle culminated in *The First Men in the Moon* (1901). It has the merit of summarizing and explicating openly his main motifs and devices. The usual two narrators have grown into the contrasting characters of Bedford, the Social-Darwinist speculator-adventurer and Cavor, the selfless scientist in whom Wells manages for once to fuse the cliché of absent-mindedness with open-mindedness and a final suffering rendered irremediable by the cosmic vistas involved. The sharply focused lens of spatial pinpointing and temporal acceleration through which the travelers perceive the miraculous growth of Lunar vegetation is the most striking rendering of the precise yet wondering scientific regard often associated with the observatories and observation posts of Wells's stories. The Selenites not only possess the Aesopian fable background and an endearing grotesqueness worthy of Edward Lear's creatures, they are also a profound image of sociopolitical functional overspecialization and of an absolute caste or race State, readily translatable from insect biology back into some of the most menacing tendencies of modern power concentration. Most Swiftian among Wells's aliens, they serve a double-edged satire, in the authentic tone of savage and cognitive indignation:

> . . . I came upon a number of young Selenites, confined in jars from which only the fore limbs protruded, who were being compressed to become machine-minders of a special sort. . . . these glimpses of the educational methods of these beings have affected me disagreeably. I hope, however, that may pass off and I may be able to see more of this aspect of this wonderful social order. That wretched-looking hand sticking out of its jar seemed to

appeal for lost possibilities; it haunts me still, although, of course, it is really in the end a far more humane proceeding than our earthly method of leaving children to grow into human beings, and then making machines of them. (chap. 23)

The usual final estrangement fuses biological and social disgust into Bedford's schizophrenic cosmic vision of himself "not only as an ass, but as the son of many generations of asses" (chap. 19). Parallel to that, Cavor formulates most clearly the uselessness of cosmic as well as earthly imperialism, and articulates a refusal to let science go on serving them (had this been heeded, we would have been spared the Galactic Empire politics and swashbuckling of later SF). Finally, Bedford's narration in guise of a literary manuscript with pretenses to scientific veracity, combined with Cavor's narration in guise of interplanetary telegraphic reports, exhibit openly Wells's ubiquitous mimicry of the journalistic style from that heyday of early "mass communications"—the style of "an Associated Press dispatch, describing a universal nightmare."[8]

Yet such virtuosity cannot mask the fundamental ambiguity that constitutes both the richness and the weakness of Wells. Is he horrified or grimly elated by the high price of evolution (*The Island of Dr. Moreau*)? Does he condemn class divisions or simply the existence of a menacing lower class (*The Time Machine*)? Does he condemn imperialism (*The First Men in the Moon*) or only dislike being at the receiving end of it (*The War of the Worlds*)? In brief are his preoccupations with violence and alienation those of a diagnostician or of a fan? Both of these stances coexist in his works in a shifting and often unclear balance. For example,—to translate such alternatives into an immediate determinant of narration—Wells's central morphological dilemma in the years of his first and best SF cycle was: which is the privileged way of understanding the world, the scientifically systematic one or the artistically vivid one? Faced with the tension between "scientific" classification and "artistic" individuation, a tension that remained constant (albeit with different outcomes) throughout his life, Wells had already in 1891 satirized the deterministic rigidity in his essay "The Universe Rigid" and gone on to find a first compromise in his "The Rediscovery of the Unique" and its successive avatars in "The Cyclic Delusion," "Scepticism of the Instrument," and *First and Last Things* (1908). These articles attempt to formulate the deep though unclear pulls which Wells at his best reconciled by opting for representativeness, for fusing individuum and species into socially *and* biologically typical figures like the Time Traveller, but which he often left unreconciled.

Wells's SF makes thus an aesthetic form of hesitations, intimations, and glimpses of an ambiguously disquieting strangeness. The strange novum is gleefully wielded as a sensational scare thrown into the bourgeois reader, but its values are finally held at arm's length. In admitting and using their possibility he went decisively beyond Verne, in identifying them as horrible he decisively opposed Morris. Wells's SF works are clearly "ideological fables,"[9] yet he is a virtuoso in having it ideologically both ways. His satisfaction at the destruction of the false bourgeois idyll is matched by his horror at the alien forces destroying it. He resolutely clung to his insight that such forces must be portrayed, but he portrayed them within a sensationalism that neutralizes most of the genuine newness. Except in his maturest moments, the conflicts in his SF are therefore transferred—following the Social-Darwinist model—from society to biology. This is a risky proceeding which can lead to some striking analogies but as a rule indicates a return to quasi-religious eschatology and fatal absolutes. Wells expressed this, no doubt, in sincerely Darwinist terms, but his approach is in fact marked by a contamination of echoes from a culturally sunken medieval bestiary and a Miltonic or Bunyanesque color scheme (dark and red, for example, as satanic) with the new possibilities of scientific dooms (compare the Ruskinian Angel of *The Wonderful Visit* [1895], presented as an alien from a parallel world). The annihilation of this world is the only future alternative to its present state; the present bourgeois way of life is with scientific certainty leading the Individualist *homme moyen sensuel* toward the hell of physical indignity and psychic terror, yet this *is* still the only way of life he can return to and rely on, the best of all the bad possible worlds. Thus Wells's central anxious question about the future in store for his Everyman—who is, characteristically, a bright, aggressive, White, middle-class male—cannot be resolved as posed. His early SF can present the future only as a highly menacing yet finally inoperative novum, the connection with its bearers (Time Traveller, Moreau, Griffin, Martians, Selenites, or Cavor) being always broken off. Formally, this impasse explains his troubles with works of novel length: his most successful form is either the short story or the novelette, which lend themselves to ingenious balancings on the razor's edge between shock and cognitive development. In them he set the pace for the commercial norms of most later SF (which adds insult to injury by calling such works novels).

Wells's later SF abandoned such fragile but rich ambiguity in favor of short-range extrapolations. His first attempt in that direction, *When the Sleeper Wakes* (1899), was the most interesting. Its picture of a futuristic megalopolis with mass social struggles led by demagogic leaders was "a nightmare of Capitalism triumphant" and an explicit polemic against Bellamy's complacent optimism about taming the organizing urge and the jungle of the cities. In Wells's complex corporate capitalism "everything was bigger, quicker and more crowded; there was more and more flying and the wildest financial speculation."[10] Since Wells's sketch of the future was full of brilliant and detailed insights (as, for example, those about competing police forces and stultifying mass media) that turned out to be close to actual developments in the twentieth century, this novel became the model for anti-utopian anticipation from Zamyatin and von Harbou to Heinlein and Pohl. But Wells's imaginative energy flagged here at the crucial narrative level: the observer-hero waking after two centuries behaves alternatively like a savior (suffering his final passion on an airplane instead of a cross) and vacillating liberal intellectual. The jerky plot concerns itself primarily with the adventure of a beautiful soul in the future, and is thus coresponsible for a spate of similar inferior SF with more rugged heroes who are given wonderful powers and who experience sentimental entanglements. "A Story of Days to Come" (1899) and "A Dream of Armageddon" (1903), told wholly from inside the same future, are not much more than an exploitation of that interesting locale for sentimental tales seen from the bottom, respectively the top, of society. Wells's later SF novels—though even at their worst never lacking flashes of genuine insight or redeeming provocation—do not attain the imaginative consistency of his first cycle. In *The Food of the Gods* (1904) the fundamental equation of material and moral greatness is never worked out. His series of programmatic utopias, from *A Modern Utopia* (1905) to *The Holy Terror* (1939), has interesting moments, especially when he is describing a new psychology of power and responsibility such as that of the "Samurai" or the "holy terror" dictator. However, its central search for a caste of technocratic managers as "competent receivers"[11] for a bankrupt capitalist society oscillates wildly from enlightened monarchs or dictators, through Fabian-like artists and engineers, to airmen and Keynesians (in *The Shape of Things to Come,* 1933): millennium has always been the most colorless part of Christian apocalypse. What is worst, Wells's fascinated sensitivity to the uncertain horizons of humanity gives only too often way to impatient discursive scolding, often correct but rarely memorable. A visit to young Soviet Russia (where his meeting with Lenin provided an almost textbook example of contrasts between abstract and concrete utopianism) resulted in the perhaps most interesting work in that series, *Men Like Gods* (1923), where Wells gave a transient and somewhat etiolated glimpse of a Morris-like brightness. But his work after the first World War vacillated, not illogically for an apocalyptic writer, between equally superficial optimism and despair. His position in the middle, wishing a plague on both the upper and the working classes, proved singularly fruitless in creative terms—though extremely influential and bearing strange fruit in subsequent SF, the writers and readers of which mostly come from precisely those "new middle classes" that Wells advanced as the hope of the future.

With all his strengths and weaknesses Wells remains the central writer in the tradition of SF. His ideological impasses are fought out as memorable and rich contradictions tied to an inexorably developing future. He collected, as it were, all the main influences of earlier writers—from Lucian and Swift to Kepler, Verne, and Flammarion, from Plato and Morris to Mary Shelley, Poe, Bulwer, and the subliterature of planetary and subterranean voyages, future wars, and the like—and transformed them in his own image, whence they entered the treasury of subsequent SF. He invented a new thing under the sun in the time-travel story made plausible or verisimilar by physics. He codified, for better or worse, the notions of invasion from space and cosmic catastrophe (as in his story "The Star," 1899), of social and biological degeneration, of fourth dimension, of future megalopolis, of biological plasticity. Together with Verne's *roman scientifique,* Wells's "scientific romances" and short stories became the privileged form in which SF was admitted into an official culture that rejected socialist utopianism. True, of his twenty-odd books that can be considered SF, only perhaps eight or nine are still of living interest, but those contain unforgettable visions (all in the five "romances" and the short stories of the early sociobiological-cum-cosmic cycle): the solar eclipse at the end of time, the faded flowers from the future, the invincible obtuseness of southern England and the Country of the Blind confronted with the New, the Saying of the Law on Moreau's island, the wildfire spread of the red Martian weed and invasion panic toward London, the last Martian's lugubrious ululations in Regent's Park, the frozen world of "The New Accelerator," the springing to life of the Moon vegetation, the lunar society. These summits of Wells's are a demonstration of what is possible in SF, of the cognitive shudder peculiar to it. Their poetry is based on a shocking transmutation of scientific into aesthetic cognition, and poets from Eliot to Borges have paid tribute to it. More harrowing than in the socialist utopians, more sustained than in Twain, embracing a whole dimension of radical doubt and questioning that makes Verne look bland, it is a grim caricature of bestial bondage and an explosive liberation achieved by means of knowledge. Wells was the first significant writer who started to write SF from within the world of science, and not merely facing it. Though his catastrophes are a retraction of Bellamy's and Morris's utopian optimism, even in the spatial disguises of a parallel present on Moreau's island or in southern England it is always a possible future evolving from the neglected horrors of today that is analyzed in its (as a rule) maleficent consequences, and his hero has "an epic and public . . . mission" intimately bound up with "the major cognitive challenge of the Darwinist age."[12] For all his vacillations, Wells's basic historical lesson is that the stifling bourgeois society is but a short moment in an impredictable, menacing, but at least theoretically open-ended human evolution under the stars. He endowed later SF with a basically materialist look back at human life and a rebelliousness against its entropic closure. For such reasons, all subsequent significant SF can be said to have sprung from Wells's *Time Machine.*

Notes

1. Preface to *Seven Famous Novels by H. G. Wells* (Garden City, N.Y.: Knopf, 1934), vii.

2. Unsigned review [by Basil Williams] in *Athenaeum,* 26 June 1897; reprinted in Patrick Parrinder, ed., *H. G. Wells: The Critical Heritage* (London: Routledge & Kegan Paul, 1972) 57.

3. H. G. Wells, "An Experiment in Illustration," *Strand Magazine* February 1920; quoted in Geoffrey West, *H. G. Wells* (New York: W. W. Norton, 1930), 112.

4. H. G. Wells, "The Rediscovery of the Unique," *Fortnightly Review*, n.s. 50, July 1891; reprinted in Robert M. Philmus and David Y. Hughes, eds., *Early Writings in Science and Science Fiction by H. G. Wells* (Berkeley: University of California Press, 1975), 30–31.

5. Jules Verne's interview is from *T. P.'s Weekly*, 9 October 1903; reprinted in Parrinder, *Heritage*, 101–2; Wells's rejoinder is from the Preface cited in note 1 above, vii.

6. Christopher Caudwell, "H. G. Wells: A Study in Utopianism," in *Studies and Further Studies in a Dying Culture* (New York: Dodd, Mead, 1971), 76, 93.

7. V. S. Pritchett, *The Living Novel* (London: Chatto & Windus, 1960,) 128.

8. Unsigned review in *Critic*, 23 April 1898; reprinted in Parrinder, *Heritage*, 69.

9. Patrick Parrinder, *H. G. Wells* (New York: G. P. Putnam's Sons, 1977), 18.

10. Wells, first quotation from his "Author's Preface" to *The Sleeper Awakes* (London: Collins, 1921); second quotation from his *Experiment in Autobiography* (New York: Macmillan, 1934), 551.

11. Wells, *Experiment in Autobiography*, 206.

12. Patrick Parrinder, *News from Nowhere, The Time Machine*, and the Break-Up of Classical Realism," *Science-Fiction Studies* 3 (1976): 273.

[From "Technique as Discovery"]

MARK SCHORER

Technique alone objectifies the materials of art; hence technique alone evaluates those materials. This is the axiom which demonstrates itself so devastatingly whenever a writer declares, under the urgent sense of the importance of his materials (whether these are autobiography, or social ideas, or personal passions)—whenever such a writer declares that he cannot linger with technical refinements. That art will not tolerate such a writer H. G. Wells handsomely proves. His enormous literary energy included no respect for the techniques of his medium, and his medium takes its revenge upon his bumptiousness. "I have never taken any very great pains about writing. I am outside the hierarchy of conscious and deliberate writers altogether. I am the absolute antithesis of Mr. James Joyce. . . . Long ago, living in close conversational proximity to Henry James, Joseph Conrad, and Mr. Ford Madox Hueffer, I escaped from under their immense artistic preoccupations by calling myself a journalist." Precisely. And he escaped—he disappeared—from literature into the annals of an era.

Yet what confidence! "Literature," Wells said, "is not jewelry, it has quite other aims than perfection, and the more one thinks of 'how it is done' the less one gets it done. These critical indulgences lead along a fatal path, away from every natural interest towards a preposterous emptiness of technical effort, a monstrous egotism of artistry, of which the later work of Henry James is the monumental warning. 'It,' the subject, the thing or the thought, has long since disappeared in these amazing works; nothing remains but the way it has been 'manipulated.' " Seldom has a literary theorist been so totally wrong; for what we learn as James grows for us and Wells disappears, is that without what he calls "manipulation," there *is* no "it," no "subject" in art. There is again only social history.

The virtue of the modern novelist—from James and Conrad down—is not only that he pays so much attention to his medium, but that, when he pays most, he discovers through it a new subject matter, and a greater one. Under the "immense artistic preoccupations" of James and Conrad and Joyce, the form of the novel changed, and with the technical change, analogous changes took place in substance, in point of view, in the whole conception of fiction. And the final lesson of the modern novel is that technique is not the

First published in *Hudson Review*, 1, no. 1 (Spring 1948). Reprinted by permission.

secondary thing that it seemed to Wells, some external machination, a mechanical affair, but a deep and primary operation; not only that technique *contains* intellectual and moral implications, but that it *discovers* them. For a writer like Wells, who wished to give us the intellectual and the moral history of our times, the lesson is a hard one: it tells us that the order of intellect and the order of morality do not exist at all, in art, except as they are organized in the order of art.

Wells's ambitions were very large. "Before we have done, we will have all life within the scope of the novel." But that is where life already is, within the scope of the novel; where it needs to be brought is into novels. In Wells we have all the important topics in life, but no good novels. He was not asking too much of art, or asking that it include more than it happily can; he was not asking anything of it—as art, which is all that it can give, and that is everything.

A novel like *Tono-Bungary,* generally thought to be Wells's best, is therefore instructive. "I want to tell—*myself,*" says George, the hero, "and my impressions of the thing as a whole"—the thing as a whole being the collapse of traditional British institutions in the twentieth century. George "tells himself" in terms of three stages in his life which have rough equivalents in modern British social history, and this is, to be sure, a plan, a framework; but it is the framework of Wells's abstract thinking, not of his craftsmanship, and the primary demand which one makes of such a book as this, that means be discovered whereby the dimensions of the hero contain the experiences he recounts, is never met. The novelist flounders through a series of literary imitations—from an early Dickensian episode, through a kind of Shavian interlude, through a Conradian episode, to a Jules Vernes vision at the end. The significant failure is in that end, and in the way that it defeats not only the entire social analysis of the bulk of the novel but Wells's own ends as a thinker. For at last George finds a purpose in science. "I decided that in power and knowledge lay the salvation of my life, the secret that would fill my need; that to these things I would give myself."

But science, power and knowledge, are summed up at last in a destroyer. As far as one can tell Wells intends no irony, although he may here have come upon the essence of the major irony in modern history. The novel ends in a kind of meditative rhapsody which denies every value that the book had been aiming toward. For of all the kinds of social waste which Wells has been describing, this is the most inclusive, the final waste. Thus he gives us in the end not a novel, but a hypothesis; not an individual destiny, but a theory of the future; and not his theory of the future, but a nihilistic vision quite opposite from everything that he meant to represent. With a minimum of attention to the virtues of technique, Wells might still not have written a good novel; but he would at any rate have established a point of view and a tone which would have told us what he meant.

Tono-Bungay and *Mr. Polly:*
The Individual and Social Change

PATRICK PARRINDER

Wells's powers as a social novelist are most fully realised in *Tono-Bungay* (1909) and *The History of Mr. Polly* (1910). Formally the two novels are in open contrast. *Tono-Bungay* is a social panorama, a "description," as Edward Shanks put it in an admirable survey of Wells (1923),[1] "in a multitude of instances, of how human nature expressed itself in England in the twentieth century." It is cast as the autobiography of a complex, stubbornly intellectual engineer. *Mr. Polly* is a poetic comedy built around the most memorable of Wells's simple heroes, and exhibiting some highly singular instances of human nature. In *Tono-Bungay,* the Ponderevos, uncle and nephew, are always moving forward on their social journey, and the narrative sweeps along with a mounting exhilaration. It ends aboard a destroyer racing out to sea. Mr. Polly becomes a tramp wandering about the countryside, and he finally attains to a tranquil dignity, having moved through an emotional cycle which has the stately frequency of a human lifetime. The two novels of Wells's artistic maturity have several themes in common, but they offer a striking confirmation of V. S. Pritchett's remark that "Wells, as an artist, thrived on keeping his seeds of self-contradiction alive."[2]

In *Tono-Bungay* he was concerned, perhaps more directly than any other twentieth-century novelist, with the nature of social change. "An old and degenerating system, tried and strained by new inventions and new ideas";[3] Wells detected only shifting uncertainties behind the Edwardian façade of permanence, and soon after *Kipps* appeared he began the elaborate planning of a major novel diagnosing the social condition and exploring the typical expression of human value within it. In the opening sections of *Tono-Bungay* George Ponderevo indicates the vast areas of experience which seem to him relevant. The only limit to his ebullience seems to be spiritual exhaustion:

> I suppose what I'm really trying to render is nothing more nor less than Life—
> as one man has found it. I want to tell—*myself,* and my impressions of the
> thing as a whole, to say things I have come to feel intensely of the laws,

From Patrick Parrinder, *H. G. Wells* (Edinburgh: Oliver & Boyd, 1970). Copyright © Patrick Parrinder, 1977. Reprinted by permission of the author.

traditions, usages, and ideas we call society, and how we poor individuals get driven and lured and stranded among these windy, perplexing shoals and channels.[4]

After *The New Machiavelli,* James wrote to Wells remonstrating about "the bad service you have done your cause by riding so hard again that accurst autobiographic form which puts a premium on the loose, the improvised, the cheap and the easy."[5] He had evidently felt the same about *Tono-Bungay.* George warns that the novel will be "something of an agglomeration," and adds that his "ideas of a novel all through are comprehensive rather than austere."[6] Recent critics have been divided as to whether the novel Wells actually wrote with "restraint and care"[7] is the one that George warns us to expect. Mark Schorer, Arnold Kettle, and Walter Allen all find a lack of inner artistic unity; Kenneth B. Newell and David Lodge, on the other hand, have discovered an extraordinary amount of thematic integration, repetition, and intensification, and my own reading supports their view.[8] If *Tono-Bungay* was to present a panoramic vision of a changing society, it needed a sound and extensive basis of social analysis. David Lodge, who sees it as a "Condition of England novel" in the tradition of Disraeli, Mrs. Gaskell, and the Dickens of *Hard Times,* gives a brilliant exposition of the taxonomic view of society developed in the narrative. George's descriptive commentary both links the multitude of experiences and phenomena which he encounters, and animates them with "a strange and sinister life of their own."[9] It is a diseased life; Wells creates a network of pathological images of growth, decay, hypertrophy, and malignancy, radiating from a central organic metaphor for the condition of England—cancer. One of the many passages expressing the idea of sinister and malignant growth is George's survey of the newly swollen London of his time. He concludes a splendid topographical evocation by relating the formless tracts of the suburbs to an organic conception of the city (the "affected carcass") as a whole:

> All these aspects have suggested to my mind at times, do suggest to this day, the unorganised, abundant substance of some tumorous growth-process, a process which indeed bursts all the outlines of the affected carcass and protrudes such masses as ignoble, comfortable Croydon, as tragic, impoverished West Ham. To this day I ask myself will those masses ever become structural, will they indeed shape into anything new whatever, or is that cancerous image their true and ultimate diagnosis?[10]

The idea of social cancer has a considerable nineteenth-century history, from Cobbett (the "Great Wen") and Carlyle to Gissing, and it has re-emerged more recently in Norman Mailer's theories of the hipster. Wells had hinted at it in "The Days to Come," when Denton raved against civilisation as a "vast lunatic growth."[11] There are precedents, too, for the rhetorical technique of

Tono-Bungay in Dickens, Zola, and in the images of the class system in *Kipps*. Wells's earlier novel is full of oppressive institutions: the Emporium, the Royal Grand Hotel at which Kipps stays in London, *Manners and Rules of Good Society* (his guide-book), Chester Coote his chaperon, and the Anagram Tea with its bewildering crowd of people wearing incomprehensible labels. These are drawn together in the titanic symbol of the Labyrinthodon at Crystal Palace, and the System is summed up at last, with a Dickensian staginess, in an even more generalised image of an obsolete monster:

> As I think of them lying unhappily there in the darkness, my vision pierces the night. See what I can see! Above them, brooding over them, I tell you there is a monster, a lumpish monster, like some great clumsy griffin thing, like the Crystal Palace labyrinthodon, like Coote, like the leaden goddess of the Dunciad, like some fat, proud flunkey, like pride, like indolence, like all that is darkening and heavy and obstructive in life. It is matter and darkness, it is the anti-soul, it is the ruling power of this land, Stupidity. My Kippses live in its shadow. . . . And the claw of this Beast rests upon them![12]

This is a drastic oversimplification; it is the whole system, and not parts of it, that Kipps encounters at every stage, and Wells has only to pin it down, encircle it and destroy it with rhetoric in order to rescue his hero from the enchantment. Name the system as Stupidity—a prehistoric monster which will perish of its own accord—and it is already half-extinct. There is a more genuine social insight in an incidental passage from the chapter entitled "The Housing Problem." Kipps and Ann, looking for a house to buy, are appalled by the avoidable domestic drudgery imposed by basement kitchens, crude plumbing, and the narrow, dangerous stairs up which coal and water have to be carried:

> All the houses they saw had a common quality for which she could find no word, but for which the proper word is "incivility." "They build these 'ouses," she said, "as though girls wasn't 'uman beings."[13]

Incivility; the word penetrates at once through the comedy of polite manners in which Kipps has so earnestly engaged. His experience gives a very complete account of the travesties of "civility."

In *Tono-Bungay* the monster Stupidity is replaced by a historical analysis of English society, which is superbly recapitulated in the final scene, as the destroyer sweeps down the Thames cleaving a section through all the strata of English history. The last hundred years have seen the withering of the organic society represented by Bladesover, the country house in which George spends his boyhood, and the atrophy and hypertrophy brought by the spread of commercialism and profiteering. The condition of England, as George surveys it, is compared to "an early day in a fine October."[14] The underlying rot and decay are thinly masked by the Edwardian Indian summer. The new forces of socialism, science, and technology point ahead to the winter and spring, but the society they will create remains an enigma. This alone leads to an outlook very different from that of *Kipps* and *Mr. Polly,* where society is a constant pressure upon the individual. George moves in an area of flux—the sea across which his destroyer drives, or the air across which the rocket of Tono-Bungay, the patent medicine, flashes. He is one of the new men, and he owes his social opportunities to his uncle Edward Ponderevo, inventor of Tono-Bungay, the jumped-up "little man" who becomes a great financier, and whose rise and fall provides both the novel's broad shape and comic vitality, and George's most intimate and revealing insights into the rot in English society. George begins as an orphan, and is whirled up into the "pseudo-morphous" commercial aristocracy; for him, as for Wells himself, the world of confinement and submission is located back in his childhood. Under the Bladesover system, he recalls, "every human being had a 'place' "[15] in a graded hierarchy. Bladesover was an organic society because its members co-operated to support one another's sense of function and station. The point is made in the sly observation of Lady Osprey behaving "rather like an imitation of the more queenly moments of her own cook,"[16] and it is forced home in one of Wells's greatest comic scenes, the servants' tea at Bladesover, which is the epitome of genteel stuffiness. Wells's organic society makes a pointed contrast with that of D. H. Lawrence, who wrote approvingly in *The Rainbow* of the imaginative enrichment brought to women of Cossethay by the lady of the Hall, whose "life was the epic that inspired their lives."[17] For Wells the relation is a dead one, and the mental images it provides are hung with cobwebs:

> "Sir Roderick used to say," said Mrs. Mackridge, "that the First Thing"—here Mrs. Mackridge paused and looked dreadfully at me—"and the Second Thing"—here she fixed me again—"and the Third Thing"—now I was released—"needed in a colonial governor is Tact." . . . "It has always stuck me that that was a Singularly True Remark."[18]

The country-house system has determined the shape of English society as a whole, and anyone outside it is "perpetually seeking after lost orientations." George is a natural child of Bladesover and an instinctive rebel, but he never despairs of making his escape, as Kipps and Polly do. He sees that the "old habitual bonds"[19] have weakened, and the system is in open decline.

This slackening of social bonds leaves the way open for the adventurer riding a "transverse force" of his own creation, and the principal personal conflicts in *Tono-Bungay* do not begin until the release has been achieved. The first stage in the Ponderevos' emancipation is their discovery of the city. Edward, a chemist in a typical country town of the Bladesover system, is forced to move to London by impending bankruptcy. George follows him in order to become a science student. At first he is deeply disillusioned. His first move after leaving Bladesover took him to Chatham, where he was appalled by the dingy squalor of industrialism. He observed that the surplus of population from the landed estates were herded into places which reminded him strongly in colour and smell of the Bladesover dustbins;[20] industry "in a landlord's land" lives off the scraps and sewage of the organic society.

George continues to use Bladesover, the starting-point of his experience, as a key to decipher each new environment, and his "social anatomy" of London is a brilliant example of this. Central London, with its parks, West End mansions and clubs, museums, art-galleries and libraries, Bond Street, Harley Street and the City, is the consummation of the country-house culture. But it is surrounded by the vast, tumorous growths of the East End and the suburbs, threaded by the railways which have even butted their termini in among the mansions. The residential areas, the "dingy London ocean,"[21] remind George of Chatham, and the description is crowded with images of waste and dirt. But as George's knowledge of the metropolis becomes more intimate, and he ceases to be a priggish scholarship boy up from the provinces, his view changes. London is like a sea, a formless element of flux which erases fixed personal identities. He becomes socially "invisible" in an alluring, anarchic environment which will mould itself to his fantasies. The restless, ambivalent curiosity of adolescence is aroused by the hoardings, the people in the streets, the public meetings and freedom of thought, and the beckoning prostitutes: "Extraordinarily life unveiled."[22]

For George, the threat to his own identity is linked with sexual stimulation. Edward, who began playing the Stock Exchange to relieve the tedium of Wimblehurst, nourishes much grander dreams:

> "London, George," he said, "takes a lot of understanding. It's a great place. Immense. The richest town in the world, the biggest port, the greatest manufacturing town, the Imperial city—the centre of civilisation, the heart of the world! See those sandwich men down there! That third one's hat! Fair treat! You don't see poverty like that in Wimblehurst, George! And many of them high Oxford honour men, too. Brought down by drink! It's a wonderful place, George—a whirlpool, a maelstrom! whirls you up and whirls you down."[23]

This is a new world of infinite possibilities and inconceivable degradation, and Edward prepares to grab his chance. When Tono-Bungay whirls him up, he breaks into song with the words "I'm afloat, I'm afloat," and his financial ventures are known as "flotations." George too wishes to master the anarchic element, the sea, and he ends up building destroyers. The direct social analysis in *Tono-Bungay* shows England as a carcass swollen by cancer and hypertrophy. The narrative itself, following the journeys of Edward and

George, contrasts two ways of living in the turbulent and disordered regions of the organism. Here I would go further than David Lodge, who finds the frame of social analysis to be "the only constant element in a novel which is otherwise deliberately chaotic in structure."[24] Wells's network of metaphors is not confined to George's commentary. It penetrates to the core of the protagonists themselves, so that George and Edward exist both as realised characters, and as the poetic embodiments of opposing and yet not wholly incompatible values.

Edward is first or all a comic character, seen with detachment and invariably through George's eyes. He owes little to conventional ideas of the tycoon, for he remains a small shopkeeper, a typical Wellsian figure (except for his energy) who is blown up big by a social accident. He is first seen jerking in and out of his shop in carpet slippers to inspect his eccentric window-display, a thwarted little man fighting external subjection with the obscure inner compulsions of his fantasy. There is a homely and ineffectual quality about him which contrasts at all times with the social havoc he causes; George, with his habitual taxonomy, characterises this as "Teddi-ness." The justly famous death-scene, which Wells modelled on his visit to his dying friend, George Gissing, enforces the point that for all the splendour of his ascent from a Clerkenwell back-street to the huge mansions of Lady Grove and Crest Hill, Edward's greatest projects, like Mr. Polly's, are inherently spiritual. It is entirely fitting that he should leave the world babbling of cloud-capped towers and gorgeous palaces,[25] and after his death George confesses to feeling as the audience feels at the end of a play.[26] Each of Edward's appearances is a tableau. The narrative dwells at great length on the houses, the gestures, and the clothes which mark the different stages in his progress. The title of one of the earlier chapters—"The Dawn Comes, and my Uncle appears in a New Silk Hat"—is characteristic of the method, as are phrases wuch as "There he stands in my memory" and "So he poses for my picture." Edward, in fact, is revealed by a montage technique; he is an automaton, and all his projects and ideas are self-expressive, glimpses of an inner romance that by some freak fits in with the madness of the world. He is the focus of the sparkle and vitality in the novel, and yet his commercial activities provide the dramatic context for Wells's social criticism. There is always a limit to the narrative indulgence of his wilful, obsessive behaviour. The note of disapproval creeps in when he cheats George out of his mother's legacy, and his callous treatment of the admirable Aunt Susan (whose cheer-ful stoicism points to the deficiencies in both George and Edward) inevitably limits the reader's sympathy for him. Edward is called "Napoleonic" about twenty times in the novel, and although this accounts for some of his grandeur, Wells takes care to insinuate his own view of Napoleon as a monster of blind and petty egotism. *The Outline of History* (1920) is enlivened by a fierce attack on the man whom Wells now saw as the greatest of all traitors to the historical process. Humanity, in his view, was emerging slowly from a scatter of warring tribal groups towards global unity. In 1799 (much as in 1909), the old order was degenerate and dying, and "strange new forces drove through the world seeking form and direction."[27] But Napoleon, the man of the hour, was impervious to this unrivalled opportunity. Wells makes him an archetype of the purely expressive nature, the incarnation of libido: "What we all want to do secretly, more or less, he did in the daylight."[28] And what he did do was to "strut upon the crest of this great mountain of opportunity like a cockerel on a dung-hill."[29] Whatever we think of this as history, we cannot mistake the involuntary echoes of *Tono-Bungay*. Crest Hill was Edward's greatest mansion. The indictment against Edward appears in one of the best moments of the novel, a dialogue in which George's friend Ewart intuitively seizes upon the difference between nephew and uncle:

> "Your nephew, sir, is hard; he wants everything to go to a sort of predestinated end; he's a Calvinist of Commerce. Offer him a dustbin full of stuff; he calls it refuse—passes by on the other side. Now, *you,* sir—you'd make cinders respect themselves."
> My uncle regarded him dubiously for a moment. But there was a touch of appreciation in his eye.
> "Might make 'em into a sort of sanitary brick," he reflected over his cigar end.
> "Or a friable biscuit. Why *not?* You might advertise: 'Why are Birds so Bright? Because they digest their food perfectly! Why do they digest their food so perfectly? Because they have a gizzard! Why hasn't man a gizzard? Because he can buy Ponderevo's Ashpit Triturating Friable Biscuit—Which is Better.' "[30]

The general bearing of this is made clear in an acute and prophetic comment on modern advertising—"The old merchant used to tote about commodities; the new one creates values." But Ewart's assessment makes the "Romance of Commerce" no more than the adornment of waste. This connects up with the other dirt and waste images in the novel—with Chatham and the London suburbs, with the patent medicine itself (Tono-Bungay is "slightly injurious rubbish" and in his more philanthropic moments George would like to throw the whole stock down the drain), and with the "quap," a radioactive mineral which George tries to steal from the African coast. "Quap," which is explicitly compared to the degenerative processes in society, is cancerous stuff found in "heaps of buff-hued rubbish."[31] Edward's exploitation of rubbish is his exploitation of the whole society. Brilliant like the cockerel, he is an emanation from the dunghill, a specimen of human waste. This is a severe judgment on the comic hedonist, who after all is indispensable to the novel. Soon afterwards Wells was making handsome amends for his own and George's "Calvinism," by writing *Mr. Polly*.

Towards the end of *Tono-Bungay* George uses the idea of waste to sum up not only his uncle but the content of his book and the condition of England itself:

> I have called it *Tono-Bungay,* but I had far better have called it *Waste.* I have told of childless Marion, of my childless aunt, of Beatrice wasted and wasteful and futile. . . . It is all one spectacle of forces running to waste, of people who use and do not replace, the story of a country hectic with a wasting aimless fever of trade and money-making and pleasure-seeking. And now I build destroyers![32]

The final exclamation here is consciously ironical, and it is followed by another of George's momentary self-criticisms: "It may be I see decay all about me because I am, in a sense, decay." These admissions may put us on our guard, but since they call attention to the difficulties of any kind of interpretative sociology they do not have any precise effect on the way in which George is seen. The portrayal of George is the source of considerable flaws in the second half of the novel. Edward and George are plainly antithetical; the one is the sensualist embroidering life with his fantasies, the other the straightforward scientist who calls waste waste. It is George who confidently judges the people and the society around him, and who finally writes them off. His perceptions, also, provide the note of uplift which concludes the novel, as the destroyer steaming out to sea becomes a symbol of Technology driving forward through the waste. Few readers have found this affirmation—"Sometimes I call this reality Science, sometimes I call it Truth"[33]—entirely satisfactory. But it needs to be stressed that the "other note" George is now sounding, which he goes on to describe as "the heart of life" and "the one enduring thing," has been heard many times before. It is in fact the principle of George's character—the principle of drive.

Both the Ponderevos are socially displaced persons. George cannot live on his inner resources as Edward does, and he constantly searches for sources of nourishment outside himself. After the failure of his marriage he defines his temperament as a "stupid, drivingly-energetic, sensuous, intellectual sprawl."[34] This is intended as deprecating, and indeed, it describes a spiritual disorder no less than his uncle's, but George really feels that the driving energy redeems him. It *is* him, and it must be in his terms a state of grace. Yet his energy, both in his science and in his love affairs, leads him into a succession of failures. The process begins with his expulsion from Bladesover. Cut loose from life "in character," he discovers a "queer feeling of brigandage," and a compulsion to drive himself back into a station in society.[35] This initial insecurity is connected with a quality of bluntness, an impatience with pretence and concealment which informs all his attitudes. This leads to such telling social observations as his description of the suffocating respectability of the Ramboat home with its drapes and hangings. Marion Ramboat, George's girl-friend, is principally responsible for this, since it is she who has "draped the mirror, got the second-hand piano, and broken her parents in."[36] Yet he is irresistibly drawn to her. Her exterior qualities count for nothing against his urge for the "drawing back of a curtain" to reveal "the reality of love beneath."[37] He cannot help creating value where there is none; he marries her, and the only reality he finds is disappointment. There are vividly realised moments in the relationship, but it ends in formless meditations and self-indulgent confessions. From now on George's self-analysis becomes increasingly unsatisfactory, and the final claim that he has come to see himself "from the outside—without illusions"[38] is transparently false. He turns from the pursuit of sexual fulfilment to the scientific quest for truth; the value of this, it seems at one point, lies in the elusiveness of the goal, so that he need never suffer disappointment:

> All my life has been at bottom, *seeking,* disbelieving always, dissatisfied always with the thing seen and the thing believed, seeking something in toil, in force, in danger . . . something I have ever failed to find.[39]

Science has been, he says, "something of an irresponsive mistress." There is another irresponsive mistress in the book, however—Beatrice Normandy, George's aristocratic playmate at Bladesover, who returns into his life after his divorce—and his relationship with her merely confirms the sense of displacement and loss of identity. Most of the episodes are embarrassingly sentimental and unreal, but the general intention is clear; love too has been displaced from the social hierarchy, and can only exist as moments of totally unconnected privacy, a disentanglement from the world which they recognise as spiritually akin to annihilation. The failure of George's sexual relationships is symptomatic; he has been knocked out of his place in society, he has lived "crosswise" and seen through society, but he never makes a settlement and finds a role as Kipps and Polly do. Whenever he aims at a fixed point, it proves to be a chimera. Finally his drive is transferred to the destroyer, rushing on heedlessly abreast of the chaos, "on what trail even I who made her cannot tell."[40] The only faith he has is in the activity of motion itself:

> I fell into thought that was nearly formless, into doubts and dreams that have no words, and it seemed good to me to drive ahead and on and on through the windy starlight, over the long black waves.[41]

Captain or passenger, driving or drifting, he is going nowhere, except out into the open future. The conclusion of *Love and Mr Lewisham* here receives a far more dramatic and paradoxical expression. "Science, power and knowledge are summed up at last in a destroyer," Mark Schorer has commented.[42] "As far as one can tell Wells intends no irony, although he may here have come upon the essence of the major irony in modern history." It can hardly be claimed, although those who see Wells as a naïvely optimistic rationalist might wish to do so, that he had no intimations of this particular irony. He knew that you have to destroy in order to rebuild, and in all his imaginative prophecies it is through catastrophe that men are brought to their senses. The destroyer symbolises the paradoxes inherent in the two main twentieth-century ideologics of progress—revolutionary theory and scientific human-ism. To attempt to control the environment is to risk defeat, and to have reached a scientific analysis of people and society, as George's life shows, is to have cut oneself off from their sources of nourishment. The question remains to what extent *Tono-Bungay* embodies the ironies it raises. All the elements of failure and uncertainty are there in the novel, but they are subdued beside the exhilaration of the sense of change itself. A comparison may be made here with a novel on a similar theme, Scott Fitzgerald's *The Great Gatsby*. I will take the closing sentence from each:

> So we beat on, boats against the current, borne back ceaselessly into the past. (Fitzgerald.)

> We are all things that make and pass, striving upon a hidden mission, out to the open sea. (Wells.)

The last note of *Tono-Bungay* is an ambiguous one. The "hidden mission" leaves it open whether the striving is enough to overcome the current, whether it signifies control or submission. Fitzgerald, on the other hand, uses the same image for an elegant statement of futility. His studied detach-ment, which clearly belongs to the novel as art, is vulnerable to the reply which Wells's narrator made to the Time Traveller: "If that is so, it remains for us to live as though it were not so."[43] *Tono-Bungay* offers a devastating picture of commercialism and social stagnation, and Wells clearly felt the need for a final profession of faith. As a result, he both endorsed George's way of "living as though it were not so" and acknowledged some of the objections to it; the weakness, the lack of conviction which prevents *Tono-Bungay* from achieving greatness, is that he could not find a better way. George, like Edward and of course like Wells himself, has something Napoleonic about him. "We make and pass," he writes; and he, too, fights against insignifi-cance with a drivingly-energetic assertion of personality. *Tono-Bungay* re-mains a rich and exhilarating novel as long as it has two contrasted heroes; at the end, when Edward has left for his heavenly mansions, it is overwhelmed by a single, garrulous performance.

The History of Mr. Polly is a small-scale novel beside *Tono-Bungay*, but in it Wells brought his lower-middle–class hero close to perfection. Polly is a richer character than Kipps, and he lives out an inner romance like Edward. But his imagination supplies him with pastoral images and with queerly expressive idioms rather than with slogans and products, and he meets with far more resistance from the world than his predecessor. His is an ordinary life of frustration and defeat which culminates in a magnificent rebellion. But although he fights a lone battle for spiritual independence, his triumph is not purely an individual one. Wells broadens the significance of the comedy, using the interpretative narrative to show him as a socially representative figure. One of his devices is a carefully distanced exponent character, the "Highbury gentleman," who generalises about the "ill-adjusted units" produced by a "rapidly complicating society" defective in its "collective intelligence." Modern society, for him, is analogous to

> a man who takes no thought of dietary or regimen, who abstains from baths and exercise and gives his appetites free play. It accumulates useless and aimless lives, as a man accumulates fat and morbid products in his blood; it declines in its collective efficiency and vigour, and secretes discomfort and misery. Every phase of its evolution is accompanied by a maximum of avoidable distress and inconvenience and human waste. . . .[44]

Here Wells is repeating the diagnosis and the imagery of *Tono-Bungay. Mr. Polly* concentrates on the condition of the individual rather than the condition of England, but this simply means that the organic-social analogy is reversed. The metaphor of social cancer is replaced by the metaphor of Polly's indigestion. The novel begins with a picture of the hero in early middle age. He is sitting on a gate, racked with dyspepsia and cursing the world in his own idiom: "*Beastly* Silly Wheeze of a hole!" The relation of dyspepsia and the world's beastliness, of inner and outer disorder, is explored in a passage two pages later:

> To the moralist I know he might have served as a figure of sinful discontent, but that is because it is the habit of moralists to ignore material circumstances—if, indeed, one may speak of a recent meal as a circumstance—seeing that Mr. Polly was circum. . . . So on nearly every day in his life Mr. Polly fell into a violent rage and hatred against the outer world in the afternoon, and never suspected that it was this inner world to which I am with such masterly delicacy alluding, that was thus reflecting its sinister disorder upon the things without. It is a pity that some human beings are not more transparent. If Mr. Polly, for example, had been transparent, or even passably translucent, then perhaps he might have realised, from the Laocoon struggle he would have glimpsed, that indeed he was not so much a human being as a civil war.
> Wonderful things must have been going on inside Mr. Polly. Oh! wonderful things. It must have been like a badly managed industrial city during a period of depression; agitators, acts of violence, strikes, the forces of law and order doing their best, rushings to and fro, upheavals, the *Marseillaise*, tumbrils, the rumble and the thunder of the tumbrils. . . .[45]

Thousands of Pollys make up a diseased society; Polly himself is torn by internal strife. The intestinal "civil war" which controls his jaundiced view of the world is itself a consequence of social disorder—it was provoked by unwise feeding in childhood and his wife's appalling cookery—and it is turning him into a revolutionary, so that the strikes, tumbrils, and so on function as images of his coming insurrection. The interchangeability of inner and outer realities is neatly indicated by the play on "circum." The stomach and the world, in fact, reflect one another like mirrors. There is a thread of "indigestion" references throughout the book, and connected with these is another pervasive analogy, that of body and mind. Polly is torn by mental and physical conflict; both derive from the ravages of his youth, when "His liver and his gastric juice, his wonder and imagination"[46] were constantly at war with the formative and educational processes of society. A richly ironic association is suggested between the imagination and the equally useless appendix. Polly's education is grotesquely seen as an incredibly hamhanded surgical operation. The "surgeons"—a well-meaning, boldly enterprising, but rather overworked and underpaid butcher boy" and a "left-handed clerk of high principles but intemperate habits" (that is to say, a National school and a private school) are fortunately unsuccessful. The "appendix" is left "like a creature which has been beaten about the head and left for dead but still lives."[47] The wound heals up, so that he retains an obscure awareness of what Yeats called "the loveliness / That has long faded from the world"; and in time his drab outward career coexists with a furtive but richly eventful fantasy life. Once again, his imagination is seeking a capacious enough range of roles to fill. Wells expresses his aspirations through a series of lists—his boyhood fantasies, his favourite books, his meticulous preparations for his suicide attempt, and finally his multifarious duties as odd-job man at the Potwell Inn. Then there are the impotent daydreams which flow continuously through his adult life, manifesting a decorous sexuality and a romantic medievalism which are familiar escapist elements in the Victorian and Edwardian sensibility. The keynote of his imaginative individualism, however, is the active reorganisation of his world through his garbled, private language. "Allittritions Artful Aid"; "lill dog"; "Telessated pavements all right" (an obscure reflexion of his panic as he walks up the aisle to be married); "Boil it some more, O'Man": Polly's expressions become more astringent as his life increases in bitterness, and each of them is a momentary victory in his conflict with the world. He transforms the oppressive reality into the richer image of his fantasies, as Edward Ponderevo turns dung into advertising jingles. But Polly's gift also leads to disaster. He uses his linguistic gifts to fascinate his female cousins, their response goes to his head, and he finds himself trapped with fifteen years of dreary wedlock before him. Once Polly has escaped from his wife and his shop, we hear little more of his linguistic inventiveness. Having changed his world objectively, he no longer needs it.

For most of his life, Polly is the victim in a deterministic world. Wells portrayed the forces of society and nature in many remarkable shapes, and none more so than those of Mr. and Mrs. Johnson, Aunt Larkins, Uncle Pentstemon and the other characters brought together in the magnificent funeral and wedding scenes of *Mr. Polly.* The extent to which Wells's comedy is indebted to Dickens has often been noted. Wells even tried to persuade his publisher to continue *Mr. Polly* in an indefinite number of periodical parts, and as a free wanderer, having thrown off the yoke of society, Polly might have become a sort of Pickwickian tramp. This was not to be, but one of the things which Wells clearly learnt from Dickens, and adapted to his own purpose, was the symbolic power of scenes of marred festivity. Dickens shows his humbugs and scoundrels making a travesty of celebration, as in little Paul's christening in *Dombey & Son:* "The party seemed to get colder and colder, and to be gradually resolving itself into a congealed and solid state, like the collation round which it was assembled."[48] Wells shows how celebration itself, through its archaic rules and conventions, can travesty the emotional spontaneity of the individual. Polly is an outsider at his father's funeral and his own wedding. The superb description of him viewing his father's body, for example, captures the embarrassing gulf between the free, uncertain consciousness and the rigid traditional conventions of feeling:

> His cousin Johnson received him with much solemnity, and ushered him upstairs to look at a stiff, straight, shrouded form with a face unwontedly quiet, and, it seemed, by reason of its pinched nostrils, scornful.
> "Looks peaceful," said Mr. Polly, disregarding the scorn to the best of his ability.
> "It was a merciful relief," said Mr. Johnson.
> There was a pause.
> "Second—second Departed I've ever seen—not counting mummies," said Mr. Polly, feeling it necessary to say something.
> "We did all we could."
> "No doubt of it, O'Man," said Mr. Polly.
> A second long pause followed, and then, to Mr. Polly's great relief Johnson moved towards the door.[49]

There follow the ceremonial meals, and the noisy collisions of fixed personalities incapable of communication but united by kinship, the conventions and a common greed. There are similarities with the jealousy and suspicion of Polly's neighbours in Fishbourne High Street. In each case, the bickering is an external manifestation of the war in Polly's stomach.

Polly tries unobtrusively to escape from the funeral and wedding, but each time he is foiled. More desperate expedients are suggested by a vivid memory of his father, struggling to get a sofa up a narrow flight of stairs:

> For a time his father had coaxed, and then groaned like a soul in torment, and given way to blind fury; had sworn, kicked, and struck at the offending piece of furniture, and finally, with an immense effort, wrenched it upstairs, with

considerable incidental damage to lath and plaster and one of the casters. That moment when self-control was altogether torn aside, the shocked discovery of his father's perfect humanity, had left a singular impression on Mr. Polly's queer mind. . . .

A weakly wilful being, struggling to get obdurate things round impossible corners—in that symbol Mr. Polly could recognise himself and all the trouble of humanity.[50]

His father becomes a general symbol of man in an alien universe, and this prepares for the broad, allegorical reference of his own release. When it comes, his self-control is torn aside in an instinctive act of assertion linked with the death-wish. The affair of the Fishbourne fire has a grandiosity appropriate to Polly's fantasies. Ironically, however, his instincts save him, and the shock of fear which turns his suicide attempt into panic and flight brings about a spiritual resurrection. The fire is described with energy and demonic gusto, and David Lodge has rightly called it a "private enactment of the earlier visions of global destruction"[51] in the scientific romances. The result of this deluge, however, is liberation, as the deterministic world collapses around him. He "understood there was no inevitable any more, and escaped his former despair."[52]

He finally settles down in the idyllic Potwell Inn, in an idyllic and sexless relationship with the woman who owns it. It is here that he fulfils his fantasies, notably in the violence of his mock-heroic backyard scrap with the petty criminal Uncle Jim. This is a consummation of his romantic medievalism in knight-errantry, in defence of a riverside inn which itself has a strong literary and pastoral flavour. *Mr. Polly* ends, in fact, as a Thames valley romance, a late example of a favourite Victorian genre which includes Arnold's "Thyrsis" and "The Scholar-Gipsy," Morris's *News from Nowhere,* some of the verses in the *Alice* books, and Jerome K. Jerome and Kenneth Grahame. Wells was also drawing upon his own memories of a Thames-side inn, Surly Hall near Windsor, where he spent some holidays as a boy. And the tranquillity in which Polly comes to rest has a regressive element which is not only literary:

It was one of those evenings serenely luminous, amply and atmospherically still, when the river bend was at its best. A swan floated against the dark green masses of the further bank, the stream flowed broad and shining to its destiny, with scarce a ripple—except where the reeds came out from the headland, and the three poplars rose clear and harmonious against the sky of green and yellow. It was as if everything lay securely within a great, warm, friendly globe of crystal sky. It was as safe and enclosed and fearless as a child that has still to be born. It was an evening full of the quality of tranquil, unqualified assurance. Mr. Polly's mind was filled with the persuasion that indeed all things whatsoever must needs be satisfying and complete. It was incredible that life had ever done more than seemed to jar, that there could be any shadow in life save such velvet softnesses as made the setting for that silent swan, or any murmur but the ripple of the water as it swirled round the chained and gently swaying punt.[53]

It is certainly remarkable that *Kipps, Tono-Bungay,* and *Mr. Polly* all conclude with these watery scenes. But the symbolic womb into which the landscape, the sky and the whole universe now dissolve is the distinguishing feature of the passage quoted. It points to a complexity of resolved and unresolved meaning, for it ought to be understood in Wells's terms as well as Freud's. If we do so, it becomes the keystone of the arch of organic-social analogies in the book, and curiously analogous to the destroyer in *Tono-Bungay.* The destroyer suggests a dialectic of creation and destruction which has its counterpart in Wells's political projects for the future. After the fire, Polly has sloughed off the corrupted skin of training and servility which was all society had to offer him. He is back where he started; an "artless child of Nature, far more untrained, undisciplined, and spontaneous, than the ordinary savage,"[54] who is released into a world accommodated to his nakedness. Wells, I think, might have justified the mellow conclusion to *Mr. Polly* by seeing the "friendly globe of crystal sky" as the womb in which the new civilisation and the new human race could be born. This would make Polly a forebear, and his fulfilment as well as his victimisation would have a general significance. But the argument cannot be pressed too far. The friendly sky embraces a literary landscape steeped in nostalgia; the womb metaphor is cosy and soothing, with none of the bracing development of embryonic life. Life, in fact, is drawing to a close, and after an orgy of satisfying primitivism Polly has achieved the "smooth, still quiet of the mind."[55] The moral questions raised by Wells's comic hedonist are not clearly resolved. Polly is so obviously right in his anarchistic struggle for a richness of which he has been cheated except in dreams; Edward Ponderevo is equally wrong in choosing the path marked out by his obsessions. The dedicated scientist or revolutionary, however austere his imagination, is also driven to impose his will on society. It is not the wilfulness but the social acceptability of the capitalist adventurer which is so damning. There is a telling moment in the Wimblehurst section of *Tono-Bungay* when George describes his uncle's dreams of cornering quinine. George imagined then that anyone attempting this would be sent to prison; later experience teaches him that anyone who actually brought it off would be much likelier to end up in the House of Lords.[56] It is unlikely that Wells himself was ever in any real danger of being offered a peerage, and he continued to play the *enfant terrible,* coming out with a vehement attack on the monarchy only a few months before his death. But David Lodge very plausibly suggests that, although he condemned the British social system as "essentially irresponsible," he "secretly . . . felt his own success had been contingent on that irresponsibility";[57] hence his ambiguous attitude to his irresponsible comic heroes. There is nothing Napoleonic about Mr. Polly, and the indulgence of his libido could never lead him to profit by the system, so the comedy of his limited life ends in a fitting and deeply-felt individual triumph. But this ending is still not as closely linked to Wells's broad "world outlook" as he had wished the boat at Sandgate to be. The good life, he wrote in *First and Last Things,* is that which "contributes most effectively to the collective growth."[58] Polly's solution is attained on the simple and pastoral level, and it only doubtfully possesses the qualities which Wells as a moralist required on the intellectual and complex. If David Lodge is right in postulating a secret guilt about his own success, the question must be why Wells was unable to bring what could hardly have been a unique phenomenon out into the open; why, in fact, his analysis of George Ponderevo is deficient. Wells was more conscious of his intellectual assumptions than most novelists, and perhaps the weakest part of the "reconstruction of the frame" of the universe which he inherited in the eighties and nineties was its account of individual psychology. His characterisation shows him anticipating some of the main insights of modern psychoanalysis, but he was not able to develop them as fully as he might have done had he formed his imagination after Freud as well as after Darwin. After 1910 he began to lose interest in imaginative character-creation. He would still write a few social comedies—*Bealby* (1915) and *You Can't Be Too Careful* (1941) are examples—but these are of little significance. His later novels preserve the seeds of sociological and ethical self-contradiction, but they are neither tended so carefully nor allowed to grow so luxuriantly.

Notes

1. Edward Shanks, *First Essays in Literature* (London: Collins, 1923), 164.
2. "Wells Marches On," in *New Statesman,* 23 September 1966, 433.
3. H. G. Wells, Preface to *Tono-Bungay, The Atlantic Edition of the Works of H. G. Wells,* vol. 12 (London: T. Fisher Unwin, 1924), ix. This edition of *Tono-Bungay* will be cited as *T.B.*
4. *T.B.* I, 1, ii.
5. *Henry James and H. G. Wells: A Record of Their Friendship, Their Debate on the Art of Fiction, and Their Quarrel,* ed. Leon Edel and Gordon N. Ray (Urbana: Illinois University Press, 1958), 128.
6. *T.B.* I, 1, i.
7. Preface to *T.B.,* ix.
8. Mark Schorer, "Techniques as Discovery," *Hudson Review* 1, no. 1 (Spring 1948), reprinted in *Forms of Modern Fiction,* ed. W. Van O'Connor (Minneapolis: Minnesota University Press, 1948), 9ff. (reprinted in this volume); Arnold Kettle, *An Introduction to the English Novel,* vol. 2 (London: Hutchinson's University Library, 1953), 92ff.; Walter Allen, *The English Novel: A Short Critical History* (London: Phoenix House, 1954), 300ff.; Kenneth B. Newell, *Structure in Four Novels by H. G. Wells* (The Hague: Mouton, 1968); David Lodge, *The Language of Fiction* (London: Routledge, 1966), 214ff.
9. Lodge, *Language of Fiction,* 219.
10. *T.B.,* II, 1, i.
11. H. G. Wells, *The Complete Short Stories of H. G. Wells* (London: Benn, 1927), 786.

12. H. G. Wells, *Kipps: The Story of a Simple Soul, The Atlantic Edition of the Works of H. G. Wells,* vol. 8, III, 2, v.

13. *Kipps,* III, 1, ii.

14. *T.B.,* I, 1, iii.

15. Ibid.

16. Ibid., III, 3, iii.

17. D. H. Lawrence, *The Rainbow* (Harmondsworth: Penguin, 1949), 11.

18. *T.B.,* I, i, iv.

19. Ibid., I, 1, iii.

20. Ibid., I, 2, i.

21. Ibid., I, 3, vii.

22. Ibid., I, 3, vi.

24. Lodge, *Language of Fiction,* 238.

25. *T.B.,* IV, 1, vii.

26. Ibid., IV, 1, viii.

27. H. G. Wells, *The Outline of History,* rev. ed. (London: Cassell, 1972), 620.

28. Ibid., 632.

29. Ibid., 620.

30. *T.B.,* II, 3, ii.

31. Ibid., III, 4, iv.

32. Ibid., IV, 3, i.

33. Ibid., IV, 3, iii.

34. Ibid., II, 4, ii.

35. Ibid., I, 2, iii.

36. Ibid., II, 1, v.

37. Ibid., II, 1, iv.

38. Ibid., IV, 3, iv.

39. Ibid., II, 4, x.

40. Ibid., IV, 3, ii.

41. Ibid., IV, 3, iii.

42. Schorer, 17.

43. *Complete Short Stories,* 91.

44. *The History of Mr. Polly, The Atlantic Edition of the Works of H. G. Wells,* vol. 17, 7, iii.

45. *Mr. Polly,* 1, i.

46. Ibid., 1, ii.

47. Ibid.

48. *Dombey & Son* (London: Oxford University Press, 1950), 60.

49. *Mr. Polly,* 4, i.

50. Ibid.

51. David Lodge, *The Novelist at the Crossroads* (Ithaca: Cornell University Press, 1971), 217.

52. *Mr. Polly,* 9, i.

53. Ibid., 10, iii.

54. Ibid., 10, i.

55. Ibid., 10, iii.

56. *T.B.,* I, 3, i.

57. Lodge, *Novelist at the Crossroads,* 61.

58. H. G. Wells, *First and Last Things: A Confession of Faith and Rule of Life,* rev. ed. (London: Watts, 1929), 79.

Self and Society in H. G. Wells's *Tono-Bungay*

Linda R. Anderson

The precise differences of opinion about the novel which fueled the quarrel between Henry James and H. G. Wells have never been adequately defined. Partly as a result of Wells's adopted role as literary philistine, partly as a result of the later triumph of modernism which enthroned Jamesian attitudes to art, their debate has been seen less in terms of specific ideas than as James's vindication of the novel form itself against someone who failed to understand "the true nature of art."[1] When James, however, summed up his own beliefs in an often quoted final letter to Wells—"It is art that *makes* life, makes interest, makes importance, for our consideration and application of these things, and I know of no substitute whatever for the force and beauty of its process"[2]—he was not just resoundingly stating the case for the literary artist, as has been commonly supposed; he was rather proposing his own partial and necessarily limited view of art.

From the very beginning of his career, as his essay *The Art of Fiction* makes clear, James's urge to develop and polemicize a serious aesthetic of the novel also involved a special manipulation of the relationship between art and reality.[3] The novel, James insisted, had to do with life—"The only reason for the existence of a novel is that it does attempt to represent life"[4]—but this dependence of fiction on the reality it represented was implicitly qualified by the necessarily subjective nature of the process as James understood it. Not only did James describe the novel as "a personal, a direct impression of life,"[5] reality having thus shifted from something "out there" to its reflection in the mind of an observer; more tellingly, experience itself was defined by James as a conscious mental process, and such a definition inevitably reduced more immediate forms of engagement with reality to what could be perceived or apprehended about them. "Experience is," James wrote, "an immense sensibility, a kind of huge spider-web of the finest silken threads suspended in the chamber of consciousness, and catching every air-borne particle in its tissue. It is the very atmosphere of the mind."[6] This should prepare us for the more extreme formulations of the later prefaces. In these James discusses his subject-matter more emphatically in terms of its relationship to a subjective view of it—"What a man thinks and what he feels are the history and the

From *Modern Fiction Studies* 26 (1980). Copyright 1980, Purdue Research Foundation, West Lafayette, Indiana 47907. Reprinted with permission.

character of what he does"[7]—moreover, the novel as he describes the technical resources which have brought it into existence, becomes an opportunity for this kind of form-giving process.[8] For James, art is a subjective order imposed on reality as an object, not finally capable of penetrating or interpreting it, but only of understanding the process of its own relationship to reality.

It is worth remembering that, like James's, Wells's critical appraisal of the novel was pre-eminently a response to the trivializing of fiction as entertainment, the "Weary Giant Theory" which Wells saw as ruling Victorian attitudes.[9] Like James, he thought that the novel could lay claim to seriousness, a real intellectual eminence, because of the kind of connections it made with life. Unlike James, however, he did not consider that this relationship with life was something which the novel enacted through supplying a subjective order for objective reality, but thought that it was something which the novel had to strive to express or contain. Wells's *Autobiography,* written some years after his quarrel with James, contains the fullest account of his own dissenting philosophy of the novel. Here Wells, unlike James, described the novel not as wholly self-contained, becoming "a great and stately addendum to reality, a sort of super-reality with created persons in it," but rather as a fiction, "necessarily fictitious through and through," referring to and commenting upon the reality of which it is a part.[10] Wells conceived of the novel as having a referential function, pointing us to the reality which exists outside it, rather than as substituting the subjective, abstract order of art for reality. His rejection of Jamesian aesthetics led to his rejection of the attitude to experience which that both implied and sprang from. For Wells, experience was not passive, subjective, or conscious, but involved the contradictory evidence of both the individual's apprehension and the concrete situation in which he is caught, and which remains forever inaccessible to his understanding—both the individual's self-image and his reality, which can never be interiorized, as a situated and determined object.

Wells saw the major change which had occurred between the nineteenth- and twentieth-century novel in terms which help to illuminate these ideas. For Wells, the nineteenth-century novel operated within a framework of social fixity and was thus able to concentrate on character as the embodiment of value and the motive force behind events; in the modern novel, however, "the frame has begun to get into the picture"; character can no longer be presented as the predominant interest but can only be fully apprehended along with the background or values which have formed him and against which he reacts.[11] What Wells means here can be better understood by referring to his earlier criticisms of naturalistic novels where he approaches the problem from the opposite point of view. As a reviewer in the 1890s, Wells often tended to find fault with this kind of novel because it provided only a documentary image of society, a view of the individual as primarily part of his context, and did not express the differences between his objective situation and his subjective response to it.

Gissing's character Rolfe in *The Whirlpool* is accordingly described by Wells as an "exponent character" who "reflects" but does not "react"; the character has acquiesced in and, therefore, become merely a part of the social reality of the novel.[12] In effect Wells is criticizing Gissing for a weakness analogous but contrary to that displayed by James's writing, that of suppressing the complex interaction between subject and object by treating character as a symptom of environment, reducing subject to object, just as James absorbed experience into subjective perception.

Wells can be seen, therefore, as formulating a view of the novel essentially opposed to that of James. Instead of seeing the novel as an agent of order which removes the complexities of existence to a different, aesthetic realm where they can be neutralized and solved, Wells's view is that the novel is an "ethical enquiry" which always returns us to the anxieties and problems of living themselves, to "matters of conduct."[13] Wells rejected the implicit subjectivity of James's novels and aesthetic—the posture of passivity before reality to which the only accommodation is through understanding—for a more engaged view of the novel which expressed the interaction between the individual and his social environment. However, the interest of Wells's ideas is not just that they suggest that he did have a more sophisticated, intellectual response to James than has commonly been realized, but also that they help us to understand his own novels. Wells, after all, did not just work out his ideas as a desultory response to James's insistent theorizing; they also reflect the interests and endeavors of his own novel-writing.

When Wells made his fullest attempt to become a novelist at the beginning of the century, turning from fantasy and romance to the realistic treatment of contemporary life, his efforts were directed, significantly, toward tracing the disparity between his characters' awareness and their lives as understood from the outside as a social and historical event. Wells describes the conflicting patterns of private desire and social necessity: his characters often live at a level of self-conception which the process of narrative then goes on to question or undermine. In *Love and Mr. Lewisham*, the first of these novels, written in 1900, this pattern is fairly simply defined: the identity as a scholar which Lewisham has built for himself in private is broken in upon by the outside world and eventually destroyed; Lewisham's accommodation to social reality means, in effect, the abandonment of his dream of himself for the very different roles that society has to offer. At the beginning of the novel, as Lewisham's attention wanders from his books and he looks out of his window on a bright spring day, it is easy to see that Wells's use of the imaginative potentialities of this image, his sense of relationship between self and world, is considerably altered from earlier Victorian counterparts. Dorothea in *Middlemarch*, by looking out of her window, transcends her own private sorrows, affirming, through the perceived connections between herself and life outside, a more satisfactory sense of identity and meaning. What Lewisham looks out upon, however, is conceived as a temptation and a threat; his sense of identity is significantly opposed to the world rather than finding its deepest fulfillment there.

This pattern, as I have outlined it in *Love and Mr. Lewisham,* is complicated by two qualifications, however. Firstly the ideal self which Lewisham constructs is an essentially impoverished conception, too rigid and abstract—significantly he devises a *schema* to order his life and study—sufficiently to embrace the potentialities of human feeling and experience; we may feel that Lewisham has gained more than he has lost when he eventually tears up the *schema* and settles into family life. Second, there is a suggestion within the novel that the intractability of society to the individual's creative efforts may be less important than the muted possibility of communal living which is thus preserved. Chaffery, justifying his own deceptions by exposing the larger ones in which everyone is involved, points out that society may be "a vast conspiracy of human beings to lie and humbug themselves and one another for the general Good" and that "lies are the mortar that bind the savage individual into the social masonry."[14] In other words society, or the obligations which society imposes, may be necessary to enable people to suppress their destructive individualism and live comfortably with others. These two considerations partially transform the sense of rigid opposition in the novel between self and society into something more problematic—their troubling and necessary dependence.[15]

The discovery that Lewisham makes in the course of the novel is that people are not totally responsible for their own lives; they cannot order their lives to satisfy their dreams, but they must accept that in part they are going to be molded by the possibilities of life they encounter.[16] In a later novel, *The History of Mr. Polly,* the protagonist, Mr. Polly, experiences a similar imbalance between his dream, the interior world of "picturesque and mellow things" developed by reading Boccaccio, Rabelais, and Shakespeare,[17] and the bleakly mundane actuality in which his life as a draper's apprentice immerses him. This central contradiction, however, does not dictate the direction of the narrative, as in *Love and Mr. Lewisham,* so that the primary effect is of dreams and aspirations being quietly circumscribed by the inevitable, simple encroachment of life. In *The History of Mr. Polly* the narrative itself, the range of possibilities which external action offers to the individual, is altered in order to satisfy the requirements of dream. Instead of the individual being eventually connected through the gradual erosion of the dream to the social reality which has surrounded and threatened his self-conception, the disjunction is healed by the author's distorting the inevitable progress of the narrative and displacing Mr. Polly from his real social milieu in Fishbourne to the pastoral Utopia of Potwell Inn. The deflation of Polly's inner disorder as indigestion at the beginning of the novel is just the kind of deflation that society has inflicted on Polly since childhood (it is analogous to the conversion to a physical disease of the "inner discomfort" suffered by his father through imagination); but just as indigestion is not a complaint originating solely in the individual but is caused by what he eats, so Polly's sense of dissatisfaction is not self-induced but a response to the quality of the external influences on his character. Clearly the remedy is not for the individual to change because the removal of conflict between individual and world in this way can only signify a deterioration on the individual's part; the real answer lies in an alteration in the condition of the world. The Potwell Inn section of *The History of Mr. Polly* functions in much the same way as the Utopian vision of Wells's sociological writings; as the projection of Polly's dream, his interior world made real, it challenges the nature of the world to which he had been forced to conform without really providing a way of bridging reality and dream except through the notion of escape. Fiction in *The History of Mr. Polly* has withdrawn from reality, become a deliberate fiction, the fashioning of an escape; and, although in this way the dream can be realized, the gap remains, in effect, just as great.

Tono-Bungay, published a year before *The History of Mr. Polly* in 1909, represents Wells's most serious attempt to confront this problem of the relationship between self-conception and lived reality, between the inner world of imagination and feeling and the outer world of social actuality. The autobiographical form of this novel, however, means that Wells's emphasis is slightly different; instead of taking the disparity between self and world as an initial premise and tracing the possibility of their reintegration through the modification of the one or the other, because the narrator, George Ponderevo, is attempting to tell the story of his own life, the duality that is felt to exist between the inner and outer view is transformed into an anxiety about the very nature of identity. Because the past does not lead to the present as its summation and fulfilment, George cannot write from a basis of inner certainty: bewilderment is a continuing state for him. "Here among my drawings and hammerings *now,* I still question unanswering problems" (p. 252).[18] In a decisive way he is cut off from the most necessary guarantee of identity—its continuity through time. Memory, for George, instead of offering a pattern—the concrete revelation of identity through past actions—can only provide evidence of the jumbled and incoherent nature of his life.

> Now I sit down to write my story and tell over again things in their order. I find for the first time how inconsecutive and irrational a thing the memory can be. One recalls acts and cannot recall motives; one recalls quite vividly moments that stand out inexplicably—things adrift, joining on to nothing, leading nowhere. (*TB,* p. 37)

The episodic nature of *Tono-Bungay,* revealed through George's various encounters with society, is clearly related to its major theme—a lack of belief in the progressive and interconnected development of character and action. Each episode is not merely acted out in the novel, however; it is also framed by George's generalizing commentary which sets his individual experiences in the context of his era. This commentary has been accorded special attention by David Lodge in an important essay about *Tono-Bungary* in *The Language of Fiction*. For Lodge, the commentary is the "chief character of the novel" and may be said to define its central motive since *Tono-Bungay* is not, as its form suggests, the fictional transcript of a life, but more importantly an analysis of the "Condition of England."[19] While it is undeniable that, as Lodge claims, George's commentary establishes a vivid picture of contemporary society, it does not merely serve this static function. Through it is also established an important narrative movement, a movement away from a sense of the individual as being uniquely responsible for his own life, to the idea of the larger social sphere which limits and conditions action. In this passage, for example, George clearly explains the relationship between place and person which the novel continually draws attention to, the way in which setting may be said to define person.

> London! I came up to it young and without advisers, rather priggish, rather dangerously open-minded and very open-eyed, and with something—it is I think the common gift of imaginative youth, and I claim it unblushingly— fine in me, finer than the world and seeking fine responses . . . But I did not realize all this when I came to London, did not perceive how the change of atmosphere began at once to warp and distribute my energies. (*TB*, pp. 123, 125)

Through his commentary George describes the social reality which has dictated the direction his life has taken; the importance of this is not just for the picture of contemporary society that it thus invokes, but the way it presents, in its substitution of the general for the particular, the individual being constrained and repressed by his social environment.

George cannot write about his life as a progress toward the present; his analyses, therefore, which deflect and divert the narrative sequence, imitate as well as describe the gradual imposition of society on the individual. For George, a sense of purpose or responsibility, the idea, indeed, of moral significance attaching to his actions, can only exist in the past; in looking back from the present his perspective has altered, as this passage illustrates, and he must accept with resignation the way he has been formed and controlled by things outside himself.

> I may be all wrong in this. It may be I should be a far more efficient man than I am if I had cut off all those divergent expenditures of energy, plugged up my curiosity about society with some currently acceptable rubbish or other, abandoned Ewart, evaded Marion instead of pursuing her, concentrated. But I don't believe it!
> However, I certainly believed it completely and was filled with remorse on that afternoon when I sat dejectedly in Kensington Gardens and reviewed,

in the light of the Registrar's pertinent questions, my first two years in London. (*TB*, pp. 152–153)

Wells's insight that there were two possible, contradictory interpretations of human life which, from their different perspectives support the notion of the efficacy of individual effort and the idea of deterministic laws governing human life, is built into the structure of *Tono-Bungay*.[20] The retrospective narrative method, which envelops past action in a present commentary, also balances, in continual counterpoise, the notion of individual freedom against the determining forces of modern society.

George begins his account, therefore, not only by tracing his emergence from childhood, a growing personal awareness, but also by describing his changing relationship with his social environment. George is exiled from the country house, Bladesover, and, as in the nineteenth-century *bildungsroman*, this transportation in space also represents, in metaphorical fashion, a significant stage in the protagonist's spiritual journey. In *Tono-Bungay*, however, this spatial dimension cannot be totally reduced to a human equivalent in this way; it has an intrinsic importance of its own. George diagnoses the qualities that he possesses that make him able to free himself from Bladesover.

> It is a little difficult to explain why I did not come to do what was the natural thing for any one in my circumstances to do, and take my world for granted. A certain innate scepticism, I think, explains it—and a certain inaptitude for sympathetic assimilation. (*TB*, pp. 23–24).

It is also true, moreover, that society is in a state of change, that the "ostensible order" is in the process of passing away and cannot offer to the individual a firm sense of public obligation and status. "The hand of change rests on it all, unfelt, unseen; resting for awhile, as it were half reluctantly, before it grips and ends the thing for ever" (*TB*, pp. 11–12). George is able to free himself from a moribund class system not just because of his own precocious individuality but because of its weakened and decaying state.

This important conjunction of intuited personal experience and social change is repeated in the next episode of George's life which enacts a freeing of himself not this time from class values but from religious ones. His cousins' religion is rejected by George because it allows for no personal assertion or creation of value; rather, their religion enjoins the total submission of the self to God's will. They were people, according to George, who

> solaced their minds on the thought that all that was fair and free in life, all that struggled, all that planned and made, all pride and beauty and honour, all fine and enjoyable things, were irrevocably damned to everlasting torments. (*TB*, p. 50)

This belief is, of course, in complete contradiction to George's growing sense of value of the self. George's confidence as a young man, his developing reliance on his own powers of understanding, is not a simple positive; for one thing, his skepticism derives from a general context of dissolution; for another, his freeing of himself from the restraining dogmas of his youth cannot lead him objectively into a new state but only back to the old where he no longer has a place and feels "the finality of my banishment" (*TB*, p. 61). In maturity George reflects that for all his youthful purposefulness, for all his energy in breaching existing rules, he has ultimately been formed by an equally oppressive, if more chaotic, world.

> I thought I was presently to go out into a larger and quite important world and do significant things there. I thought I was destined to do something definite to a world that had a definite purpose. I did not understand then, as I do now, that life was to consist largely in the world's doing things to me. (*TB*, p. 88)

The principal vehicle for this theme of how impossible it is for the individual to liberate himself from a social reality which penetrates his motives, as well as standing in stubborn resistance to his needs, is not George Ponderevo, however, but his energetic and optimistic uncle, Edward. For Edward, the importance of the individual will is paramount; he earnestly desires to free himself from all external ties and make his life solely dependent on his own unique powers. Consequently he chafes at the constraints of his middle-class, provincial environment, feeling a desire to "live," to experience life in a grander and more emphatic way than is possible in Wimblehurst (*TB*, p. 67). When he moves to London, therefore, to what is an aimless environment seemingly providing few checks on behavior and action, he is able to live out his most extravagant dreams. It is less how he achieves success than success itself which is important to Ponderevo, the assertion of the ego rather than the proof of a particular ability. He is attracted by "this Overman idea, Nietzsche—all that stuff' (*TB*, p. 331) and the example of Napoleon, by what is a Romantic conception of the self straining beyond itself to create itself anew.

> He mingled those comforting suggestions of a potent and exceptional human being emancipated from the pettier limitations of integrity with the Napoleonic legend. (*TB*, p. 331)

That his success is founded on a quack medicine, that it has no real basis, is part of its significance; it emphasizes his total reliance on self—on ambition rather than its object—as a source of value.

Tono-Bungay has no intrinsic beneficial qualities. It cannot fulfill the claims of its inventor to restore vitality and alleviate fatigue and boredom. In this sense, therefore, it provides an appropriate image for the nothingness underlying Ponderevo's achievements. But, in another sense, the particular desires and needs it appeals to are also significant—its success depends upon a powerful general urge to create identity through the intensification of individual experience. Ewart, who functions as a detached observer for much of the novel and who is able to offer a lucid and penetrating exposé of the real motive forces of society, identifies the relevance of Tono-Bungay to the contemporary condition:

> The real trouble of life, Ponderevo, isn't that we exist—that's a vulgar error; the real trouble is that we *don't* really exist and we want to. That's what this—in the highest sense—muck stands for! The hunger to be—for once—really alive—to the fingertips! (*TB,* p. 193)

Ponderevo, in his search for a more intense and fulfilling way of life, invents a supposed cure for this same disease of unsatisfied longing from which he also suffers.

It is in this, indeed, that the central irony of Ponderevo's career resides; in his urge to prove his unique individuality he demonstrates, on the contrary, his ability to corroborate and appeal to the unformed desires of others. Instead of projecting himself above and beyond his society, he reveals an aptitude for blending with his environment.

> But much more was it a curious persuasion he had the knack of inspiring—a persuasion not so much of integrity and capacity as of the reciprocal and yielding foolishness of the world. One felt that he was silly and wild, but in some way silly and wild after the fashion of the universe. (*TB,* p. 168)

George eventually sees his uncle not as a highly individualistic adventurer but as a spectacular image of contemporary life, his desire to accumulate wealth no more than reflecting the selfishness and materialism of his age.

> What a strange, melancholy emptiness of intention that stricken enterprise seemed in the even evening sunlight, what vulgar magnificence and crudity and utter absurdity! . . . It struck me suddenly as the compactest image and sample of all that passes for Progress, of all the advertisement-inflated spending, the aimless building up and pulling down, the enterprise and promise of my age. This was our fruit, this was what we had done, I and my uncle, in the fashion of our time. We were its leaders and exponents, we were the thing it most flourishingly produced. (*TB,* pp. 437–438)

Not only is Ponderevo a product of his society, but his ambitions being essentially those derived from his age, his endeavors also depend on society in the sense that he needs its collaboration in order to succeed; the withdrawal of public support inevitably brings about the destruction of Ponderevo's financial empire. Ponderevo firmly embodies the whole paradox of egoistic striving; his urge to project himself beyond his society is not just futile in the sense that it is impossible to achieve, but it must also inevitably collapse back into the emptiness from which it springs.

Although George's is a much more moderate effort to find meaning in the creative efforts of the individual, it inevitably involves a similar ambiguity, the desires of the self and the claims of society frequently coming into conflict. George continually feels that contradictory pressures operate on him; he must both sustain himself against the forces that threaten him, the "great new forces" of the industrial city (*TB,* p. 121), and adjust to what objectively exists. He is both a subject that wills and an object which is controlled and restricted by his environment. These contradictions are located in the following passage where George, using the interesting juxtaposition of verbs, "thrust" and "fit," seems drawn between breaking through constraints and adjusting to their mold.

> Such was the world into which I had come, into which I had in some way to thrust myself and fit my problem, my temptations, my efforts, my patriotic instinct, and all my moral instincts, my physical appetites, my dreams and my vanity. (*TB,* p. 123)

George describes a world in which things seem to have gained mastery over man as subject and transformed him as well into an object. His memorable evocations of London, frequently expressed through lists of unconnected elements—seemingly defeating the observer's attempts to relate them to each other or to himself—suggest an encircling chaos, suffocating and subordinating the passive human perceiver at its midst, imposing its own being on him so successfully that he feels that he is invisible (*TB,* p. 125). George, of course, necessarily struggles against this, trying to preserve the illusion that he is personally in control of what is happening to him, even though he is really being driven by forces he cannot understand or control.

This ambivalence, the presentation of experience as both humanly willed and externally determined, is well illustrated in the incident of George's attempt to fly. Whereas George dwells on his own daring efforts, he is finally dependent on natural laws which exist independently of him. In this passage, George records his gradual achievement of self-control, an achievement which contrasts strikingly with the act of flight itself which requires self-abandonment, a leap into the unknown.

> It is curious that I remember that shame and self-accusation and its consequences far more distinctly than I recall the weeks of vacillation before I soared. For a time I went together without alcohol, I stopped smoking altogether and ate very sparingly, and every day I did something that called a little upon my nerves and muscles . . . If I didn't altogether get rid of a certain

giddy instinct by such exercises, at least I trained my will until it didn't matter. (*TB,* pp. 350–351)

Of course, the image of flight is also a suggestive one in terms of the narrative pattern of Ponderevo's career and is clearly used as such in the episode of the escape across the channel by balloon, before Ponderevo's final defeat and death. Ponderevo, as he thinks, propels himself into the giddy spheres of success; his business venture really means, however, surrendering to market forces, the whims of the buying public, things which he cannot control, and which, in due course, bring him crashing down.

These contradictions also pervade George's private life. His inability to control the outcome of his affair with Beatrice is focused in an incident which, like George's flying, juxtaposes the illusion of individual creativity against the reality of the external forces which direct his life. George plays Beethoven's *Kreutzer Sonata* on the pianola to Beatrice; he pretends to play an instrument which is in fact playing itself. The Romantic notion of self-expression which Beethoven seems to suggest is sharply at variance here with the realities of George's age and the mechanical process which requires the human only as an operator, its instrument.

In these incidents it is not only the superior vision of the mature George which highlights the contradictions; the incidents themselves are made to contain them. This is also true of Wells's treatment of science in the novel. Increasingly towards the end of the novel, in the wreck of all his plans and hopes, George turns to science as a goal; he sees in scientific truth the only fixed and certain principle that can exist in the surrounding atmosphere of decay and change. "I idealized Science. I decided that in power and knowledge lay the salvation of my life, the secret that would fill my need" (*TB,* p. 280). Later he claims that by doing scientific research the individual is liberated from the anxiety and futility of modern life.

> It is a different thing from any other sort of human effort. You are free from the exasperating conflict with your fellow-creatures altogether—at least so far as the essential work goes—that for me is its peculiar merit. Scientific truth is the remotest of mistresses, she hides in strange places, she is attained by tortuous and laborious roads, but *she is always there!* Win to her and she will not fail you; she is yours and mankind's for ever. She is reality, the one reality I have found in this strange disorder of existence. (*TB,* p. 346)

George has here effected a curious reversal of the relationship between truth and existence, a reversal which is also instanced in his language, the personalizing of science as it assumes, in George's scheme of things, the place of human relationships. Instead of truth being a reflection of a human situation, arising naturally out of a condition of being, truth is opposed to life; it has no relevance to human existence. At the end of the novel the destroyer, which is what, in concrete terms, George's scientific research has brought into being—it is the inner impulse given form—is described as "irrelevant to most human interests." It is a human achievement which is yet "the most inhuman of all existing things" (TB, p. 491). Instead of being controlled and directed by George, X2 is like "a black hound going through reeds—on what trail even I who made her cannot tell" (TB, p. 487). In the failure to reconcile self and social role, the intimacies of individual living and the formulations and patterns of society, George turns with relief to truth as an object rather than as a system of relationships; paradoxically, however, by doing so, he more fully embraces the condition he has sought to avoid—he objectifies himself, he accepts his own "dehumanization."[21] "I have come to see myself from the outside, my country from the outside—without illusions," he writes (TB, p. 493). He can only see himself without illusions by refusing to admit of the gap between individuality and society which the rest of the novel has so convincingly demonstrated, by suppressing the personal intricacies from which the illusions sprang. At the end of the novel, therefore, we withdraw to a perspective above George. Throughout most of the novel he exposes the effects of a modern society which traps and diverts the individual's efforts to find fulfillment; at the end of the novel, despite his own claims to have found a solution in this way, George has finally surrendered himself; he has discounted the importance of his own dreams and plans for living in favor of an abstract concept of science which has no other justification than its own inner necessity.

The pessimism which has been implicit throughout the novel culminates in George's rejection of his writing as empty and irrelevant. "All this writing is gray now and dead and trite and unmeaning to me" (TB, p. 482). For George it is redolent of the failure of living it records. The situation, indeed, as he has presented it allows for no solution and no change. This is the final discovery of the process of writing and the lucidity of his point of view as writer which sees beyond the individual endeavor to its eventual futility within the scheme of society, in a decisive way, therefore, cutting off the possibility of a hopeful vision of the future. George ends the novel with the words, "We are all things that make and pass, striving upon a hidden mission, out to the open sea" (TB, p. 493). George has become one of many, a part of the society which he sees objectively as wasteful and empty. In attempting to possess the past and tell his story, George relives the process by which society takes over the individual's purposes and energies and makes them its own.

In a sense it is important to recognize that both James and Wells attest in their novels to the same historical moment; they both write out of an experience of acute imbalance between the inner world of the individual and the narrow and incompatible forms of society. At a novelistic level this means that the original desires of their protagonists cannot find an objective satisfaction in the outer world, that these two realms are never reconciled. Whereas James turned to art to find a solution to the problem—indeed, in that he defined his art as the subjective contemplation of an objective reality from which it is, therefore, always separate, his novels vindicate and support the experience of duality—Wells attempts to locate the problem in a social and historical context. For Wells the fixing into a pattern, the determination of experience, is effected by history, not by art. In *Tono-Bungay,* by contrasting present and past, he attempts to show this process at work, the movement of history towards its own fulfillment of meaning. For Wells, therefore, while art could reflect a historical condition, it could not offer an alternative solution of its own without, as in *The History of Mr. Polly,* a radical distortion of the realistic function. It should not surprise us, therefore, that, while James could overcome the pessimistic implications of his vision by emphasizing with increasingly solipsistic subtlety the formal possiblities of art, Wells turned away from the novel to prophecy and sociology, to visions of a future in which society has been transformed into an adequate home for the self.

Notes

1. Introduction to *Henry James and H. G. Wells,* ed. Leon Edel and Gordon Ray (London: Rupert Hart-Davis, 1958), 39.

2. James's letter, dated 10 July 1915, is quoted in *Henry James and H. G. Wells,* 267.

3. For an interesting discussion of the origins and significance of this essay see Mark Spilka, "Henry James and Walter Besant: 'The Art of Fiction' Controversy," *Novel* 6 (1973): 101–19.

4. "The Art of Fiction," in *The House of Fiction,* ed. Leon Edel (London: Rupert Hart-Davis, 1957), 25.

5. Ibid., 29.

6. Ibid., 31.

7. Preface to *The Princess Casamassima,* in *The Art of the Novel,* ed. Richard P. Blackmur (London: Charles Scribner's Sons, 1935), 66.

8. For a discussion of this point see Leo Bersani, "The Jamesian Lie," *Partisan Review* 36 (1969): 53–79.

9. "The Contemporary Novel," in *An Englishman Looks at the World,* (London: Cassell, 1914), 149.

10. *Experiment in Autobiography* (London: Victor Gollancz and Cresset Press, 1934), 2:494, 493.

11. Ibid., 494–95.

12. "The Novels of Mr. George Gissing," *Contemporary Review* 72 (1897): 192–201.

13. *Experiment in Autobiography,* 2:488, and "The Contemporary Novel," 2:168.

14. H. G. Wells, *Love and Mr. Lewisham* (London: Harper and Brothers, 1900), 205.

15. This echoes T. H. Huxley's argument that "animal man" exists in complete opposition to "ethical man" and that society depends upon modifying and containing individual action according to its own moral laws. See Huxley's essay "The Struggle for Existence in Human Society," in *Collected Essays* (London: Macmillan, 1894–95), 9:211.

16. *Love and Mr. Lewisham,* 72.

17. *The History of Mr. Polly,* (London: Thomas Nelson, 1910), 66.

18. *Tono-Bungay* (London: Macmillan, 1909). All further references are to this, the first edition, and are cited in the text as *TB* with page references.

19. David Lodge, "*Tono-Bungay* and 'The Condition of England,' " in *The Language of Fiction* (London: Routledge & Kegan Paul, 1966), 219.

20. The clearest expression of this idea by Wells occurs in *Anticipations* (London: Chapman & Hall, 1902), 285.

21. Bernard Bergonzi is surely right to connect George's ideas about science here with modernistic theories about art; both accept the same goal of "dehumanization." See "*Tono-Bungay*" in *The Turn of a Century* (London: Macmillan, 1973), 90.

The Mood of *A Modern Utopia*

DAVID Y. HUGHES

H. G. Wells's distinctive manner of predication in *A Modern Utopia* takes the subjunctive mood. "Suppose that we were indeed . . . translated even as we stood,"[1] says a Voice in a lecture hall; whereupon the realm of utopia and its adventures depend throughout upon what the Owner of the Voice insistently "supposes" that he and his companion, the botanist, "would" see, feel, say, and do in that imaginary world. So far as I know, the experiment is unique. There is no doubt that Wells carries it off fluently, skilfully, but it is surprising to see the conventions of utopian realism deliberately flouted. Why did Wells experiment in this direction? What aim does the method serve? Van Wyck Brooks thought *A Modern Utopia* "a beautiful utopia, beautifully seen and beautifully thought," and found it "artistic in method and diagnostic in aim."[2] So far as the imaginative narrative goes, I agree, and I would add "therapeutic in effect."

An appropriate critical approach to *A Modern Utopia* will take account of author-intention and reader-response. William Bellamy refers to "the central Edwardian fiction [of Wells, Bennett, and Galsworthy] as an art characterized by its overt interest in therapy—not simply therapy in the shape of social reform, but . . . [therapy as] direct remedial action undertaken on behalf of the self."[3] This judgment is aimed at somewhat later works, such as *Tono-Bungay* and *The History of Mr. Polly*, but applies to *A Modern Utopia*, whose art, surely, is concerned with therapy, both outwardly as social reform and inwardly as psychic self-mastery; and, as Bellamy implies, of the two, the psychological concern is the "direct," controlling one, and social reform, if it followed, would simply accrue to such a transformative state of mind.

In this context, a subjunctive quotation of some length may serve to get in touch with Wells's psychological intent. At the point in question, the Owner of the Voice and the botanist have been translated without their knowledge into utopia, a world geophysically the double of our own—even to its sister, the moon—but located "out beyond Sirius." Only the utopian social body, made up of the utopian double of everyone on earth, is visibly different from our own social body and our own social environs. And since the "turn about" to utopia befalls the two travellers as they are still very high

Reprinted from *Extrapolation*, December 1977, by permission of the editor.

up returning from an Alpine walk, at first they have no clue to the incredible enlargement that has been thrust upon them. Thus, descending unawares:

> Before nightfall we should be drenched in wonders, but still we should have wonder left for the thing my companion, with his scientific training, would no doubt be the first to see. He would glance up, with that proprietary eye of the man who knows his constellations down to the little Greek letters. I imagine his exclamation. He would at first doubt his eyes. I should inquire the cause of his consternation, and it would be hard to explain. He would ask me with a certain singularity of manner for "Orion," and I should not find him; for the Great Bear, and it would have vanished. "Where?" I should ask, and "where?" seeking among that scattered starriness, and slowly I should acquire the wonder that possessed him.
>
> Then, for the first time perhaps, we should realise from this unfamiliar heaven that not the world had changed, but ourselves—that we had come into the uttermost deeps of space. (p. 16)

In this passage, typically enough, the subjunctive both invites the reader to an act of participatory imagination, wonder, reconstruction, and at the same time alerts his critical faculties because subjunctives question what they seem to state. That is, the process of reading implicates one in the process of discovery.

Since form in *A Modern Utopia* is only a means to larger psychological or social ends, a purely formal-aesthetic analysis would be misplaced. Yet that approach—in this case by an often illuminating critic of utopias, Robert Elliott—does bring out the principles of Wells by assuming their opposite. After acknowledging *A Modern Utopia* to be "a bold, and in many ways an effective, conception," Elliott states that Wells "allowed the narrative sections of the work to be hampered by a clumsy entanglement with the subjunctive mood," perhaps because of a failure of nerve, "as though he were not willing to commit himself completely to the fictional reality of Utopia— as though Utopia were a hypothesis rather than a place."[4] But Wells did not write "Utopia," he wrote a utopia, which is the same kind of difference as between a Platonic Idea and an idea. "Utopia," in the sense Elliott uses it, would be for Wells a negative term—Nowhere—which, with others, such as the Absolute, the Infinite, he would "describe as being off the stage or out of court, or as the Void without Implications" (pp. 385–86).

In a sense, Elliott is right. Wells's notion of a utopia more nearly approaches to a hypothesis awaiting testing than to a "place" (i.e., No-place). Wells elsewhere said: "the creation of Utopias—and their exhaustive criticism—is the proper and distinctive method of sociology."[5] He was arguing that sociology should acknowledge itself to be less a science than an art, because statistics are delusory and "all real objective being [is] individual and unique." This idea of the uniqueness of all things from atoms to ethics was a favorite notion of Wells's, about which more later. Applying it to the problem of utopias, it has at least three obvious implications. A utopia is an individual vision properly addressed to readers as individuals in the hope of persuading them to the same vision, or to the same methods of vision, or at any rate to retort in kind with their own utopias. A utopia ought to be a vision that includes the individuals of utopia because the individuals of innovative character will be its makers and leaders, and the impossibility of success in this area is a weakness of the genre. But if enough utopias were written by enough individuals, the individuality of the utopias themselves would, in a sense, people the progress of the world toward a perfecting of utopia in reality and in this "place."

On the other hand, Wells's very insistence on the importance of the individual—as author, as reader, as projected citizen of utopia—throws him back onto a non-sociological aim in the end, so that the "place" of his utopia finally lies in "what it does"—in its enlarging and yet critical cognitive thrust for the reader—and not as such in the social blueprint it offers.

The trouble with the blueprint is "a certain effect of hardness and thinness about Utopian speculations" (p. 9) as Wells conceived of them. Since nothing less than a World State could satisfy him for size, the State is the main character, the citizens are "no individualities, but only generalised people" (p. 9), and the State, from the point of view of the reader's individuality, appears monolithic. At the very beginning of his career (1891), Wells wrote two essays, "The Rediscovery of the Unique" and "The Universe Rigid," which set forth already the two extremes of his world view: free will and determinism. On the one hand, extrapolating from Darwinian biology, he affirmed the primacy of the unique (because evolution is the accumulation of individual variations), and then generalized uniqueness in the world, down to the level of atoms and up to the level of morality and aesthetics. A revised version of this essay forms the "Appendix" to A Modern Utopia, "The Scepticism of the Instrument." On the other hand, extrapolating from physics, if "one began with a uniformly distributed ether in . . . infinite space . . . and then displaced a particle . . . the character of the consequent world would depend entirely, I argued along strictly materialist lines, upon the velocity of this initial displacement."[6] Despite Wells's hopes and intentions, the World State, from the reader's eye view, looks "rigid." The sociology is totalitarian. (The sense of the "unique," strong as it is, issues almost exclusively from the elaborate framing narrative, to which I return later).

The World State is a macro-biological metaphor of formidable sweep. In the metaphor, the life of the earth, the whole "tangled bank" of Darwin developing through the ages—the evolutionary process—is seen as an undying organism perpetuating and improving itself by means of all the past and present variety of its individual, innovating life forms; and, by analogy, the World State is seen as an undying organism perpetuating and improving itself by means of the innovations of single, prepotent individuals. The first organism is unconscious, the second is conscious. Swapping terms freely,

Wells manages to force the hopeful conclusion that both organisms exist, really, "for" their individuals.

> Biologically the species is the accumulation of the experiments of all its successful individuals since the beginning, and the World State of the Modern Utopist will, in its economic aspect, be a compendium of established economic experience, about which individual enterprise will be continually experimenting, either to fail and pass, or to succeed and at last become incorporated with the undying organism of the World State. This organism is the universal rule, the common restriction, the rising level platform on which individualities stand. . . . The energy developed and the employment afforded by the State will descend like water that the sun has sucked out of the sea to fall upon a mountain range, and back to the sea again it will come at last. . . . Between the clouds and the sea it will run, as a river system runs, down through a great region of individual enterprise and interplay, whose freedom it will sustain. In that intermediate region between the kindred heights and deeps those beginnings and promises will arise that are the essential significance, the essential substance, of life. From our human point of view the mountains and the sea are for the habitable lands that lie between. So likewise . . . the State is for Individuals, the law is for freedoms, the world is for experiment, experience, and change: these are the fundamental beliefs upon which a modern Utopia must go. (pp. 89–91)

Thus, all of nature and all of human nature exist "for" individuality and free enterprise (like an ad for General Electric). But since, as a trained biologist and a strong admirer of T. H. Huxley, Wells really knew that the sole apparent "purpose" of the evolutionary process—purpose or behavior—is self-perpetuation, it inevitably turns out that the World State he builds upon the evolutionary metaphor behaves (all his disclaimers notwithstanding) as if it existed not for individualities but for and in itself.

The logic of the metaphor as it unfolds is "rigid" indeed. The well-being of the "undying organism" requires a strong directive will. There is the disciplined class of the Samurai, modelled directly on Plato's Guardians, which holds all real power. The organism requires a nerve center and memory bank. The vital statistics of each of the one and a half billion people are maintained in a colossal card-index in Paris, classified by thumb-print, so that the State has "organised clairvoyance" (p. 165). The organism requires nerves and muscles. "The old Utopias are sessile organisations; the new . . . [has] a migratory population . . . a people as fluid and tidal as the sea" (p. 162). The organism requires a circulatory system. That goes back to sea-cloud stream: money "is the water of the body social" (p. 73) and the utopians are learning to reduce the monetary standard to units of physical energy because economic production and distribution is "a problem in the conversion of energy" (p. 78). The organism requires body parts and functions. Four classes of people are recognized in utopia, corresponding well to an organic hierarchy: the Poietic, the Kinetic, the Dull, the Base. Above all, the organism needs to maintain, renew, and improve itself. Marriage, mother-hood, hygiene, child-rearing, and elimination of inferior human stock are matters of the most particular interest and extensive state control in utopia. Furthermore, design, technology, "the ways and means of the modern men," assure the ordered, cerebralized progress of man forward through all the hinterland of time down to "the Night of this World—the time when our sun will be dull, and air and water will lie frozen together" (p. 307).

In *A Modern Utopia,* Wells completed a long, gradual reversal of view without, however, abandoning a basic metaphor (which I have elsewhere called "the garden").[7] He had once regarded man as an experiment made by nature. In *The Time Machine,* the bio-system of the Thames Valley—a river system again—is perpetuating itself in the year 802,701 while incidentally accommodating the symbiotic cannibalism of the races of man, Morlocks and Eloi. In *The Island of Dr. Moreau,* evolution is personified by the mad doctor and his plastic creation. But Moreau, besides representing nature and/or God, represents science emulating nature. This signals the beginning of Wells's coming reversal whereby in *A Modern Utopia* nature becomes passive under the guidance of man for as long as the sun burns. Next, in *The War of the Worlds,* the Thames Valley (once again) stirs, as it were in its sleep, under the "poisoned dart" of the invading Martians—practically mere brains—who, before their deaths, nearly master the earth (i.e., cerebralize it, uto-pianize it). Then, in *The First Men in the Moon,* through the narrator, Cavor, Wells assumes an air of naive, "scientific" detachment in reporting the "natu-ral history" of the Selenite formicary, where every citizen is a "perfect unit in a world machine."[8] Finally, in *A Modern Utopia,* in the garden where nature made man, man has become the gardener of the garden of himself and the world. But from Eloi to Samurai, the individuals remain barely differenti-ated: "Ever and again," says the Owner of the Voice, "come glimpses of . . . the scheme of a synthetic wider being, the great State, mankind, in which we all move and go, like blood corpuscles, like nerve cells, it may be at times like brain cells, in the body of a man" (p. 372).

All this and the Third Reich, Oceania, and Watergate, too? We need either less sociology or a better one.

Even so, the fiction *A Modern Utopia* redeems Wells's "rigid" sociology. In the framing narrative, reinforcing the use of the subjunctive, Wells em-ploys an ingenious structure of infinite regress, the effect of which is to open to the reader an enlarging sense of the relativity of himself and of the world through time, tempered by an opposite sense of their intractability.

The outer frame of front and back matter comprises a signed "Note to the Reader" and a philosophical "Appendix" by "H. G. Wells"; the book then begins and ends with several pages of italic print said to be by "the ostensible author," also called the chairman; the latter explains that the body of the work, part narrative, part lecture, should be conceived of as spoken by

the Owner of the Voice; in turn, his narrative contains intermittent squabbling with the botanist, who "gets no personal expression in this book"
because the Owner of the Voice delivers both sides of the dialogue; and at the
end of the chain is the ultimate receiver, the reader, whom the Owner of the
Voice directly addresses whenever he ceases from portraying himself and the
botanist.

This regress of script and dramatis personae is reinforced by a regress of
scene: "the image of a cinematograph entertainment is the one to grasp." The
residual scene is a public hall or theater, where the chairman introduces the
Owner of the Voice. Seated at a table on the stage, the latter addresses the
hall at large, at times lecturing with the lights up about what "would be" in
utopia and about the trends on earth that point that way, and at other times
becoming a mere Voice in the dark in accompaniment to a film. What film?
The projector is faulty but occasionally shows "a momentary moving picture
of Utopian conditions." Somehow an actual image of utopia fitfully material-
izes on the screen in the hall. And by means of the screen and an effort of
imagination, "you" (reader) "will go with him through various and interesting experiences," beginning when he and the botanist are walking in the
mountains and "behold! in the twinkling of an eye" the mountains are those
of "that other world" (p. 14).

To see that such a frame shapes A Modern Utopia into a doubly imaginary
"imaginary voyage" or, as Wells says, into "a mere story of personal adventures among Utopian philosophies" (p. 372), is to recognize Wells's synoptic
intent of synthesizing earlier utopias (of whom he had studied many), but at
the same time it may be to neglect his intent to implicate the reader. One
might well argue, however, that Wells's use of a series of *gradations* from "H.
G. Wells" through various personae to the reader, and from the reader's
armchair through various imaginary agencies to the "Alps" of utopia, is both
a way of establishing that utopia is not a place but a mode of thinking and a
way of placing that mental habit into the fabric of the reader's world.

Turning briefly again to Wells's "rigid" sociology, the notion of gradation here, too, guides his conceptions. The utopia he imagines is not perfect
or even the best possible (that utopia is *Men Like Gods*) but it is "better," a
better double of our world. As such, it is still actively evolving, and its
conscious evolutionary intent is reflected in its stepwise classification of the
Base, the Dull, the Kinetic, and the Poietic Personalities, the first two of
which "the ways and means of the modern men" are gradually diminishing
("island monasteries and island nunneries" [p. 144] are mentioned). Meanwhile, personal upward striving is encouraged. A class that anyone may
aspire to is the ruling class, the Samurai—"voluntary nobility"—to which
anyone willing and able to carry out the strenuous discipline of the order may
belong. Even in utopia, potentialities are partly unfulfilled and "the Thing in
Being" (pp. 366–67) claims its due; yet mankind progresses and the individual may if he will.

As a political system, such a set of hierarchies as this would impose unacceptable physical and moral compulsion, but viewed as a ladder of personal commitment and activist self-discipline it has its appeal. In this latter light it appears in the Owner of the Voice, struggling with himself, as he does, both to overcome those tender-minded egoisms that blind the botanist, and to achieve the tough-minded altruism of his own utopian double, a member of the Samurai. Indeed, if one identifies with the Owner of the Voice, one may even discern, as a possibility, a sort of personal Jacob's ladder from the base and terrestrial to the poietic and utopian, though it is a possibility which in the end of the book recedes to a mere ideal hope.

The story of *A Modern Utopia* is autobiographical in its concerns in the period it was written (1905), and the Owner of the Voice, his utopian double, and the botanist are three versions of Wells. The Owner of the Voice is the public figure, "plump," "a little under the middle size and age," bearing himself "as valiantly as a sparrow," and speaking in "an unattractive tenor that becomes at times aggressive" (pp. 1–2). One pictures Wells addressing the Fabian Society. By the time of *A Modern Utopia,* he had already raided deeply into sociology. Patrick Parrinder points out that his first major effort in the field, *Anticipations* (1901), "caused an intellectual sensation," and William Archer, the noted journalist, had even suggested his prophesying be endowed at public expense.[9] Coming before the great British public as a freelance thinker belonging to no regular profession or established class, Wells cut across compartmentalized interests and his appeal appeared broadly capable of shaping the future which he meant it to serve. To Wells himself, indeed, it must have seemed a possible thing to achieve the stature of his utopian double. Proleptically, this was already Wells the interlocutor recording dialogues with Theodore and Franklin Roosevelt, Lenin and Stalin.[10]

On the other hand, Wells also saw himself in the botanist. The botanist is thirty-nine, about Wells's age, and bears the marks of a "rigid" scientific, emotional, and cultural conditioning. Science means to him classification: "he knows his constellations down to the little Greek letters" and "thinks and argues like drawing on squared paper" (p. 124). Emotion means to him a doglike attachment to an unreconstructed image of his early love, who jilted him: "the story of a Frognal heart" (p. 26). Culture means to him scientific professionalism. That Wells could not shake off the anxieties of similar early training and experience appears, for example, from a letter of 1904 to Frederick Macmillan: "My public is a peculiar one, and the electro-technical publications, scholastic papers . . . medical and nursing publications . . . truck up sections of it. The women don't read me."[11]

The women have a chapter to themselves in *A Modern Utopia,* reflecting awakened interest in the feminist cause. He combines economic equality with sexism. A woman is to have a state-supported career of Motherhood, her special sphere, where she will not be at a disadvantage because of "her incapacity for great stresses of exertion, her frequent liability to slight illnesses, her weaker initiative, her inferior invention and resourcefulness, her relative incapacity for organisation and combination, and the possibilities of emotional complications whenever she is in economic dependence on men" (p. 187). This reconstruction of the roles of the sexes the botanist's "Frognal heart" of course repudiates, passionately. As for Wells, it was another thirty years before he publicly dissected "the dead rabbit" of his former self and laid bare in relation to his first wife the anatomy of his motives and constraints, like a plot-outline: "hidden garden of desire," "primary fixation," "humiliation," "evasion" and "enterprising promiscuity," and, nevertheless, "irrational organic jealousy." In fact, he records that early in 1904, twelve years after he left her, when he learned of her remarriage, jealousies he thought he had buried overwhelmed him, he burned all her pictures, and in an earlier age "would have taken his axe of stone and set out to find and kill her."[12]

Through the muddled rhythms of his own sexuality projected upon the botanist, Wells poses the problem of revolt in utopia, the major problem of the twentieth century (especially sexual revolt), whether in dystopias such as *Brave New World* or utopias such as *Island*. But these are works of a novelistic realism, so that the utopia, the enveloping frame of the action, "heals" the protagonists. With Wells, the protagonists frame the utopia and everything that "would be" there. From this point of view, it comes as no surprise that, having travelled to London (via a 200 mile an hour train from the Alps and under the English Channel), the Owner of the voice delightedly interviews his utopian self, or that the botanist happens to encounter the double of his "Frognal love" on the arm of "that scoundrel" for whom she had jilted him. At sight of those two (the man is one of the Samurai), the botanist's sexual fixation overcomes him—"he waves an unteachable destructive arm" (p. 357—and utopia vanishes, "the bubble bursts."

But the narrative is not quite finished, and in the end one is left with a sense of return and renewal. Back they are in earthly London, with "no jerk, no sound, no hint of material shock," standing in "the grey and gawky waste of asphalte—Trafalgar Square" (p. 358). Here, partly because utopia is a recapitulatory genre and partly because Wells in this sequence slips into the present indicative, the transformation to "reality" strikes the Owner of the Voice (and the reader) with an effect of desolation, just as it had Bellamy's Julian West in his nightmare return to nineteenth-century Boston, and just as it would Skinner's Burris walking in squalid streets after leaving Walden Two. But the redemptive power of utopia reawakens West into the twenty-first century, and it returns Burris to Walden Two. The method of *A Modern Utopia* is different. Suddenly the italic print takes in again, and with it the city disappears—the Owner of the Voice is last seen whirling away on an omnibus still talking of utopia (like the Time Traveller disappearing on his machine)— and the scene is once again the theater where it all began. What lingers is a sense of potentiality. Which "London" is real? What self is real? Back in the theater, all are equally mental constructs; the utopia that is not, may be; and "for measured moments . . . the wider aspirations glow again with a sincere emotion, with the colours of attainable desire . . ." (pp. 373–74).

At the last, Wells explicitly waves away "clear resolves . . . lists of names, formation of committees, . . . commencement of subscriptions," instead ending "in dust and doubt, with, at the best, one individual's aspiration" (Wells means the Owner of the Voice). Yet *A Modern Utopia* was soon to be swept up into history, its merely literary aims overwhelmed. Wells himself, at first surprised and irritated by the disposition of younger readers to implement his ideas, underwent a change of heart in 1906, aided, it seems, by an American trip and the Liberal sweep in the General Election, and, ironically, by 1907 was attempting (futilely) to turn the Fabians into an order of the Samurai.[13] Thus, it turns out that Virginia Woolf's famous literary epitaph of 1924 for Wells, Bennett, and Galsworthy—("It seems necessary [after reading one of their books] to do something, to join a society, or . . . write a cheque. That done . . . it can be put upon a shelf, and need never be read again")[14]—had come to be true of the whole corpus of Wells only as he had been absorbed into the propagandist image he later made for himself.

H. W. Fowler glosses "Subjunctive" in part as follows: "*Were that true there were no more to say;* . . . [the] reference [here] is to present or to undefined time, or more truly not to time at all . . . but to utopia, the realm of non-fact." Were that true there were no more to say. But if "that" is not true but occupies a range of possibility, then there may well be much to say. That is the mood of *A Modern Utopia*.

Notes

1. H. G. Wells, *A Modern Utopia*, ed. Mark R. Hillegas (1905; reprint ed., Lincoln: University of Nebraska Press, Bison Books, 1967), 13; hereafter cited parenthetically in my text.

2. Van Wyck Brooks, *The World of H. G. Wells* (New York: Mitchell Kennerley, 1915), 73.

3. William Bellamy, *The Novels of Wells, Bennett and Galsworthy: 1890–1910* (New York: Barnes & Noble, 1971), 22.

4. Robert C. Elliott, *The Shape of Utopia: Studies in a Literary Genre* (Chicago: University of Chicago Press, 1970), 114–15.

5. The "The So-called Science of Sociology," in H. G. Wells, *An Englishman Looks at the World* (London: Cassell and Co., 1914), 204.

6. H. G. Wells, *Experiment in Autobiography: Discoveries and Conclusions of a Very Ordinary Brain (since 1866)* (New York: Macmillan, 1934), 172.

7. "The Garden in Wells's Early Science Fiction," in *H. G. Wells and Modern Science Fiction*, ed. Darko Suvin and Robert M. Philmus (Lewisburg, Pa.: Bucknell University Press, 1977).

8. H. G. Wells, *The Atlantic Edition of the Works of H. G. Wells*, 28 vols. (London: T. Fisher Unwin, 1924–26), 3:255; 6:237.

9. *H. G. Wells: The Critical Heritage*, ed. Patrick Parrinder (London: Routledge & Kegan Paul, 1972), 13.

10. Wells, *Experiment,* 646, 680, 687.
11. Parrinder, 2.
12. Wells, *Experiment,* 350–60.
13. Wells, *Experiment,* 563–64.
14. Quoted by Bellamy, 215.

[From "The Splintering Frame"]

William J. Scheick

Two Novels

. . . . *All Aboard for Ararat* (1941) (*AA*) is Wells's third [to] last fictional work, a dialogue novel without a strong plot. An escapee from a mental asylum who calls himself God instructs Noah Lammock to build an ark in preparation for a world-wide devastating deluge (World War II). Noah demurs, but after he delivers (while in a trance) a monologue to a vole, he begins to construct the ark, which apparently is the very text of the incomplete novel we are reading.

Although *Ararat* might seem less accomplished than the best of his fiction written during the Thirties, it displays several basic traits of Wells's mature artistry. Most appropriate, for example, is the designed incompleteness of its exterior structure, the frustration of any reader expectation of closure. The novel trails off with these final words about the protagonist: "His sentence remains unfinished. The final pages of this story do not appear to be forthcoming. They never may be. As there is so much current interest in it, it has been decided to print and publish the expanding narrative so far as it goes now. So that this is not so much the end as a colophon" (*AA*, 103; italics deleted). The non-conclusion of this novel makes the reader think about the origins of the book, in a sense returns the reader to the beginning of the story. Such a manner participates in a tradition deriving from Spanish picaresque works like *Don Quixote,* but Wells is discovering it for himself *vis-à-vis* the work of Sterne and Fielding.

The incomplete narrative of *Ararat,* we are told, is *expanding.* In this novel there is no clear starting or finishing point, only an endless round of intensified ebb and flow in an increasingly expanding sea of Noah's mental activity. "Nowhere was there any finality," thinks the protagonist of the novel, who later concludes: "This new-born religion, *this religion of the perpetually increasing and renascent truth,* carries with it an inner compulsion to live, or, if need be, die, as it dictates, directly its apprehension becomes com-

From William J. Scheick, *The Splintering Frame: The Later Fiction of H. G. Wells,* ELS Monograph Series No. 31 (Victoria: University of Victoria, 1984). This selection comprises the last two sections of the opening chapter. The omitted subsections are entitled "The Shape of a Literary Career," "The Fourth Dimension," and "Typological Characterization." Reprinted by permission of the author.

plete. . . . Enquiry replaces dogma. You grow" (*AA,* 10, 79). *You* speaks to the reader. The use of direct address by Noah and by the narrating anonymous editor of the text finally directs the reader beyond any disappointment with the novel's non-ending to a sense that he or she is to some extent responsible for furthering the story toward closure.

This pattern is reinforced by remarks in the account that draw attention to the reader reading and to the text as artifice. This pattern surfaces, for instance, when we are told that consideration of the "everlasting sequence of the Universe" is "like dealing with an interminable history in an interminable book. You may open the book anywhere; or close it anywhere. This history goes on in spite of you" (*AA,* 44). The narrative of *Ararat* expands whenever it transgresses its borders as an act of fiction, whenever it splinters its frame by swelling outwards to include the reader within the expanded margin of the text; for just as all of "expanding" history is like a book, so also each reader, as a life in that history, is textually enclosed in a work like *Ararat,* which retells a story from one of the oldest histories, the Bible. Moreover, the narrative of *Ararat* enlarges in the sense that this embracement of the reader, through the splintering frame of the novel, constitutes self-awareness in that reader, an enlargement of the reader's previous range of thought; his realization of personal responsibility is in fact the very mechanism of his inclusion. This reader who experiences the splintering frame of the expanding text, which is also his own expanding thought, will go from the unfinished end of *Ararat* to a reconsideration (as it were, a second reading) of the text of the novel (now transformed through character typology into the text of his or her self). The resultant enlarged insight from this reconsideration comprises one more new start in an interminable human mental evolution of such beginnings. This perception of individual relativity to the whole comprises, as well, the fourth dimension of the novel. Reader and text dialectically interact (as do, in Wells's ideology, the "essential complements" of spirit and matter, freedom and fate). In the process of interacting they mutually develop deeper meaning.

This pattern is reinforced by the novel's protagonist, Noah Lammock, a modern-day "evolved" version of the Old Testament Noah, son of Lamech. Facing World War II, which he consistently images as an inundation (*AA,* 26, 55, 102), Lammock contemplates human destiny. He concludes that mythical stories, historical events, and cardinal personality types in both these stories and events repeat themselves. Even the most elevated artistic vehicles for the transmission of these stories, events and types are repetitive. The "Bible is *the* fundamental book," Lammock observes, "*our* literature is just a footnote to it" (*AA,* 58). The Bible is, as *Ararat* demonstrates, an inexhaustible sourcebook for mythical, historical and personality types. In a "splintering-frame" remark God specifically cites *The Time Machine* and *The Work, Wealth and Hapiness of Mankind* (1932)—the span of Wells's Noah-like career—when he tells Lammock, "*You* have written every book with the idea of a world reconstruction in it for the last hundred years. You may not know it, but you have. Under various names. If you did not actually write it at the time, you absorbed it all. There are too many books now for us to talk about individual authors any more" (AA, 56–57). There is, in short, the type specimen.

There is also a series of variations. So this expression of the Noah-impulse, predominant in certain reappearing personalities like Wells and characteristic of the human collective self, is not static. History expands, as should the aesthetic dimension of each successive literary embodiment of scriptural patterns and the increasingly clarifying insight of each successive embodiment of fundamental personality types. God tells Noah, "History, Sir, has a way of repeating itself—with variations. Always with variations" (AA, 12). Later Lammock echoes this idea (AA, 30)—quite similar to Giovanni Vico's approach to history—eventually realizing that even the concept of God must evolve from the Old Testament notion, through the New Testament image, to the (essentially Romantic) belief that "revolution is the living God" (AA, 70). This belief, in conjunction with the concept of the infinite relativity of human perception, explains the meaning of the gnomic statement in the novel, that "the apprehension of Being is a three-dimensional consciousness system falling through a fourth dimension" (AA, 41). This remark summarizes the reader's ideal experience of "expansion" in the novel.

The "revolution [which] is the living God" refers to a circular repetition and a change, a recurrence with variation. Graphically this pattern may be depicted as a spiral, a three-dimensional locus moving through space around a fixed center at a monotonically increasing or decreasing distance from the center. This spiral pattern, which Wells employed in previous works, echoes Plato's use of the image in *The Republic* as a model of the universe. Principally it likely derives from Wells's familiarity with nineteenth-century astronomical interest in such patterns. A specific source might be Arthur S. Eddington's early twentieth-century treatments of the concept of an expanding universe (explicitly remarked in *Experiment in Autobiography* [EA], *Babes in the Darkling Wood* and *The Conquest of Time*) and of spiral forms in the universe. In *Stellar Movements and the Structure of the Universe* (1914) Eddington observes: "The form of the arms—a logarithmic spiral—has not as yet given any clue to the dynamics of spiral nebulae. But though we do not understand the cause, we see that there is a widespread law compelling matter to flow in these forms."[1] In the arts, a dialectic of spiral return informs much nineteenth-century Romantic poetry; and interest in this form as a symbol of primitive generation and of human progress—"a pattern of hope"—was expressed just prior to World War I and shortly thereafter by members of the Vorticist movement, including the poet Ezra Pound, the painter Wyndham Lewis, the sculptor Henri Gaudier-Brzeska, and the contributors to the short-lived journal *Blast,* which published T. S. Eliot's "Preludes."[2]

A spiral pattern comprises the emerging inner structure splintering the outer structure of *Ararat*. This spiral pattern, evoked through imagery and complementing the typological (repetitive yet evolving) manner of characterization, vies with the external structure; it expands from within the latter's narrative sequence and its implicit promise of closure or finish. Moreover, it implies two motions. As the intrinsically four-dimensional human mind increasingly clarifies, it expands the circumference of the preceding framework circumscribing that mind's thought; this enlarged ring, as it were, becomes the new framework, which in turn is to be splintered outwardly, and so on *ad infinitum* with no real beginnings or endings. Applied to this capacity of the human mind for "different dimensions of thought" (*The Bulpington of Blup* [1932] [*BB*], 72), the spiral pattern endlessly increases its distance from the center. It opens outward into fourth-dimensional possibility as that mind moves through time, or history; this spiral movement of the mind is the expression of spirit paradoxically achieving a fated freedom equivalent to the function of expanded insight in the reader of *Ararat*. The ideal readers of *Ararat* will expand, evolve mentally, as does Noah Lammock, and so will repeat with slight but significant variation basic human personality types.

But as the collective human mind enlarges its metaphorical circumferences intellectually, the human race experiences the spiral pattern as a steady diminishment of distance from a mystical center, as a resolution of three-dimensional fragmentation, as a transformation of the fate of matter correspondent to the text of *Ararat*. This text expands in aesthetic value only in terms of the relativity of a reader's broadening perception; it is a self-consuming artifact pointing away from itself to the reader. No Yeatsean widening gyre, Wells's dynamic spiral is another version of his notion of "essential complements," the paradoxical integration of such apparent oppositions as mind (reader) and matter (text), freedom and fate. As the collective human mind expands in its quest for freedom, the fated destiny of the race contracts, for ill or for good. And Ararat, the mountain, objectifies this spiral pattern informing the internal structure of Wells's novel. In its essential configuration a mountain is a spiral, and at the receding distant point of diminishment at the spiral's central axis, at the top of Ararat—the opposite extreme of the increasingly open-ended lower part representing the collective human mind—humanity, as the collective ark (*AA*, 76), seeks rest and fulfillment. This approach to the summit remains asymptotic, as each "Ark of to-day has to become the world of to-morrow" (*AA*, 80). Hence Wells's conception of repetition with variation is here expressed by means of an old symbol used with variation; this same concept informs Wells's reliance on evolved character types and on an expanding dynamic (always inconclusive) inner structure splintering the frame of the external structure of *Ararat*.

Twenty-two years earlier, in *The Undying Fire*, Wells reflected a similar view of time without the collateral technique of the splintering frame evoking an aesthetic fourth dimension. In 1934 he referred to this novel as "one of the best pieces of work I ever did. I set great store by it still" (*EA, 420*). We might wonder why. A dialogue novel, *Fire* retells the biblical story of Job, now a school master whose friends visit him prior to his (successful) operation for cancer and plague him to no avail with numerous challenges to his opinions. Certainly there are skillful passages in this book: Huss's long, energetic po-lemic on evil in the world demonstrating malignity, carelessness, or mere indifference in creation; the Poesque description—Poe is mentioned—of death in a U-Boat as a metaphor for the human condition. Perhaps it satisfied Wells's early attraction to the theatre, for the novel is dramatic, its manner more like that of a play than of a novel of the time, its dialogue excellent, and its focus on the protagonist's bout with cancer and on a pending operation sufficiently generative of suspense. Also the book advances with admirable clarity Wells's arguments on behalf of education and the development of a "world brain" as crucial to the improvement of humanity's collective will. Each of these contributes a good reason for Wells's high regard for this work. His autobiography provides a clue to still another factor in the book's appeal to its author so late in his career: "in *The Undying Fire,* I was at last fully aware of what I was doing and I took a new line" (*EA, 419*). Wells treasured this work because it marked an important stage in his developing self-awareness as a thinker and writer, a transition he generally attributed, we should recall, to the year 1920.

This self-awareness infuses the entire book: assessed in its light small details can suddenly radiate meaningful implications. In one minor scene, for instance, Sir Eliphaz, a governor of the school where Job Huss teaches, arrives at the institution and vaguely suffers a slight disorientation: "His eye seemed seeking some point of attachment, and found it at last in the steel engraving of Queen Victoria giving a Bible to a dusky potentate, which adorned the little parlour" (*The Atlantic Edition of the Works of H. G. Wells* [1924–27] [*Works*], 11:82). This trifling gesture indicates authorial disap-proval of Eliphaz's standards, recalls Wells's antagonism to the framework of Victorian values and fictional conventions, and points to the biblical source of the novel itself. Departing from his earlier manner, however, Wells does not merely react against what he identifies as the prevailing attitude of his time. In *Fire* he attempts a "new line," the adaptation and advancement of the Old Testament story of Job. Expanding and clarifying the framework of values of this traditional account, the novel becomes a contemporary biblical text; or, in Wells's words, "*The Undying Fire* is that great Hebrew imitation of the Platonic Dialogue, the Book of Job, frankly modernized" (*EA, 419*). This evolution includes a revision of the religious positions of the biblical Job and his acquaintances, a secularization of theology, and a modification of the protagonist.

Job Huss is a modern version of the human type depicted in the Old Testament Job of Uz. Now both Job's circumstances and his mind have advanced. Huss's core belief is reflected in a letter to him from a former student. "You made us think and feel that the past of the world was our own history; you made us feel that we were in one living story" (*Works*, 11:167; italics deleted). One living story: *Fire* suggests that every human life manifests a repetition of character types. This view, somewhat Romantic in its intimation of past and present existing in simultaneity,[3] contrasts with the convictions of Mr. Dad, a school governor who asks, "What's history, after all? At the best, it's over and done with" (*Works*, 11:34). For Wells, not history per se but the human patterns within it are important, patterns obscured by the historian's usual emphasis upon particularization and upon uniqueness of event and participant. Uniqueness is certainly there; so also is the type. Job Huss, then, parallels and at the same time realizes more fully a version of Job of Uz. "Job has become mankind" (*Works*, 11:9): Uz>Huss>Us. And like its protagonist, *Fire* is typical yet unique; it parallels and also advances the biblical story. Whereas *Ararat* fully manifests an aesthetic fourth dimension evoked by the technique of the splintering frame, *Fire*, written just before the onset of Wells's mature literary experimentation, displays no tension between outer and inner structure. It proceeds primarily by means of an innovative development of the original account. Still, its approach to time, as implied in its presentation of evolved character and textual types, anticipates Wells's subsequent interest in fictional structure and an aesthetic fourth dimension.

In light of his creator's reliance upon the typical in text and character in *Fire*, Huss's approach to history as "one living story" also looks forward to Wells's use of the spiral pattern to objectify human evolution or devolution in his later work. Huss intends his concept to refute the human tendency to stress the particular and the unique. To see only these aspects of reality is to be like a person who looks back (or down, if the spiral is conceived of as vertical) from the edge of a tier or circuit of the spiral of human history. Since the degree of gradation is very small, the spiral may appear cylindrical from this perspective, which impression might lead to such cyclical interpretations of history as those of Oswald Spengler. On the other hand, perception of gradation might lead to notions of progress that in effect isolate each time period as complete in identity; this would be especially true of the time-tier of the viewer, which tier might appear distinctive in several aspects from the dreamlike lower concentric rings of history. In Wells's opinion, as we have seen, either impression is mistaken because it is made independently from its essential complement; the larger truth includes uniqueness and typicality (repetition). The trouble is that a look into the spire from any of its circuits fails to disclose how the tiers connect. Furthermore, the viewer cannot see into the forward or upper levels—the future—where dreamlike possibilities exist, even as one in time cannot know heaven, which may be "some other dimension of space, [a] world arranged in planes" (*Works*, 11:94). What is required, and what no person can achieve since no part can know the whole of which it is a part, is an absolute overview. Such a perspective would reveal the entire spiral, near-beginning to near-end, and how each circuit is not only joined to the one preceeding and succeeding it but also in fact exists in perfect continuation with these tiers, is one with them as the locus of developing collective human consciousness moves through time around a fixed mystical center. That fixed center is will.

THE COLLECTIVE WILL

Will, a radical concept in Wells's thought and art, is also a significant concern in Victorian fiction. As Victorian fiction develops, it has been suggested, the quality of volition tends to define its characters.[4] Indeed, Jane Eyre in Charlotte Brontë's novel (1847) and Dorothea Brooke in George Eliot's *Middlemarch* (1871–72) learn to exert will in opposition to rigid social norms and, perhaps, in the process demonstrate the belief, as expressed by John Stuart Mill, that education in the broadest sense fulfills will. Eyre and Brooke, however, discover as well the egotism which excessive will can engender, and their example indicates the need to forge a balance between individuality and society. In the case of Eliot, moreover, an adaptation of the Feuerbachian theory of general consciousness in *Middlemarch* hints at something like a Collective Will providing, as it were, a benign Over-Soul for the individual expression of volition. Such a notion is turned on its back, its Schopenhauerian underside thrust up, in the late-Victorian novels of Thomas Hardy.

Like Hardy, Wells also applied a Schopenhauerian understanding of will, most directly very late in his career and then only in modified form. Schopenhauer's influence aside, Wells's interest in will appears in his earliest writings. In Wells's system, the individual will operates in consort with the imagination, which rejects "the thing that is" and inclines toward prophecy. In his fiction both faculties are consistently associated with images of light and fire,[5] for they define for Wells the animating center of human identity. This animating center, as the images also imply, is inherently divine, an early Romantic notion which Wells held to the end of his life and which would not endear him to those of the postwar modern generation who believed they had witnessed the demise of religion and tradition. In *The Undying Fire* Huss shares the biblical Job's belief in "the Will of a God of Light" pervading creation (*Works*, 11:78). He also revises this belief by identifying this divine Will as the fiery animating principle of the human heart:

> All the brighter shines the flame of God in my heart. If the God in my heart is no son of any heavenly father then he is Prometheus the rebel; it does not shake my faith that he is the Master for whom I will live and die. And all the more do I cling to this fire of human tradition we have lit upon this little planet, if

it is the one gleam of spirit in all the windy vastness of a dead and empty universe. (*Works,* 11:80)

Nothing antinomian is implied here, only a sense of the intrinsic divinity of the combined force of individual wills working, as in George Eliot's vision, toward positive collective human purposes. God is the united effort of these wills, of the "concentration of will" that defines "the pattern of the key to master our world and release its imprisoned promise" (*EA,* 12).

Wells's concept of a Collective Will became most pronounced during the 1930s when he specifically adapted Jungian, Schopenhauerian and Spenglerian ideas in his fiction. Appearing at least as early as *The History of Mr. Polly* the Wellsian version combines a Christian faith in divine providence and pagan trust in natural process. As a radical concept informing Wells's typology of characterization, it fuses a biological emphasis upon the unique and a religious emphasis upon the mystical All. Each individual will is a singular variation within this All, this Collective Will somewhat like Wordsworth's or Emerson's Romantic notion of an Over-Soul. This idea integrates, as essential complements or mutually constitutive oppositions, two notions which intrigued Wells as early as 1891. Then he described how from "the absolute standpoint" natural laws appear to determine the universe inexorably, while from the subjective human standpoint individual effort appears to some extent to shape the future.[6] By 1942 this idea not only recalled Romantic and Jungian notions but also suggested to Wells Einsteinian implications: "From the standpoint of the space-time-continuum there is no movement; the whole system is rigid"; "the four-dimensional universe is rigid, Calvinistic, predestinate; the personal life is not a freedom, though it seems to be a freedom; it is a small subjective pattern of freedom in an unchanging all. There is no conflict between fate and free will" (*The Conquest of Time* [1942] [*CT*], 84). The Collective Will is similar to an absolute view of human reality, which no individual can know as a whole, though each participates in it. Sometimes Wells's protagonists experience intuitive sensations of this unifying divinelike force comprised of essential complements. They glimpse, in or as if in a dream, other dimensions of human knowledge, other more encompassing planes of human self-awareness, control, and potentiality. They henceforth actively and "freely" will their cooperation with this ultimate benign "fate"—a fate microcosmically reflected in their manifestation of a "typical" personality—like Huss, who feels "summon[ed] . . . to live the residue of his days working and fighting for the unity and release and triumph of mankind" (*Works,* 11:148).

None of Huss's goals are attainable in any ultimate sense. The endless process of expansion underlying his effort is what matters. In struggling against the framework of the current givens of human existence, Huss and others like him press against fate, splintering the frame of its present manifestation. This is freedom, though what is achieved in time is always merely an extension of the "space" within a fate ever circumscribing human destiny. In exercising his unique individual will in this way, Huss conforms to the "typical" or predestining Collective Will. The identity he attains in the process is precisely like that of the Christian saint who renounces self in order to achieve wholeness through voluntary cooperation with the divine Will. So freedom is fate, fate freedom—a pivotal paradox or essential complement informing at the most fundamental level Wells's spiral image of time and his coincident employment of a typology of texts and characters.

And it defines his experimentation with fictional structure. In fact it determines the dominance of structure over characterization in his novels. Structure reflects a larger truth for Wells than does individual perception. He agrees with Kant, and those Romantic writers influenced directly or indirectly by Kant, that the human mind creates its own structures and that all forms are descriptions of individual truth. But he converts this fate of subjectivism into its opposite, a freedom insofar as these very structures are transcendentally infused, so that through *time* they comprise the noumenon, or thing-in-itself, the Collective Will.

Like George Moore, George Gissing, Henry James and Thomas Hardy, Wells turned to the craft of fiction as a response to the dying values of society,[7] but he could never endorse, like Nietzsche, William James, Henri Bergson, Joyce and Woolf, the individual as the standard and source of reality. His attitude agreed with Walter Pater's observation that "modern thought is distinguished from ancient by its cultivation of the 'relative' spirit in place of the 'absolute' ";[8] in contrast to Pater's anxious conclusion, Wells's position never endorsed relativism as a sufficiently accurate means of assessing human existence or as an appropriate response to human existence. Beyond Bergsonian *durée,* characterizing each person's experience of time, there exists for Wells the larger relativity of the expanding Collective Will of humanity as it interacts and mystically becomes one with an expanding universe. Just as space and time, in Einstein's theory, comprise a continuum, so do, in Wells's system, Universe and Will; so much so that their identities transpose (in Romantic fashion, perhaps), even as do the unique and the typical, freedom and fate, matter and spirit in Wells's thought. Each of these identities alternate with their opposite in the flowing spiral of time, which is the manifestation of the expanding Collective Will and which constitutes the ever-emerging structure of reality for humanity. Wells's novels, it follows, emphasize structure more than characterization, which consequently is determined by structure in his work. That structure, however, will be expressed as a splintering frame, suggesting both the interaction of life's essential complements and, especially, the eternal emergence of an incomplete potential structure expressing a Collective Will processively evolving from within the present framework. In this way Wells sought to make his art reflect reality.

Notes

1. Arthur S. Eddington, *Stellar Movements and the Structure of the Universe* (London: Macmillan, 1914), 244. Eddington's theory of relativity, incidentally, differs from Einstein's, but Wells does not indicate any awareness of the distinctions.

2. See M. H. Abrams, *Natural Supernaturalism* (New York: Norton, 1971); and Timothy Materer, *Vortex: Pound, Eliot, and Lewis* (Ithaca: Cornell University Press, 1979).

3. George Poulet, "Timelessness and Romanticism," *Journal of the History of Ideas* 15 (1954): 3–22.

4. J. Hillis Miller, *The Form of Victorian Fiction: Thackeray, Dickens, Trollope, George Eliot, Meredith, and Hardy* (Notre Dame: University of Notre Dame Press, 1968), 33.

5. Documentation of this point is provided in my "The Thing That Is and the Speculative If," *English Literature in Transitions* 11 (1968): 67–78.

6. Robert M. Philmus and David Y. Hughes, eds., *H. G. Wells: Early Writings in Science and Science Fiction* (Berkeley: University of California Press, 1975), 6.

7. See Donald David Stone, *Novelists in a Changing World: Meredith, James, and the Transformation of English Fiction in the 1880s* (Cambridge: Harvard University Press, 1972). See also Rubin Rabinovitz, *The Reaction against Experiment in the English Novel, 1950–1960* (New York: Columbia University Press, 1967).

8. Walter Pater, *Appreciations,* in *Works* (London: Macmillan, 1915), 5: 66.

Brynhild

ROBERT BLOOM

*B*rynhild (1937) represents a startling departure from the critical positions
that Wells had maintained for almost forty years in his battle with Henry
James. It is, within the framework of that battle, a Jamesian novel, or at least
the most Jamesian of Wells's novels. Perhaps the five-year hiatus between it
and Wells's last full-length work of fiction, *The Bulpington of Blup,* in which
he had vented his distaste for an aestheticism that James always partly
embodied for him, disposed Wells to feel that he should now, if he was to
return to novel-writing at all, put the more strictly imaginative side of his
talent to a test, if only to see what was in it, what he had all along been
denying, and what he might hope to find or convey in the novel as James
understood the form. The deepening interest in character that he confessed in
the *Autobiography* must have made the occasion, since he had already moved
significantly in this direction with the fashioning of Theodore Bulpington,
seem all the more propitious. So too, no doubt, did his last major love affair,
beginning a few years earlier when he was in his mid-sixties with the woman
upon whom Brynhild, his heroine, is modeled.[1]

In any case, there are numerous accommodations to James's procedures.
The time scheme, for one, is not that of the characteristic Wellsian chronicle,
which took the hero, and would again take him in novels that followed, from
birth to some catastrophic middle of the journey of his life. Instead, we have
a Jamesian dramatic transaction, centered on a single major action and requir-
ing less than a year of narrative time. In the "Envoy" with which Wells
concludes *Brynhild,* he expressly indicates that any typically Victorian interest in the ultimate fates of all the characters is quite out of place in his work,
even if he does manage to provide some indications sub rosa.

In place of the life of the protagonist as the essential organizing principle, there is a Jamesian principle of theme, or subject: *Brynhild* is a novel
about contrived appearances, façades, masks, pretensions and their relation
to reality and integrity. Hence, not the squeezed orange of life-likeness, but a
pattern of meaning lies at the center of the book, and Wells's consciousness of
the shift—his pride in it too—is discernible in the same "Envoy." With
uncharacteristic owlishness and aesthetic pretension he writes, "In New Zea-

From Robert Bloom, *Anatomies of Egotism: A Reading of the Last Novels of H. G. Wells* (Lincoln: University of
Nebraska Press, 1977). © 1977 by University of Nebraska Press. Reprinted by permission.

land, as Mrs. Ettie Hornibrook showed so ably and interestingly in her *Maori Symbolism,* the decorations on a beam or a pillar may be expanded by an understanding imagination into the most complete and interesting of patterns, and so it is with this book. It is a novel in the Maori style, a presentation of imaginative indications."[2] Whether the claim is serious or playful, it points faithfully enough to Wells's unprecedented concern with imagination, patterning, and completeness in the work. For the theme of appearances, which is first announced in the subtitle of the novel, *The Show of Things,* is reinforced by symbolic charades, pageants, and Miltonic allusion, by a tight plot structure which creates thematic connections and recurrences, and by motifs linked through reflection, diction, and metaphor. Everywhere Wells seems intent on allowing art to make the life of the book.

More specifically Jamesian still is the relative absence of general ideas in *Brynhild.* There is hardly a single pressing problem connected with the survival of civilization in it; Wells seems remarkably content to portray the world instead of wishing to change it. He works within the framework of personal life and personal relations and is concerned more with the feelings that ideas evoke than ideas themselves, insofar as the two are separable. Such large ideas as do enter are always dramatically functional, serving to reveal the character and motives of the speaker advancing them. This is feasible because authorial intrusion is held to a minimum and almost everything is seen, thought, and felt through the characters. The point of view is technically omniscient, yet Wells chooses to limit himself largely to his characters' assessments of things, employing Brynhild most extensively as the observing consciousness. We recognize here the method of as late a James novel as *The Wings of the Dove,* for the master did not always use only the one central consciousness that he commended. The high point of this technique in *Brynhild* comes in the long ninth chapter, which is almost entirely given over to the heroine's meditation on her husband, her marriage, her delusions about both, and her speculations about the future. It is formally and functionally reminiscent of the famous vigil scene in *The Portrait of a Lady,* although it has none of the climactic intensity of Isabel Archer's recognitions. Like both the *Portrait* and *The Golden Bowl, Brynhild* is one of the rare instances, before our own vexed era, of a novel devoted more to the anguishes of marriage than to those of courtship.

The commitment to character, especially Brynhild's as a focal interest is thus very strong and puts us in mind of Wells's declaration in the *Autobiography* that exhaustive character study is an adult and philosophical occupation. It is true that Wells had always exaggerated characterization as an end in James, who actually abided throughout his career by the rhetorical questions he asked in "The Art of Fiction": "What is character but the determination of incident? What is incident but the illustration of character?" However, the balance that James achieved, where character becomes a constituent, along with incident, of a larger design, is precisely the balance that Wells achieves in *Brynhild,* even though a new psychological astuteness, a new sensitivity to emotional disposition and interaction, is present.

That larger design in *Brynhild* is elaborated on a field of egotism, another Jamesian preoccupation. Like Dr. Sloper of *Washington Square,* Gilbert Osmond of *The Portrait of a Lady,* and John Marcher of "The Beast in the Jungle," Rowland Palace, Brynhild's husband, is obsessed with himself, a writer who sees the whole world largely as an instrument of his own well-being and distinction. It is he who after suffering an imaginary embarrassment seeks to put appearances at the service of egotism by means of that peculiarly modern instrument, public relations. Here again Wells, who had himself been one of the greatest journalists of his time, utilizes an unmistakably Jamesian horror and loathing of publicity and newspapers, the violators of privacy, decorum, integrity, sanctity, and all value, as a major element of his "subject."[3] And with a quite Jamesian delicacy, he delineates for us not only the vulgarity of the newspapers, but the vulgarity that tempts the elegant Rowland Palace into making use of them in behalf of his own egotism. In Brynhild Palace he also provides us with a figure of Jamesian sensitivity and refinement, equal to Jamesian reaches of perception, through whom to measure the tawdriness of her husband's endeavor.[4]

Palace himself fairly seethes with refinement, but it is for Wells the specious, hypocritical refinement of the aesthete, one of the more reprehensible guises of vanity. The link between aestheticism and sterile pride, though Wells associates it with James, notably in *The Bulpington of Blup,* is not so much a personal as a categorical observation. He never accused James of personal vanity—it would have been thoroughly unjust to do so—but of futility, misguidedness, lack of proportion, the hippopotamus retrieving the pea. James himself was, of course, immensely sensitive to the dangers of aestheticism, as the cold egoism of Osmond and the Wildean frivolity of Gabriel Nash in *The Tragic Muse* amply testify. In a sense, Wells finds Palace guilty of standard Jamesian crimes—of insufficient awareness, of a presumptuous skepticism and irony that invite Wells to treat Palace with a larger, more conscious, and more just irony, which Brynhild, in turn, is privy to. The matter is complicated—again, newly complicated—by a mingling of Wellsian as well as Jamesian features in Palace's situation. Like Wells in the thirties—and like James through most of his career—Rowland Palace has a smaller public for his novels than he could wish, is being displaced by rising young novelists, and has not been offered the Nobel Prize. Yet he is treated with very little sympathy and with no significant psychic or emotional identification by Wells, who has learned in these late novels to create mixed figures. These may share situations, impulses, even ideas with him, yet not necessarily serve as spokesmen and surrogates. They are instead firmly placed and scrupulously judged. Indeed, Wells fashions for his presentation of Palace an ironic narrative voice which establishes a distance between character and novelist that almost no similarities could bridge. James had utilized the same ironic perspective in the narrative style of *The Bostonians,* though oddly enough, with less consistency, at least in connection with Miss Birdseye, who moves irresistbly through the course of novel from some comic Coventry into the very center of her creator's heart, and with Basil Ransom as well, who stands in an ironic half-life of repudiation and approval.

The question of impersonality is further complicated by the presence of the most Wellsian figure in the book, the one character who could not be a part of James's world and is more or less charged with keeping things recognizably in Wells's, Alfred Bunter. Like young Wells he is a lower-middle-class writer who has come to literary London from the provinces at the beginning of a most promising career, full of ideas—he does indeed have some—and of passions and aspirations. Like Wells, he remains an outsider even as he is fashionably taken up by the best circles, and he is eventually undone by aesthetic vanity and ill-will. At the same time, Wells's identification with him is actually rather limited: Bunter is a Welshman living under an assumed name and, it turns out, under suspicion of having murdered his brother-in-law. In fact, Bunter's wife, Freda, who figures minimally but brilliantly in the novel, is not the only thing about him that suggests D. H. Lawrence. Bunter represents, then, like Palace, a mixture of things. Nonetheless, through Bunter Wells manages to intrude some of his own characteristic reality, not of ideas only, but of class and career, upon the Jamesian one. Much of the charm of the book resides in this impingement of worlds, the exploration of what, for Wells, had hitherto been, with the somewhat different exception of *Bulpington,* the other side of the wall. This rich union of Jamesian and Wellsian possibilities, with a resulting modification of each, produced one of the best things Wells achieved in his last years.

The thematic substance of the novel, which Wells was at pains to secure on this occasion, is drawn from his four central figures and then elaborated and modulated around them. As they first appear these figures are paired socially and culturally. Rowland and Brynhild Palace, husband and wife, belong to the upper world of taste and refinement, while Immanuel Cloote, the public relations man who takes charge of Palace's affairs, and Alfred Bunter, the rival poet, come from below, bearing an odor of disreputability with them. Yet almost at once in Palace's case we are made to recognize anomalies.

Though an eminent writer with an aesthetically enviable reputation, at the book's beginning he is discovered fretting at three in the morning over some photographs taken of him in bardic costume—scarlet robe, gold fillet, and bay leaves—at a May Day festival and published around the world. Against his better judgment, certainly against his wife's as he discerned it in a fleeting glimpse, he had allowed himself to be seduced into dressing up and awarding some literary prizes by a most Jamesian invitation:

"A bard, a soothsayer," cried the vicar. "Merlin almost. You come, *cher maître,* apt to our occasion." (p. 7)[5]

Palace frets because he feels that the photographs make him appear undignified, ridiculous. "The scarlet robe wasn't a bit splendid. It was just a big dark robe obviously much too big for him and making him look stumpy—stumpy was the only word for it. The fillet of gold was askew, if ever it had been straight; it came down over his forehead and rested over one eyebrow. The bay leaves were crooked too; they gave him dark pointed ears. His genial expression was dradfully overdone. (That perhaps was his own fault.) The harp got in edgeways—obviously pasteboard. He looked like one of the less respectable and less expensively dressed boon companions of the Emperor Nero" (pp. 9–10). In Palace's finicky, excessive distress Wells gives us the anomolous side of his protagonist's participation in a world pretending to grace, ease, and light. He is, in fact, beset by egotism, insecurity, and irritability: "Like so many men who make their way to positions of importance in the world of thought and letters, Mr. Rowland Palace was a man of acute sensibilities and incessant anxieties. . . . His conception of himself was of a reserved, slenderish figure, delicate but opaque, observant, amused, kindly but enigmatical. His bearing, like his work, was pervaded by a gentle irony. (But Mrs. palace knew better.) He carried his faintly smiling face a little on one side. Few of his intimates suspected his phases of irritation and neurasthenia" (pp. 2–3).

These passages serve to convey Palace's instinctive devotion to appearances. His concern over looking stumpy, over the dreadfully overdone genial expression, the obviously pasteboard harp, together with his mask of reserve, kindliness, and gentle irony calculated to disguise the irritation and neurasthenia within, gives us in short compass—Wells is working with great economy here at the outset—the disparity between what Palace is and what he would like to appear to be that governs his life. In addition, the May Day incident that gives rise to Palace's distress is a rich emblem of the permutations of the motif of appearance that lie ahead in the novel. Although he feels his bardic costume has gone tragically awry and misrepresented him, Palace was at least in donning it pretending to be what he actually is, a writer of some distinction. Yet even what he actually is turns out at the next moment to be elusive, a kind of appearance within to match the appearances without: "His intellectual pose was to acquiesce in everything and believe in nothing. His dexterous depreciation could be turned left or right or where you would. He undermined and destroyed with a polished civility. His style was a witty style. This endeared him to youth, full of youth's natural suspicion that it is being dreadfully put upon and not quite clear how and why. He believed nothing; he clung to nothing. No trustful infantism for him, he intimated. They envied that tremendously ripe grown-up attitude of his beyond measure" (pp. 3–4). As a result of this near nihilism, he gains a reputation as a liberator and comes to accept the role with characteristically meaningless, irresponsible, futile urbanity: "But there was nothing anarchic or revolutionary about the liberation he purveyed; it was the liberation of a man of the world. It left you free to do anything—or nothing" (p. 4).

Brynhild, on the other hand, possesses the integrity and candidness that sorts with her station. Beautiful, quiet, and wise, she is the daughter of a country rector, a fine classicist who "had not so much educated her as made up his old classical clothing for her mind to wear. It fitted very loosely but it kept her out of contact with vulgar ideas" (p. 36). Her upbringing has made her a gracious antithesis of her husband, for her father had done his utmost to impress upon her "that though sin was highly reprehensible, meanness and mental disingenuousness were far more hateful to both God and man. One was in the world, of course, but that was no reason why one should mix oneself up with it in an indiscriminating way" (p. 36). Much later in the novel, the point is made even more explicitly and forcefully as Brynhild recalls words of her father that she had long ago committed to memory:

> "The one precious thing in life, my dear, is integrity—an inner integrity. The hard, clean, clear jewel, the essential soul. No matter where it takes you. . . . What I pray more and more frequently nowadays, Bryn, is this: May the Almighty damn and destroy me utterly and for ever, if I compromise in one particle when I am thinking in my own private thoughts. You think that over. You remember that. That's what I want to get over to you, my dear, somehow." (pp. 179–80)

Consequently, though she is sympathetic with Palace in his distress over the photographs, she cannot quite agree with his estimate of the situation or the remedy that he eventually proposes. At three in the morning—the chapter is ironically called "Nocturne"—she patiently suggests that his concern is exaggerated, that writers are after all to be known by what they are and what they write. Palace, however, will have none of it and begins instead to elaborate a theory of the indispensability of façades, public identities, keeping up appearances. Warming to it, he insists that the world has always dressed up to dramatize identity and authority—crowns, robes, the wig of the judge, the mask of statesmen—and that all life is a "vast tumultuous masquerade, a clamor for attention," that "no one has ever really *seen* a human being." Having relieved himself intellectually and invited her to comfort him sexually, Palace retires. But after ministering to him, Brynhild sleeps no more that night, contemplating instead a world of artificial faces, artificial bodies, and the question of what both Rowland Palace and she herself might really be behind the arras of their apparent selves. The "Nocturne" of Palace's song of himself and Brynhild's nightmarish brooding ends with one of

Wells's rare authorial intrusions in this novel, justified by his intentness on stating the theme, the interest, the center of the whole book:

> And so the rediscovery by Mr. Rowland Palace of Schopenhauer's realization of the importance of Show (*Verstellung*) sent him and his wife off in diametrically opposite directions, for while it started him upon the idea of the extreme importance of enlarging and strengthening the façade he presented to the world, a façade obviously perilously vulnerable at present, it sent her inquiring into all the neglected possibilities that might be pining and fretting behind the façade she had hitherto unquestioningly supposed to be herself. (pp. 23–24)

Wells here charts the course of the entire novel. From this point, Palace moves in the direction of wider and deeper appearances, engaging Immanuel Cloote as his "impresario" to fashion a suitable public personality for him and to organize illusion to Palace's advantage. Cloote, a man of some genius in the infant art of public relations, is Palace's alter ego from below, his brother in vulgarity, stripped of all polite pretensions. His success in fashioning a public identity for Palace as a great man of letters and a likely candidate for the Nobel Prize is total and represents a considerable advance in sophistication and insidiousness over the promotional tactics of such an early work, dealing with such a simple time, as *Tono-Bungay.* His task is made easier by Palace's limitless unscrupulousness and essential emptiness, despite his pretensions.

As Brynhild has suspected even from the days of his courtship, there is a hollowness at the heart of Palace. On one occasion very early in their relationship presented in flashback, after hearing him declare that his aim as a writer was to release people, she asks, "Release from what?" When he replies "From all the clotted nonsense, new and old, in which they are—imbedded," she pursues him with "And, dearest, what *then?*"

Palace's aim is recognizable to any reader of Wells as Wells's own. But his reply to Brynhild's question about the next step is Jamesian, aesthetic—and hollow: "Art, freedom, a sufficient life." For what Brynhild begins to see at this early stage, and what Wells develops with great force throughout his portrayal of Palace, is the reprehensibleness of Palace's engaging in universal, "liberating" criticism, yet having nothing—certainly nothing like a Wellsian program for the salvaging of civilization—to recommend in place of what he decries. The posture is for Wells quintessentially aesthetic; and it is the hollowness of Palace's endless aesthetic sneering that cries out to be filled with the illusions and impositions of a "planned, controlled, and effective publicity." Even at this early time Brynhild, in a passage framed typically within her own consciousness, sees more of the pretension within Palace than she quite wishes to:

> Was he embarrassed at expounding the obvious or was he evading the inexplicable? Art, freedom, a sufficient life? She felt, but she did not know

how to say, that these words meant nothing until they were defined. But her mind suddenly bristled with questions like a hedgehog's quills. And as immediately it came to her that not a single quill could be shot at him profitably. What was this "art," what was this "freedom," what was this "sufficient life" that justified his widespread scorn for the rest of humanity and in particular the rest of humanity which wrote and practised the arts? She had better not ask it. Somehow it wasn't the time. And yet there she was thinking it. This realization gave her her first twinge of disloyalty. (p. 38)

On their honeymoon the difficulty arises again in another flashback as Brynhild says with somewhat ironic humility, "Very often you seem to be condemning. Just condemning. When really, if I knew your standards, I should understand why you look down on so many people." Palace's response this time is hollower still, consisting of downright bad poetry: "Am I nothing more than bitter tongued? Maybe. I thought you understood me better, Bryn. Perhaps I don't even understand myself. . . . The haunting, impalpable presence of an infinite desire" (pp. 42–43). As Brynhild stores the remark up to gnaw over in private, Palace sees, like Osmond with Isabel, that she will never feed his egotism with the plenitude he had envisioned: "She didn't quite know how to take things like that. She was joining up one thing he said with another and keeping an account for reference. He did not want her to remember; he wanted her to sympathize and accept. And pass on."

Finally, after nine years of marriage during which he has found it impossible to answer Brynhild's haunting question, "Liberation for what?" Palace resolves the problem, for himself, at least. Meditating on it he concludes, "You can't invite inspectors into the Holy of Holies." As Brynhild had earlier resorted to Milton's "safest and seemliest by her husband stays" to quiet her own doubts about a spouse for whom "even the Alps never rose to their highest" and who generally "thought the sun might have set with a better grace," so too does Palace invoke the poet. "It is plain I am a Mystic," he comes to see. "Mystics cannot explain. Mystics cannot be called upon to explain. But nevertheless they can have the clearest sense of value. They are not merely justified in condemning and deprecating certain things; it is their duty. To some of us is given the spear of Ithuriel." Milton's angel sets him free to join sheer negation and public exploitation in a triumph of narcissism:

And now having found his essential self and his essential function and defeated and dismissed that long-rankling doubt, that nine-year-old doubt, about his fundamental self, having assured himself that at heart he was not practically empty and envious but mystically full, he could deal with the problem of putting himself over to the public with a steadfast and confident mind. (pp. 50–51)

Now, having released himself from all ties to reality—Wells's image, "not practically empty and envious but mystically full," is perfect—Palace is ready for Cloote, who will undertake to locate his employer's existence in the public mind. One overriding irony of this chapter of reflections and flashbacks tracing Palace's eventual abandonment of all integrity, all genuine selfhood, is that it is accurately enough entitled "Mr. Rowland Palace in Search of Himself."

Even at this still early point in the novel Wells's treatment of Palace, making its amused transit from displeasure to disdain, is a remarkable instance of disinterestedness, or at least of impersonally complex comic portraiture. For Palace shares a good deal with his creator. Like Wells he is interested in women. When an extremely good-looking housemaid pauses after passing him to look back, Palace reflects, "It meant nothing. It meant everything." When he is suddenly kissed by a lady during the intermission of a performance of *Tristan* "in a mutuality of appreciative exaltation" he savors it: "Such little things confirm a man." But later in the novel our suspicion that he is really rather different from Wells in this regard is made clear as we discover that it is precisely confirmation of his own peculiar sort that he seeks from women, or through them, and little else; and it is a confirmation that does not even require him to have affairs. This too becomes an aspect of the show of things, for what Palace wants is only the appearance of sexual prowess in order to "confirm" an illusion about himself. Nonetheless, Wells feels free to ascribe needs and inclinations to Palace that come at least suggestively close to his own.

This is clearer still with the literary considerations that arise in the chapter on "The Science and Art of Publicity" as we follow Rowland Palace about, "brooding still on the untilled field of his personal fame." Not the least of Wells's techniques for creating yet controlling distance, for making judgment hover between dismissal and sympathy, is the use of such metaphors as this, with an irony and exaggeration fine enough not to destroy all sense of Palace's plight. Wells's related interest in the mode of specious metaphor that pervades literary promotion emerges elsewhere as Cloote, groping for images, describes his aim to Palace; the genuine, incisive metaphor by which Wells himself describes Cloote's gestures affords just the contrast between reality and humbug, between Cloote's behavior and what he is saying, that Wells wants here: " 'You want building up. To me, Mr. Palace—you mustn't mind my saying it—to me you have to be the Clay that I can make into a Living Speaking Image. Perhaps not exactly Clay. No—that has associations!' He cut up the space before him with gestures of his hands. It was as if he cut out bits of it and threw them away. The piece he kept was: 'Glorious living material, fine and subtle. But there it is—you see what I mean. It is an adventure which—I can only say'—he hesitated for a moment seeking the right word, and produced it at last with an air of triumph—'fascinates me' " (p. 94).

As we follow Palace about in this chapter, we find him voicing a number of complaints about the literary situation, and about neglect especially, that

Wells himself expressed elsewhere.[6] It is almost as if Wells is able to exorcise his own grievances, as a novelist at least, by having the indignant but discredited Palace utter them. We have, at any rate, a complex, almost eerie, sense of home truths spoken by one whom we thought disqualified from all reality: " 'There is no longer a reading public; there are innumerable little transitory reading publics. They come and go. They are attracted with more difficulty, they forget more readily, and they misunderstand—swiftly' " (p. 58). " 'But now,' said Mr. Palace, 'a personal reputation is infinitely more exposed and precarious; it has to be sown, watched, fostered, protected from wilting, protected from parasites and enemies of all sorts, developed, guarded, magnified' " (p. 59). In this speech the satirical and egotistic color is more discernible and somewhat undermines the position as it undermines Palace; but when Palace calls on his publisher, Schroederer, to complain about insufficient promotion and publicity, Wells treats Schroederer with such open satirical distaste that the episode reinstates, rather complexly, the near-legitimacy of Palace's demands.

Wells initiates this shift by momentarily adopting Schroederer as point of view and presenting the publisher's hard-nosed fantasy: "Schroederer was a realist and his concern with his firm. Authors were merely the material you arrange upon your list so as to make the pattern of Schroederer clear and bright. They rose somehow to fame and you paid for them; they declined and you dropped them. The thing to do was to put them all in uniform mauve-green wrappers with red and buff covers underneath, so that ultimately the public would recognize these chromatic signs for good reading and bother no more who the authors were. 'I read Schroederer books,' the public would say, and then there would be an end to authors and their airs and graces, and he would get intelligent female labor at reasonable rates to write the stuff inside under his direction."

The climax of Wells's involved noninvolvement comes in Cloote's exposition to Palace of a cardinal error in the tactics of literary promotion. Here we find Wells obtruding his own painful situation on our notice as though his account of Palace's yearnings were being written by someone else altogether: "You must not harp too much on one aspect of a writer's quality. Gissing, for instance, was handicapped by his irony; they called him depressing; Chesterton was pigeon-holed as paradoxical even when he was doing his simple utmost to speak plainly; Wells was pinned down by his being always linked with 'The future of—this or that.' (But Wells at the best was a discursive, intractable writer with no real sense of dignity. A man is not called 'H. G.' by all his friends for nothing.)"

Brynhild, on the other hand, is impelled by the Nocturne episode, with its evocation of Schopenhauerian Show, truly to take the long journey into herself in order to seek out the reality of what she is. As Cloote is Palace's alter ego, Alfred Bunter becomes Brynhild's secret life, rising up from below socially, psychically, intellectually, emotionally, and spiritually for her to discover and embrace.

They meet on a country weekend at the estate of Lord Valliant Chevrell, where literary figures like Palace and Bunter are interspersed as sources of interest among the aristocratic guests. Wells sets the tone of the occasion instantly by allowing Brynhild to overhear an exchange between Lady Cytherea Label and Palace:

> "You mahst settle, Mr. Palace. You're just in taim. You know everything. Can a chimpanzee be crossed in love?"
>
> "It's the only way you *could* cross a chimpanzee," said Mr. Palace, right on the spur of the moment and wondering what on earth he meant.
>
> It was accepted as suggestively brilliant. (pp. 104–5)

In this setting Bunter, Brynhild sees, is "cast for the rôle of The Stranger," the "newly arrived, the last social mouthful," who "does not assimilate from the outset and gradually . . . becomes inassimilable." Since she thinks of herself as "cast for the rôle of a Quiet Lovely," she is sympathetically drawn to the young writer. As they converse, she finds the note of Wellsian out-siderism winning: " 'I had no idea,' he said, 'what these places were like and how many there seemed to be. I've lived in England all my life and I've never suspected what lay behind the gates and the palings and the notices about Tresspassing. It's amazing' " (p. 109). Before long he is speaking to her in the garden of the estate with some intensity about his career and his ideas, anticipating attitudes that were to become familiar on the British literary scene decades later: "This place is a wonder because it is rare. And yet we could make all our island a garden, an estate like this and as mellow as this. . . . We don't. that makes me Angry. . . . I am an Angry Man. . . . Almost professionally. You don't know my books? No? But that is what they say of me—the Angry Man. The world angers me. . . . I get angry and shout. I don't write books, I shout them." In a moment, without knowing that Brynhild is Mrs. Rowland Palace, he says, "I can't tell you how I envy at times the coolness, the empty, self-satisfied self-possession of that damned façade, Palace." Brynhild identifies herself to Bunter and gracefully disposes of most of his embarrassment. The remark serves only to bring them closer together and to prompt further private reflection on Brynhild's part about her relation to both men.

Wells has thus begun his extensive development in this chapter of a theatrical echo of his theme of shows and appearances. On the one hand there is the Wildely witty, but empty, dialogue of "that damned façade," Palace and his crossed chimpanzee, on the other, Brynhild's consciousness of Bunter's and her own less flamboyant roles, Stranger and Quiet Lovely. Bunter himself has come forward as the Angry Man. But this is only a beginning, for Wells soon moves past these intimations heartily into the dimension of the play within a play with Lord Valliant Chevrell's invitation to the entire company to play charades. This sequence is worth examining in some detail as an illustration of Wells's extraordinarily deliberate concentration on thematic considerations and on Brynhild's crucial relation to them.

The game is first introduced with appropriately erotic overtones: " 'Charades,' Valliant Chevrell would say, 'mix people nicely,' and there is no doubt that charades as they played them under his direction mixed them a good deal. There was a considerable amount of going off together and going off apart, necessary whispering and conspiring close to the pink receptive ear, a running about passages for needed properties, much dressing up and undressing and helping to dress and undress." The actors, moreover, have only partial knowledge of their endeavor: "Everybody knew the one or two letters in which they acted, but only their host alone or with some chosen confederate was supposed to know the 'Whole.' " For the first charade "Pluto" is the Whole, and Palace, along with Lady Cytherea and others, is charged with the letter P. They decide upon the Judgment of Paris, with Palace as the hero and Lady Cytherea as Venus. Once again, as in the pageant that had begun the novel, Palace is richly, if dubiously, costumed, once again purporting to be what he is and is not. And once again the ludicrousness of this contrived appearance is laid on by Wells:

> The three young ladies had undressed Mr. Palace very thoroughly. In place of a Phrygian cap they had put a red ribbon round his hair. He was wearing his bathing shorts under an arrangement of sheepskin rugs held together by brown luggage straps, and he carried a long alpenstock to which a crook-handled walking stick had been tied. A pair of plimsolls had been deprived of their uppers and converted into sandals with the aid of a tape measure which ran up his two shins and round his calves saying 23, 24, 25, 26, and 58, 59, 60 respectively. He had been slightly rouged and his hair arranged for him and he carried himself as though he had recently been told— as indeed he had been told—that he was "aw'fly handsome." (p. 121)

On this occasion, the Apple of Discord is a large orange, "ripe to bursting and not to be thrown about." One would never sense, in the ridicule of Palace, or in Wells's whole skeptical comic handling of the charade sequence, how passionately fond he was himself of such domestic entertainments and games in his own home, Easton Glebe.[7] Brynhild watches her husband with some distaste, and self-reproach for feeling it, as his comportment recalls "all the worst excesses of all the pseudo-Russian ballets she had ever seen." Palace's role as Paris, connoisseur of beauty and sower of discord, even without his graceless exaggeration of it, is quite an apt mythological counterpart of Palace's flirtatious behavior with Lady Cytherea and others throughout the evening, none of it lost on his wife. Following the Judgment of Paris, Bunter participates in the letter L tableau, a Laocoön group which is done "with dignity and decorum." Now it is Brynhild's turn. She is charged with representing the third letter, U, by playing the part of Undine, the water nymph, and wishes to do more than merely mope under water for her lost soul and her lost knight. As a result of Palace's attentions to others, his own charade of philandering, she "felt far too much like the part to want to display herself in that fashion" Instead she decides to do it as a scene of exorcism with Undine's knight present. She seeks to reclaim Rowland by asking him to play her redemptive knight, but when, with Lord Valliant Chevrell at her elbow, she invites Palace to do so, he displays yet more of his objectionable behavior:

> He was saying something in an undertone to Florrie Caterham, who had to direct his attention to Brynhild. He looked up startled and grasped the situation. His expression became defensive.
>
> "You mustn't make me do all the acting, Bryn," he said, as if he addressed an unreasonable child. "No."
>
> For a moment Brynhild felt that she and Rowland held the stage and that every one was observing them.
>
> "This, my dear," said her guardian angel within her, is going to be a Scene—unless you hold tight. So hold tight." (pp. 126–27)

Acting with magnificent restraint in this unscheduled drama—a kind of play within a play within a play—Brynhild shuns the obvious retaliatory move and deliberately avoids inviting Bunter, who like everyone else is watching the scene, to take the place of her husband and summons two other men instead. The exchange is an extraordinarily adroit piece of evocation on Wells's part. Here in the very midst of organizing appearances for dramatic illusion, for "show" in the theatrical sense, his characters uncover realities of feeling.

In addition, Wells is flirting with symbolic, mythological purport in an unobtrusive but suggestive way—a good deal less obtrusive, for example, than his deliberately self-conscious employment of the Delphic Sibyl in *The Bulpington of Blup*. Just as Paris emblematizes Palace's deportment at Valiant Chevrell's, and Laocoön, who denounced the Trojan Horse, represents, like the angry young writer Bunter, a figure warning against what threatens a civilization, so too Undine prefigures an important aspect of Brynhild's experience and its significance, one that in this case lies considerably ahead in the novel, so that the mythological implications have an anticipatory, prophetic force. The Undine legend is about a water nymph who could obtain a soul only by marrying a mortal and bearing a child. Brynhild's adventures, late in the novel, take something very like this form. Wells achieves a similar prophetic intimation with Bunter by having him return in another charade to play Pluto at the moment when Persephone takes leave of him on her annual trip to the upper world. Bunter "waved off her farewell embraces, indicated irritably that she must not keep the car waiting, featured all the natural relief of a husband who is seeing off a too attentive spouse, and then with an expression of impish sadism, a god left free at last to do as he pleased, bent forward, glanced over his shoulder to be sure she had really gone and prodded his scepter into young Bates with the gusto of a long-deferred pleasure. . . . Then Pluto, clawing his face with a glare of incredible malignity, considered what he should do to the two lady damned" (pp. 129–30). Although we do not at this point know these things about Bunter, he does in fact have a wife of sorts whom he has eluded in Scotland and another in Wales, and he will eventually cuckold Palace by having an affair with Brynhild. Yet neither of these prophetic parallels is forced on our attention by Wells at this juncture, precisely because they are prophetic. The enrichment that they bring to the novel is retrospective. Not so, however, the intimation of ludicrousness in certain forms of show that arises from Palace's participation, from such props as the Orange of Discord, and from the extensive treatment of household items pressed into absurdly exalted service as costume and décor. Employing a light touch throughout the sequence, Wells is able to mock symbolism at the same time that he utilizes it.

With Brynhild still looking on, Palace contrives another dramatic performance outside the charade framework. She notices that Palace has been deserted by Lady Cytherea and her friends in favor of Bunter. Desperately seeking to regain attention, Palace finally manages to detach Lady Cytherea. We remember now, if not before, that hers is another name for Venus:

> He must have made a direct appeal, because when about midnight the next charade (Nero) was over . . . he and Lady Cytherea disappeared through a door in the corridor in the most concerted manner possible and reappeared ten minutes afterwards from the direction of the front entrance, with a cleared-up expression on their candid faces.
>
> The pair of them took the center of the stage.
>
> "It's the mahst wonderful moon!" cried Lady Cytherea.
>
> "It's magic out there," said Rowland.
>
> Evidently it had been magic out there and he wanted everyone to realize it. There was something proprietorial in his bearing, there was an assertion. Whatever had happened in the garden out there was as nothing to him in comparison with the dramatic assertion of close association conveyed by this entry.
>
> Brynhild stood with a glass of barley water in her hand, marvelling quietly at life.
>
> It had become necessary to both these remarkable people to intimate that in moonlight anyhow they were of importance to each other. . . . They were playing this at Alfred Bunter, at the company generally, at Brynhild and at themselves, and why they were moved to play this small drama and make this show, Omniscience only knew. (pp. 131–32)

Alone in her bedroom later that night, standing nude before her mirror, comparing herself to the false Aphrodite, Lady Cytherea, Brynhild reflects: " 'A secret beauty is nothing to him,' she said to the living Venus before her. *The show's the thing. . . .*' " Thus her emotional and moral alienation from Palace is established by means of the same metaphors that have been at play throughout the evening. Wells has gone a long way toward releasing her for an affair with Bunter. As she reads the young writer for the first time that night in bed, she estimates his work with extraordinary critical sensitivity. It might be young Wells or young Lawrence that she is reading: "It was an extremely turgid story about hampered and defeated people. . . . They lived in London as well as in the country; *The Cramped Village,* it seemed, was not a place, but life. They paralyzed each other. Dreams tormented them from above and lusts and savage passions from below. . . . The style was rough and yet stimulating. . . . She knew quite well how prose becomes patchy if you worry it too much. How it works into raw places and holes. . . . He was plainly trying to get more into his narrative than his narrative prose could stand. 'It's a splutter,' she thought. . . . 'Like a cat with its head in a bag. . . . A man trying to say something more than *can* be said. . . . But he never fakes.' " Then the deeply contrastive word linked with her husband rises in her mind from her conversation with Bunter earlier in the day:

> She mused along these lines for a while and then she uttered one word out loud—because wanted to hear it.
> "Façade!"
> "Yes, Mr. Bunter," she reflected, "you can hit upon the just word at times. The precise word. . . . Among others. Among quite a lot of others."
> (p. 136)

And so, one of the novel's leitmotifs, first introduced by Palace himself, now newly applied to him with some abhorrence, returns. Like the word "show," or the word "debonair" with which Cloote annoints Palace later on, it serves to reinforce our awareness of the extraordinary thematic concentration and design of the novel. It also, of course, comports with Palace's very name, being the false face of the edifice of egotism that is his life. Brynhild's mood toward her husband softens before she sleeps as she wonders what he might be doing in his room: "In through those two doors there was perhaps a real Rowland now. Perhaps the Façade like a discarded garment was hanging over the back of a chair." Finally, as she shuts the light, tenderly but unyieldingly extending the metaphor, she whispers "Good-night, Façade."

Wells's extraordinary consciousness of theme and his extraordinary devotion to a personal framework of thinking and feeling in the charade sequence—his Jamesian gestures—continue, unabated, in the major action of the novel. In the chapter wryly called "Exploring the Laurel Grove," Cloote effectively takes charge of Palace's career and person by setting before his client the irresistible gloriously engineered future of his Predestined Career. As Cloote speaks of prestige, public appearances, photographs, non-events, the motive terms "show" and "appearance" reverberate through the conversation. When he proposes an occasional visit to "some little country grammar school" to say something "deep and moving to those boys which they will remember, which their mothers will remember" and Palace objects to seeming to wear his heart on his sleeve, Cloote's reply is magically apt: " 'You don't. And I don't want you to. But—Wear your heart *up* your sleeve. Give them a glimpse of it and then—Presto! It's gone, and you get that enigmatical Palace smile' " (p. 148). As they talk, Palace also entertains the possibility of "a rather frequent, recurrent appearance with Lady Cytherea, for example. . . . There would be nothing in it and yet everything would be implicitly there."

Before long the essential brotherhood of the two men forces itself upon Palace's attention:

> "We differ in our manners, we differ in our gifts," said Mr. Cloote, "but we think alike. We are going to be a great combination."
> (It seemed horribly true.) (p. 143)

But later, as he observes Cloote's uncouth behavior at table, Palace comforts himself with the illusion of a distinction, at once real and negligible: "Curiously enough this [crudity] gave no offence to Mr. Palace. He liked it. It opened a gulf between them; it mitigated that disagreeable sense of intimacy, of kindred, of something unpleasantly like being searchingly mirrored and told immodestly about oneself. A man who eats as one eats oneself is a friend and brother. But a man who scoops and engulfs food is an instrument. Cloote was much more endurable, Mr. Palace was realizing, as an instrument" (p. 151).

Palace deceives himself here, for beneath the appearance it is he who becomes Cloote's instrument and toy. We discover the process in this same chapter first as a piece of linguistic and psychic susceptibility on Palace's part. Cloote vouchsafes Palace a word:

> "I see you," Mr. Cloote raised his eyes to heaven and for a time spoke after the manner of one who sees visions. "I see you. . . . May I use a word—a key word, Mr. Palace? About you. A quality. The word—Debonair! . . ."
> He calmed Mr. Palace with an extended hand, deprecating any interruption while his vision continued. "Let me make myself perfectly clear. Debonair. You could easily be *very* debonair, Mr. Palace. I've always thought Il Re Galantuomo a most attractive title. Il Scrittore—No!—Lo Scrittore Galantuomo. A man just a little aloof—aloof in his soul and yet not too aloof. Smiling but never mingling, friendly, assured, kindly. Capable of immense seriousness,

but carrying it easily, lightly. Capable of—adventures. And naturally he was to be seen *unposed*—in transit—in action—caught unawares. A man rather heedless of his public. No standing at attention to be photographed." (p. 145)

The word takes, giving to all the suppressed yearning of Palace's life a name. Later that evening we discover him in his exalted, translated state:

It was a Florentine nobleman who towelled himself in Mr. Palace's bathroom.

At dinner that night he was unusually debonair. Brynhild couldn't imagine what had got hold of him. (p. 156)

And later still, indeed through the remainder of the novel, the word "debonair" rings out again and again in connection with Palace's conceit of himself, as the very emblem of his almost Malvolian folly. It also becomes Wells's arch means of indicating, in the Envoy, that not all of Brynhild's children are Palace's: "She developed an increasing social confidence and dignity and brought a bright and various family of three sons and two daughters into the world. Two at least of these offspring were quite debonair" (p. 302).

But another, more important instance of Cloote's control over Palace's life and illusions, quite crucial for the action of the novel, also appears in this chapter. While Palace pretends to be above such considerations, Cloote announces an ominous unilateral program for eliminating all literary competitors, Bunter especially. " 'This,' he said, 'is a service I do you and nothing I ask you to do. In fact the word for you here is—pardon me—"keep out." But we have to be chary of the growth of other reputations. A false reputation, shot up in the night, fungoid, that might take the wind out of our sails. . . . We can't ignore it.' " In thus becoming the autonomous agent of Palace's secret wish, Cloote initiates the action that throws Bunter and Brynhild together as lovers and that opens up the deepest and darkest exploration of the theme of appearance and reality in the novel.

Cloote's subsequent malicious investigation of Bunter uncovers the sordid truth beneath the young writer's promising career. We learn of it not from Cloote, though we sense him relentlessly closing in on his quarry, but from Bunter's long and moving confession to Brynhild in the tenth chapter. Bunter, whose real name is David Lewis, had thought himself married to a girl he had lived with for a week in Scotland during the First World War. After a time he left her and took up a career as a house agent in Wales. Here he was prevailed upon by an overpowering woman named Freda to marry her, thus becoming guilty, he thought, of bigamy. Worse yet, Freda's brother, Gregory, a cocaine addict, having discovered the Scots wife in Bunter's past, proceeded to blackmail him. Finding life with both Freda and her brother intolerable, Bunter dreamed of getting away, publishing the novel he had been working on and beginning a new life as a writer under an assumed name. One night when he found himself alone with Freda's brother, who had returned dirty and disheveled from a trip, the dream realized itself. After giving Gregory a hot bath, discarding his tattered garments and dressing him from head to foot in old clothes of his own, and supplying him with food, plenty of whiskey, and some money, Bunter accompanied him across a patch of open country toward the local railroad station. On the way, singing drunkenly and taunting Bunter, Gregory fell down a hole and drowned. Bunter was ten yards behind but felt that he might somehow have pushed Gregory. Frightened, he seized the opportunity to make off to London, hoping that when the body was eventually discovered it would be identified as his, David Lewis's, because of the clothes, and that having thus killed off his old self, he could assume a new identity as Alfred Bunter, the novelist.

But for Cloote, the plan would have succeeded totally, for Freda, after first identifying the body as her brother, reverses herself and pretends it is David Lewis. " 'From the indignant Deserted Wife her pose changed in a night into that of the Desperate Woman protecting her Love,' " says Bunter. Even the insurance company, though it knows better, decides to pay up on Lewis's policy for the publicity value. " 'Under protest, they said. As an advertisement. Five hundred pounds.' " The lie compounds itself, threatening to prevail.

But there is Cloote. His campaign against Bunter produces book review after book review discrediting Bunter as a writer of extremely limited social experience, inquiring insistently about his origins and credentials. Responding to this pressure and fear of exposure, Bunter makes his halting, anguished confession to Brynhild. Eventually, as Cloote gains possession of all the facts, Bunter is compelled to act. Returning to Cardiff as David Lewis, he clears himself of suspicion of murder, makes restitution, then vanishes. Very late in the novel we learn that having grown a beard—no doubt resembling Lawrence more than ever—he has been able to "rematerialize" himself as Alfred Bunter, living quietly abroad and resuming his writing.

Thus the angry young writer who at the outset embodies for Brynhild all the integrity and reality that her husband lacks, emerges at the end as the figure most deeply implicated in appearances, the charade of David Lewis's death and Alfred Bunter's life constituting appearances of a decidedly forbidding and disturbing kind. Like the Brynhild of the *Volsunga Saga,* the Brynhild of Wells's novel has been awakened by her Sigurd-Bunter from the enchanted sleep that her Odin-Palace had thrown her into, only, in this case, to discover that her young redeemer is also an illusion. But not quite. For she is also Undine and manages to win her soul, shape her own life, as a result of the child that she has by her knight, Bunter. We see this movement begin when after hearing Bunter's story, meditating on it, she dwells not on his deception of others but on his honesty with herself, "his passionate effort" to be sincere. "It was that passionate effort appealed to her most; it was as though something in him was wanting to get born through her. In her, he had intimated, for the first time he had found a chance of self knowledge. It made her feel incubatory" (p. 247).

The paternal birth image is striking, as is Brynhild's apt incubatory participation in it. For Bunter, despite the deceptions of the past, is, like Brynhild, and through Brynhild, profoundly concerned with knowing and abiding by the truth of his own real nature. In his case, his novels, as well as his intimacy with Brynhild, are the expression of that truth. Consequently, when Cloote's disclosures are about to destroy both his career and his opportunity to remain with Brynhild, when he has determined to return to Cardiff as David Lewis, he speaks of the return as a fiction: " 'I don't want to spend months, years perhaps of pretending and play-acting. All this is more than a calamity; it's devastation.' " Brynhild is immediately totally aware of the extraordinary inversion of categories, as Wells is of the radical modulation of primary thematic terms. Recognizing that the life that Bunter left behind him as David Lewis in Cardiff is really now the life of another man who did in a sense die when Gregory died, Brynhild expresses it for herself and for the novel: " 'You go back to reality,' reflected Brynhild. 'And you go back to falsehood. As if falsehood *was* reality' " (p. 265).

So it is that the Undine part of her prevails as Brynhild remains faithful to the newborn reality of Bunter's life and by means of it finds the basis of her own. She gives herself to him compassionately and consolingly as he faces the crisis of complete exposure by Cloote—the chapter is called "Mr. Alfred Bunter Goes to Pieces"—and afterward, alone, she amends her most fundamental ideas. In an access of self-knowledge, scrutinizing herself once again in a mirror at her dressing table, she says to herself, to her image in the glass, that she has always been simple because she has never done anything unexpected; that she never thought anything could surprise her or that she could surprise herself; but that now she can realize how life can be complicated and how other people are affected by it. Wells suggests that at this stage her confrontation with herself is not complete by employing a delicate extension of the mirror imagery: "She looked down at her hand mirror which was prone on the table as though hiding its reflections from her" (p. 272). It is to the less intimate dressing-table mirror that she addresses herself. Before long, however, the confrontation is completed and the Undine motif fulfilled, with flickers of the Brynhild-Odin-Sigurd story playing over it.

Carrying Bunter's child and reflecting on Palace's amusing willingness to play the role of father—Palace who is "extraordinarily married to her, about whom he would never know anything at all, about whom he didn't want to know anything at all"—she thinks that while thoroughly married herself, now "she was escaping—going away from all that had held her paralyzed for seven years—to something profoundly her own, profoundly secret in its essence and profoundly real. She had become real. Her priggishness had been reft from her. She was a cheat now—like everybody. She was a secret behind a façade. And altogether human. She had grown up at last . . ." (p. 297). Thus Bunter, her knight and her Sigurd, has dragged her down into humanity and made her real by making it necessary for her to be false. The reappearance of the façade image, now newly applied to Brynhild, makes the moral egalitarianism complete, throwing us back to the nightmarish brooding on universal deception and disguise of the early Nocturne chapter. But there is a difference, an exception. There is Brynhild's child, Undine's child, as there was Brynhild, the child of her own passionately, if conditionally, honest father: "Her thoughts flicked off at a tangent. The child? The child, though, was going to be different. Her child would never cheat like this, never humbug any one. Her child was going to be something better than had ever been before. In some way . . . this sort of thing wouldn't do for her child. That was what she had to see to. . . ."

Thus Wells, working almost totally within the frame of Brynhild's consciousness and allowing both the powers and limitations of her vision to enter in as yet another intricacy, brings the theme of appearances into its climactic phase. It is the maternal conceit of things that speaks through Brynhild at the last: the impulse to validate her own existence by giving birth to realities in the form of offspring. But here as Brynhild dreams of their difference from her, from her passive, feminine will, and of their legacy from their father(s), the Wellsian note, unobtrusively enough, creeps in:

> She felt, as she had never felt before, that she knew her own mind. And that instead of being the most aimless thing in the world, she now conceived her essential business plain before her.
> "Not one child but *children,* and the best I can get. . . .
> "What I was made for. . . .
> "A stormy little rebel to begin with who will batter at the façades. With trouble and stubbornness in those brown eyes of his. . . .
> "When all that is fairly under way, then surely at last I shall take an intelligent interest in—say—education. And politics. So that they don't kill or waste or starve my children or leave them alive with nothing sensible to do. . . .
> "If there *is* any sense in things at all." (p. 299)

As there had been something in Bunter that wanted to be born through Brynhild (p. 247), so there is something in Brynhild that wants to be born through her children. As readers of Wells, we are not surprised to find that it is partly a new world, where education and politics will not "kill or waste or starve my children or leave them alive with nothing sensible to do"—all that Wells really wanted from any future society. His grafting that hope, merely in passing, on to the pregnant Brynhild has an entire maternal, emotional propriety. We almost fail to find Wells in it at all.

But primarily what wants to be born in Brynhild through childbearing, what is already being born, is herself. This rebirth is connected with the vocation of motherhood, but it also has to do with the most fundamental forms of biological and sexual self-realization. She has had to surrender her vitality in order to gain it: "It was her love for that gracious slender body of hers that had helped her to consent not to use it. But now it did not seem to matter to her at all if that grace departed from her. Perhaps, said the Great God Pan in her, behind every lovely thing is the possibility of something lovelier. If things hadn't happened as they had happened, she would have kept that beautiful figure and it would have grown stale and fruitless upon her. From being a fresh young body it would have become a preserved body" (p. 300). Her ecstasy is Lawrentian, for the possibility of something lovelier behind every lovely thing is not only, in this case, her child, though it is partly that, but also herself quickened, herself carrying and nurturing her child. Studying her body in her mirror, Brynhild delights in the little blue veins that have appeared on her changed throat and bosom. She has the sense of living anew in generating life. Her "stormy little rebel" will need, in the future, to "batter at the façades," and in her own life now "Façade she had to be. Every self-conscious behaving thing must be a façade, must turn a face to the world and be aware of itself." But a new reality has emerged deep in her, beneath all shows, feminine, undeniable, sustaining:

> All the same these juices in her blood that had taken possession of her, and filled her with this deep irrational satisfaction, had a very imperious suggestion about them of being real. (p. 300)

At the next moment, in the very last words of the novel proper, before the Envoy, Wells has her pull back, so as to keep the thematic tension intricately poised even at the last; but it is almost too late, at least for Brynhild: "If indeed there was in human experience as yet any such thing as reality." For the skepticism belongs, by this time, more to Wells than to his heroine. The distance between them is measurable in a phrase from the Envoy that recalls some of the mystical fullness of Palace's emptiness: "Mrs. Brynhild Palace's new half-mystical self-devotion to the physical rebirth of our world." We dwell, however, not on Wells, but on Brynhild, the fully realized, fully represented, fully felt Yeatsian mother worshipping, with Lawrentian fervor, images that animate her reveries. That some of her hopes, some of her dissatisfactions, even some of her reservations may be Wells's doesn't matter, for not the least of her victories is her managing to wrest her new life away from her creator's.

    Brynhild is, then, unmistakably a novel about The Show of Things, but it is also in the end a novel about the reality of the self, either as Brynhild finds it in compassion, perception, and procreation, or as Bunter does in his work. Moreover, it is about the ways in which the lovers help one another to discover that reality. Bunter speaks of this process of self-defining communion to Brynhild in words that account for his experience and, incidentally, the wholly other experience of Palace and Cloote: " 'And never have I wanted to be known by anyone as I want to be known by you. . . . If I can get you to know me I feel that I shall begin perhaps to know something about myself' " (pp. 244–45). Such a validation of the self by means of another's accurate knowledge of it is precisely what Palace has been avoiding all his life and precisely what Cloote is hired to keep from happening. Cloote's method is to substitute a totally illusory self and make that known. The irony of the novel's structure is that Cloote makes use of the truth about Bunter's life in order to promote the deceptions about Palace's, but that in doing so Cloote eventually assists Bunter to purge himself. In the world as it is, unredeemed by sense, revolution, or good will, Wells allows Palace and Cloote their Nobel Prize, Brynhild and Bunter their façades. But he has also made it clear that the latter two are fortunate enough to have that within which passeth show.

Even this extensive treatment of the degree to which *Brynhild* is organized around its thematic center does not exhaust the matter. There are innumerable other instances, such as the various roles that Cloote has Palace play, including those on an extensive tour of Europe where Palace must first be the attentive husband, but later travel alone as the wild, lecherous man of genius; Cloote's striking description of the pretenses connected with the orderly sensuality of the French; Bunter's dodges at the newspaper room of the British Museum as he seeks to discover news about Cardiff without being himself detected; Brynhild's hiding her pregnancy from Palace for a time, and her posing with Bunter in the midst of his impassioned confession to her. Thematic resonance is everywhere in the novel. Yet at no time does it become tiresome or oppressive. Indeed, at no time does it become noticeable as an imposition on the novelistic substance, the power of the narrative and the characters to concern us, move us, engage us, however much my analytic isolation of, and concentration on, the pattern of appearance might suggest otherwise.

In fact, Wells is able to achieve a more than Jamesian unity at the same time that he provides a more than Jamesian variety. Much of this is owing to style. James typically has all his figures adopt his own voice and idiom, thus bathing his novels, the late ones especially, in a unity of language and sensibility, as well as one of "subject," action, value, and symbol. Even Kate Croy, Charlotte Stant, Mrs. Brookenham, and Gilbert Osmond have Jamesian sensibilities. As a result, we become imprisoned without recourse in the intensive unitary dimension that gives us our characteristic sense of the James novel, of one mind suffusing, animating, but also delimiting others. In *Brynhild,* on the other hand, Wells creates real distinctions among his characters' voices. There is the methodical extravagance of Cloote's public relations schemes, the outrageous yet pathetic hauteur of Palace, the impassioned, eloquent groping of Bunter, the demure, touching exploration of Brynhild, and, over all, the riddling, sympathetic irony of the narrator's voice. And each of these styles marks its possessor's relative grasp of the real.

Yet that grasp is never a matter of ideology or even ideas. These matter far less than the emotion and intent with which characters talk to one another and the degree of response they awaken. At one point Bunter speaks with enormous distress and power about life as a form of fear, about war as a form of life "hurried up, intensified, underlined, made plain by exaggeration," and about the pressing need for rebirth. But nothing that he says, indeed almost nothing that he ever says, is there for its own sake as an idea. When he breaks off, suddenly, rejecting it all, Brynhild offers the book's general intimation about such discourse:

> "Why should I spend our last moments talking this rubbish," he said, and left his sentence incomplete.
> "It's not rubbish," said Brynhild. "Everything that is worth saying seems almost impossible to say." (p. 269)

The action of *Brynhild,* like that of a James novel, consists of conversations, or exists in conversations. The major incidents—the death of Bunter's brother-in-law, Gregory, the imminent exposure of Bunter's past by Cloote, Palace's tour of the Baltic nations—are all treated in dialogue as either rehearsals of antecendent action or anticipations of projected action. Even the lovemaking between Brynhild and Bunter is merely an extension, not really presented at all, of the long conversation which gives rise to it. Yet the book is very far from being a dialogue novel in the sense that Wells expounds in his autobiography or in the introduction to *Babes in the Darkling Wood.* Wells's object in *Brynhild* is not to have his characters debate with one another, presenting views which have an intrinsic intellectual interest, and then, from the clash of opposing views and the consequences of the action, to cull the surviving ideas. He is far more interested in allowing Bunter to express his agony by "philosophizing" and pontificating and in having Brynhild express her humanity and sympathy by feeling her way tenderly and patiently through Bunter's verbiage to the pain beneath. He is similarly much more interested in the revolting comedy of their intercourse, their mutual exploitation, than in anything Cloote and Palace say to each other. Wells does take a certain delight in parodying the public relations mentality in both men, but this is hardly the stuff of the novel of ideas.

It is comportment that he works with here primarily, not so much what his people formulate as what they are, what they evolve into, and what this in turn signifies for his theme. Oddly enough, by thus charging them with themselves and relieving them of all responsibility for his own general ideas and personal history, Wells was able to write one of the most vital and touching novels of his last period. It was what Henry James had been telling him all along.

Notes

1. See Antonina Vallentin, *H. G. Wells: Prophet of Our Day* (New York: John Day Co., 1950), Lovat Dickson, *H. G. Wells: His Turbulent Life and Times* (New York: Atheneum, 1969), and Norman and Jeanne MacKenzie, *H. G. Wells* (New York: Simon and Schuster, 1973), where she can be identified as Marie, or Moura, Budberg, a former secretary and companion to Maxim Gorki.

2. *Brynhild, or The Show of Things* (New York: Charles Scribner's Sons, 1937), 302. All subsequent page references are to this edition and will be cited parenthetically in the text.

3. See, for example, James's treatment of journalists and publicity in *The Bostonians,* "The Death of the Lion," and "Flickerbridge."

4. For a perceptive account of Wells's earlier flirtations with Jamesian practice, which were less extensive, less sustained, and less heartfelt, see Richard Hauer Costa, "Edwardian Intimations of the Shape of Fiction to Come: Mr. Britling/Job Huss as Wellsian Central Intelligences," *English Literature in Transition, 1880–1920,* 18, no. 4 (1975): 229–42.

5. In the *Experiment in Autobiography* Wells writes: "From [James's] point of view there were not so much 'novels' as The Novel, and it was a very high and important achievement. . . . He saw us all as Masters or would-be Masters, little Masters and Great Masters, and he was plainly sorry that 'Cher Maître' was not an English expression" (p. 411).

6. See the Prefaces to Volumes 7 and 12 of the Atlantic Edition of Wells's works. Or this, from his introduction to *The Scientific Romances of H. G. Wells* (London: Victor Gollancz, 1933): "Work of this sort [*The Autocracy of Mr. Parham*] gets so stupidly reviewed nowadays that it has little chance of being properly read. People are simply warned that there are ideas in my books and advised not to read them, and so a fatal suspicion has wrapped about the later ones. 'Ware stimulants!' It is no good my saying that they are quite as easy to read as the earlier ones and much more timely. It becomes a bore doing imaginative books that do not touch imaginations, and at length one stops even planning them" (p. x).

7. See Dickson, *H. G. Wells,* p. 261. Wells himself treats such activities quite affectionately in the heavily autobiographical *Mr. Britling Sees It Through* (1916). One wonders if Wells's Orange of Discord, in the extreme comic artificiality of the Judgment of Paris charade, bears any resemblance to James's "plump and more or less juicy orange of a particular acquainted state" "squeeze[d] out to the utmost" in the indictment of Wells's artlessness in "The Younger Generation."

Revisions of His Past: H. G. Wells's
Anatomy of Frustration

ROBERT M. PHILMUS

The opposite of a true statement is a false statement. But the opposite of a profound truth may be another profound truth.

—Niels Bohr

I

The proposition that H. G. Wells's period of literary creativity ended more or less abruptly circa 1910 has gained general acceptance as something of a truism. Though it is neither self-evident nor substantially true, the fortunes of his reputation as a writer have come to depend on it. That Wells produced his best work in the decade and a half beginning with *The Time Machine* (1894–95) and extending through *The History of Mr. Polly* (1910) can, of course, be argued without concluding that everything he wrote subsequently is unworthy of regard. Yet most critics have imagined the two judgments to be contingent upon one another, axiologically if not logically. They expressly or tacitly suppose that the criteria they appeal to or propound for rationalizing their praise of the "early Wells" oblige them to dismiss his later writings.

The standards alleged to justify the neglect of approximately three-quarters of Wells's entire output[1] have been diverse. Critics since Henry James have complained of Wells's lapsing finally and irretrievably into "journalism" and sacrificing any concern for the niceties of literary construction and the felicities of literary style to the propagandizing of his ephemeral ideas.[2] A cognate accusation would have it that Wells in time abandoned what is somewhat quaintly referred to as "the novel proper," with its "sense of society as a whole," and turned to generic forms which are, for some undisclosed reason, improper, or otherwise illicit, such as the "discussion" or "dialogue" novel.[3] Alternatively, he has been arraigned for betraying the ironic and skeptical pessimism of his early years as a writer and indulging instead in a crass and dogmatic optimism,[4] or for repudiating "intuitive impulse" by succumbing to an "obsession" with the notion of world order.[5]

Reprinted from *Texas Studies in Language and Literature* 20, no. 2 (Summer 1978):249–66, by permission of the author and the University of Texas Press.

Critics have thus agreed in positing the existence of two Wellses, whom they have variously termed the "artist" and the "journalist," or the novelist and the polemicist, or the imaginative skeptic who experimented with ideas and the closed-minded optimist with monomaniacal delusions. By their indictments of the "late Wells," they have also—and necessarily—emphasized that these two Wellses are separable and chronologically discrete. But the criteria invoked to distinguish the one from the other do not serve to define some more or less radical disjunction between the "early Wells" and the "late." In fact, they invalidate that hypothesis by pointing to the aesthetic and ideological continuities that subsist in his writings.

Aesthetic standards provide no basis for condemning Wells's later works en masse—without, that is, condemning the rest of his opus along with them. It is true that many of the books he turned out after *Mr. Polly* are slipshod affairs. But judged fairly on their individual merits, his late novels are no more perfunctory in matters of structure and style than his early ones are. On the contrary, many of the stories he wrote in his sixties and seventies exhibit a literary craftsmanship that he only begins to approach in his best work of thirty years before. *Tono-Bungay* (1909), for example, contains only the barest hint of the happiness of phrasing, the witty, often epigrammatic, incisiveness of description, that abounds in *The Bulpington of Blup* (1932), *Brynhild* (1937), and *Apropos of Dolores* (1938).[6] If the content of these late novels does not have the imaginative power of his best science fiction, that is at least partly because Wells employs his imaginative energies elsewhere, in experimenting with the form of the novel itself. Thus *The Holy Terror* (1939) begins as a conventional fictive biography; but in its movement from the past, through the present, into the future, it exceeds the temporal limits within which novelists usually confine themselves. *You Can't Be Too Careful* (1941), though awkward and finally unsuccessful, is one of the more daring of Wells's many attempts to fuse fiction with discursive prose. Conversely, in *The Anatomy of Frustration* (1936) he embodies novelistic elements in what is preponderantly a discourse.

A Modern Utopia (1905) obviously presages these late experiments. But their generic peculiarities are foreseeable in Wells's fiction as far back as the 1890s. His literary efforts from the first manifest his abiding commitment to fiction as a vehicle for ideas, and his "discussion" or "dialogue" novels are hardly a senile aberration from his earlier practice. As anyone knows who has read the *National Observer* version, *The Time Machine* originated as one, and it still retains traces of that origin through subsequent revisions.

It also owes much to Wells's "journalism," his science journalism in particular.[7] The same thing can be said of most of his other "scientific romances" and many of his novels. *The Island of Dr. Moreau* (1896) comes straight out of "The Limits of Individual Plasticity," which he incorporated almost verbatim as one of its chapters.[8] He refashioned material from "The Man of the Year Million" in *War of the Worlds* (1898), practically the sole literary survivor of the so-called *"Battle of Dorking* controversy."[9] And the import of his more or less ephemeral essays on the teaching of science and the state of education partially finds its way into *Love and Mr. Lewisham* (1900) and several subsequent novels of his.[10] Connections of this sort between his early fiction and his "journalism" offer some indication of the extent to which the latter was always a principal source of his literary creativity generally.[11] Indeed, the presence or absence of "journalistic" elements provides no reliable measure of the literary quality of any given work of his.

Nor is it possible to differentiate clearly an "early" from a "late" Wells with respect to the ideas and attitudes he expresses. A number of his books do humorlessly expound upon various aspects of the notion of his that is often labeled, somewhat simplistically, "world order"—what he sometimes called "human ecology."[12] However, as his alternative phrase suggests, "world order" epitomizes a complex of ideas. All of these relate to the need for an intelligent and cooperative effort to prevent the human species from doing away with itself, and many of them are seminally present in his literary beginnings. In some of his earliest essays, he speculates on the chances of man's becoming extinct. The cosmic process, on a collision course with man's complacent rigidity, might annihilate him; or Darwinian law might forestall that eventuality by transforming the human species through natural selection.[13] Though Wells precariously balances the two possibilities in *The Time Machine,* he pessimistically focuses on, and virtually discounts, the second in *The Island of Dr. Moreau.* There he reveals serious doubts about the short-term efficacy of biological evolution as a means of altering human nature and thus removing the internal and external threats to the survival of the species. By 1897, he has definitively given up the hope that nature itself, in accordance with Darwinian principles and without human exertion, will accomplish the radical reconstruction of *Homo sapiens* necessary if man is to have a future. Retaining the Darwinian scheme of things as a paradigm, Wells turns to what he calls "artificial evolution" and urges the need for human direction and control over the "cultural" environment on which the future immediately depends. "One may dream," he writes in "Morals and Civilisation," "of an informed, unselfish, unauthorised body of workers, a real and conscious apparatus of education and moral suggestion . . . shaping the minds and acts and destinies of men."[14]

Thus by the turn of the century he had formulated a good many of the ideas usually associated with his later years. This does not mean that he had nothing to say thereafter, or that he could only repeat himself with tiresome solemnity. It is true that at times, both before and after 1910, his didactic insistence on the necessity for planning the cultural environment becomes overbearing and strident. It is also true that in his later writings he does not concentrate his ironic awareness on that idea, or distortions of it, as he does in *A Story of the Days to Come* (1899) and *The First Men in the Moon* (1900–01). But if he does not persist in belaboring, after the fashion of the works just mentioned, the conceivable abuses of a "conscious apparatus" for social control, neither does he lose his critical faculties altogether. Always a skeptic, he defines in his late novels a different object for ironic regard: the idiosyncratic, sometimes psychopathological, behavior of the individual ego confronted by the reality of change.

His literary project for humorously dissecting human idiosyncrasy in one sense comes unexpected: it does not sort with the prevailing assumption that Wells after 1910 stagnates as a writer. Nevertheless, his undertaking does not signal an abrupt discontinuity, the date of which has simply to be readjusted. For the books belonging to his late period, notwithstanding the apparent novelty of the materials and ideas in some of them, all embody variations on a lifelong theme of Wells's. He had hinted at the fundamentals of that theme in the overall introduction to the Atlantic Edition of his works, by way of defending the "continuity" of his literary "growth":[15]

> Himself a child of change, born in a home that was broken up by failure in the retail trade, and escaping only by very desperate exertion from a life of servitude and frustration, he has been made aware of, and he is still enormously aware of and eager to understand and express, the process of adaptation, destruction, and reconstruction of old moral and intellectual and political and economic formulae that is going on all about us. Indeed all these volumes are about unrest and change. Even in his novels his characters like Kipps [1905] and Mr. Polly, are either change-driven and unable to understand, or, like Benham of "The Research Magnificent" [1915] or Stratton in "The Passionate Friends" [1913], they are attempting desperately to understand and still more desperately attempting to thrust at and interfere with change.[16]

In their transition from autobiography to art, these remarks indicate the depth of Wells's concern with "unrest and change." They do not, however, forecast the stratagems for deliberately avoiding change that he explores, for example, in *Bulpington* or *Dolores.* Nor do they specify his theme as globally and systematically as *The Anatomy of Frustration* does. There, by focusing on the meaning of "frustration," he virtually recreates himself as his own "precursor."[17] That is, he suggests new ways of looking at, and supplies new terms for speaking about, the concepts operative in his fiction—and with them, a new perspective on his development as a writer.

If the charges against the "late" Wells do not lead one to anticipate any of this, that is because they caricature rather than characterize Wells's literary career; and even as caricatures they bear little resemblance to the original. They do not portray the mental energy of the man who at the age of seventy-six submitted a doctoral thesis ("On the Quality of Illusion in the Continuity of the Individual Life of the Higher Metazoa with Particular Reference to the Species Homo Sapiens") to the science faculty at the University of London. They also drastically misrepresent the relationship between the Wells who has a sense of the moral urgency for "adaptation, destruction, and reconstruction" in human values and the Wells who is historically aware of the obduracy of the human mind. These "two Wellses" are not chronologically disjoinable. As *The Anatomy* reveals, the discrepancy Wells recognizes between the demands of "is" and those of "ought to be" results in a conflict of allegiances that he never resolves, a conflict that remains the source of his essential ambivalence.[18] Any attempt to segregate the moral "optimist" from the historical "pessimist" must distort that truth while ignoring its complement. For, as *The Anatomy* again makes plain, Wells logically derives his moral imperatives from his analysis of the existing state of human affairs.

II

The Anatomy of Frustration purports to be a synopsis of the projected fourteen volumes (only eleven of them published) of William Burroughs Steele's magnum opus of the same title. Steele himself is of course fictitious. (The choice of his surname can in part be accounted for by its Wellsian associations in sentences like: "Science, with her order, her inhuman distance, her *steely* certainties, saved me from despair."[19]) He is also a surrogate for his creator: like Wells, he surveys the "old moral and intellectual and political and economic formulae" with a view to their "destruction" and "reconstruction." Although Steele's fictive tomes do not compare in number with Wells's, their encyclopedic scope recalls Wells's many pleas for the codifying of human thought,[20] and their organizing concept is one that Wells touches upon in his above-quoted comments on the thematic unity of "all" his "volumes." "Frustration," Steele's focal term, he declares to be the "counterpart" of Robert Burton's "melancholy" in its relation to its historical age. But as a concept, frustration is also a "repudiation" of Burton in that its "anatomy" takes hope from the assumption of a fluid and ever-changing, rather than a static, reality (*AF*, I:4 ff.).[21] "In Burton's world there was . . . no idea of fundamental change"; in Steele's world there is, and he can in consequence demand that "we change things" (*AF*, I:10).

"Change" is a crucial term in Wells's vocabulary almost from his outset as a writer. It is practically synonymous with "reality" as he understands it. In one of his early essays, having impugned as a delusion the notion of cyclical recurrence, he asserts that "the main course" of the universe "is forward, from the things that are past and done with for ever to things that are altogether new."[22] *The Anatomy of Frustration* deals with the antagonism between this cosmic reality and the human resistances to accepting it and thereby gaining some degree of direction over the course of change. As Steele (i.e., Wells) defines the word, *frustration* signifies everything that stands in the way of man's realizing his strivings as an individual and as a species. The obstacles, like Blake's "Mind-forg'd manacles," are at once both external and subjective. They are obstacles to "Vision" and "Truth" and also to "Life," which in Steele's usage is another word for "Humanity" (*AF*, XXII:207; IV, 29). Where they are not wholly the product of erroneous thinking, their obstructive power comes largely from "*Confusions in Thought*."

"Confusions in thought" and "death" Steele regards as the most encompassing barriers to human fulfillment, both for the individual and for the species (see *AF*, II). The correlation Steele establishes between these two seemingly unconnected phenomena constitutes a paradigm of his method and entails his "synthesis" as a whole. Death, he argues, obtains its power over the human mind as a result of the mental confusion about the nature of immortality perpetuated by a jumble of traditional beliefs on the subject. Sorting these out, he discovers each to be an evasive illusion. But in his conspectus he also finds them all expressive of a desire to "escape from the conclusive frustration of death . . . by merger into some greater being" (*AF*, III:27). The logical question—what "greater being" best qualifies as the object of the human aspiration towards death-transcending unity?—contains its own answer: "Humanity" itself, in its collective effort to avoid the "frustration of death" and realize its own capabilities. The common goal of such an effort is implicit in the very universality of the desire for immortality, which desire the individual can satisfy by identifying himself with "Humanity." In other words, "there is no truly rational objective, no sound and sure merger-immortality . . . except a thorough-going self-identification with the human will and intelligence considered as a synthesis of the will-drives and mental-drives of the entire species" (*AF*, IV:29).

This conclusion seems to pay dearly for the tautological self-sufficiency of having individual immortality depend on the continuance of cooperative "Humanity." After all, an organized endeavor towards human fulfillment on a global scale does not in fact exist. Nor, if it did, would it be exempt from being frustrated by the extinction of the race.

These two objections, though they proceed from a failure to distinguish—and hence to recognize the connection—between Steele's empirical analysis and his moral synthesis, are nevertheless useful for appreciating the force of his reasoning. Because they in effect rationalize the status quo, the two together serve to indicate how radical Steele's way of thinking is. His analysis of the hodgepodge of traditional contentions about immortality impinges upon virtually all other "confusions in thought." So, too, his synthesis—his own version of "merger-immortality"—would in practice involve the systematic transformation of existing patterns of social behavior. His conclusions in either case are subversive because his attack on a question is global, not "piecemeal" ("one of Steele's most frequent words, used always in a condemnatory sense" [*AF*, IX:62]). "We cannot discuss money," he maintains, "without a general theory of property, . . . we cannot discuss property without a general theory of economic organization, . . . we cannot discuss economic organization without a general political and social ideal and . . . we cannot have a general political and social ideal without a comprehensive conception of human ecology" (*AF,* IX:63). In accordance with this methodological approach, his examination of the possibilities for immortality leads him to hortative theories of social "reconstruction."

To suppose that Steele hypostatizes an enlightened effort towards co-operation on the part of "Humanity" is to misunderstand his method. He does not assume that effort to be a fact. On the contrary, he urges and prescribes it as a logical and historical imperative, as an ideal he arrives at by investigating the causes of frustration. His argument, which is similar to the one that gives structure to *The Outline of History* (1920), is that the human mind has reached the point in its development where large-scale social reorganization is both appropriate and necessary.[23] Unless man undertakes a radical synthesis of his present thinking with the intent of formulating and implementing plans for "a Next Beginning," "a New Model for humanity" (*AF,* XI:83, XXV:215), "complete frustration lies before [him]" (*AF,* VII:50). Of course, the extinction of the species might preempt any plans for a "Next Beginning." But the only hope for possibly avoiding such a fate, Steele observes in answering that criticism, resides in practical ideals for reordering the conduct of human affairs. For certainly in the short run (short by standards of geological time, that is) extinction is far more likely to occur through lack of human foresight and restraint than as a result of some cosmic mishap not precipitated by man's meddling in the econological balance of the planet. "There is," he says, "no acceptable alternative" to "world revolution . . . in human organization."

> The only alternatives we can envisage [he continues] are intolerable prospects of biological disaster, chronic war, social deterioration, diseases, specific differentiation [e.g., as between the Morlocks and the Eloi in *The Time Machine*], generation after generation of distressed existences with extinction looming at the end. Either we *take hold of our destiny* or, failing that, we are driven towards our fate. (*AF,* XXIV:211; Wells's emphasis)[24]

A rational "revolution" in human thought and social practice cannot definitively dispose of the threat of extinction, but it would eliminate other, less ultimate frustrations that are some of its probable sources. The consoling truth, offered by "the biologist," is that "there is no final defeat for an individual . . . but fruitlessness and death," and "no final defeat for a species until nothing remains of it to begin again" (*AF,* X:82).

Steele cites such truths of science from time to time and continually alludes to the scientist's method and outlook. In fact, he relies on the scientific enterprise as a model for the one he proposes. "The progress of science is the exposure of inaccuracies. Its history is a history of frustration admitted, examined and overcome" (*AF,* XXII:205). His statement implies a kind of causal relationship between identifying the frustration and surmounting it. Similarly, in postulating that "no frustration" is "inevitable" (*AF*, XXIV:213), he heuristically assumes that any particular frustration is contingent upon mental and societal confusions which can be recognized, analyzed, and remedied. To be sure, the "tak[ing] hold of our destiny" is a never-ending responsibility; for no final solution exists to the problem of frustration in general. As in science, any successful "synthesis" for dealing with troublesome frustrations becomes the source for new beginnings—that is, new questions, and new frustrations. "The 'biological use' of the individual life," according to another of Steele's parallels between science and social theory,

> is not achievement but experiment, failure and a lesson, and so too are all these larger-scale efforts to organize living forces. The conscious efforts to unify and rationalize human life, which have been going on now for five-and-twenty centuries, when seen from the perspective of geological time, are no more and no less than a struggle to secure a new foothold for the race, which won, will be in itself only a basis for new and nobler discontents. (*AF*, X:80)

Thus the persistence of frustration-in-the-abstract, so to speak, should not be a cause for despair. On the contrary, it is the necessary antagonist of life which defines itself as conscious, or rational, in its struggle to overcome frustration.

As the passage just quoted indicates, the "synthesis" Steele predicates on values drawn from social psychology contains an implicit appeal to notions of biological evolution. In this regard, Wells's science journalism of the 1890s approaches and anticipates his conclusions in *The Anatomy*. In "Human Evolution, an Artificial Process" (1896), for example, he speculates about a future time when "consciously shap[ing] their moral conceptions and their lives," men may "work towards, and at last attain and preserve, a social organization so . . . balanced against exterior necessities on the one hand, and the artificial factor [i.e., enculturated values and attitudes] in the individual on the other, that the life of every human being . . . may be generally happy."[25] Again, he prefigures the translation of biological inference into the social morality of viewing individual human life as subsidiary and instrumental to the fulfillment of "Humanity" in another of his early essays, "The Duration of Life" (1895). "The business of the animal," he writes, "seems to be not to live its own life, but to reproduce its own kind."[26] And the same year, in a companion essay, he declares: "Mortal man and the immortal protozoa have the same barren immortality; the individuals perish, living on only in their descendants . . . ; the type alone persists."[27]

Steele is more circumspect than the youthful Wells in voicing confidence about the likelihood of a cooperative assault on the "exterior" and "artificial" sources of unhappiness and frustration (see *AF*, XXV). He is also less open in expressing the reservations about "merger-immortality" and its attendant ideals that Wells conveys about its biological analogue in the word "barren" and expatiates on by saying, "It is individual life that appeals to our emotions, individual death that broods over our joys." Nevertheless, the tension here implied between the emotional needs of the individual and the rational imperatives of the species does carry into *The Anatomy*, where it remains a largely unresolved conflict in Steele's "synthesis"—as indeed it does in Wells's writings as a whole.[28]

The conflict surfaces in Steele's discussion of the nature of love, which he declines to pretend is anything but "preferential" (*AF*, XIX[a]:179ff.): "By religion we become Man, by love we remain individual" (*AF*, XIX[a]:180). Steele holds out the hope that this divergence of "head" from "heart" may one day disappear. "Intellectual realizations," he remarks somewhat cryptically, "are much easier and swifter than moral [read: emotional] reconstructions" (*AF*, XIX[c]:192). Still, he acknowledges as a source of frustration the kind of clash between the restrictions imposed by society and the instinctive drives of the individual that Freud describes as the principal cause of civilized man's discontent.[29] And since the "religion" Steele talks about refers to the social norms he is advocating, he seems to be intimating that the discrepancies between the needs of the species and those of the individual may constitute a more perdurable source of frustration that do the "confusions in thought" or faulty societal arrangements that now exist.

To admit that social reconstruction makes emotional demands which are difficult for human beings to adjust to at this point in history[30] is not, however, tantamount to positing (as Freud virtually does) an essential contradiction between society and the individual, the rational requirements of the one and the self-interest of the other. The latter are mutually exclusive only for life that is not "conscious," in *The Anatomy*'s honorific sense. "Conscious" life must recognize the imperative for an intelligently directed transformation of the "artificial" environment to relieve the pressure of frustration. On this level of realization, or "consciousness," moral self-interest and the ideal interests of the species are complementary.

That complementarity is implied by the context wherein Steele, after propounding an elaborate and systematic synthesis of social ideals, confesses to "an unconquered sense of my own individuality as significant, as primary" (*AF*, XXIII:209). This he intends as an assertion of "*free will*"; but it follows immediately upon his articulating a feeling of "complete predestination": "My story . . . is really the trace of the reaction between internal and external forces, equally destined and rigid" (*AF*, XXIII:208). The juxtaposition calls to mind Wells's lecture on "The Scepticism of the Instrument" (1903), in the course of which he singles out predestination and free will as exemplifying his contention that concepts held in logic to be antinomies are really complementary in as much as they derive from totally different "standpoints" (i.e., human and cosmic).[31]

From the standpoint of the ideal, which is primary in *The Anatomy,* the individual will is in harmony with the moral exhortations of a hypothetical collective will to combat the causes of frustration by changing the patterns of thinking and social behavior. But the "confusions in thought" Steele attempts to dispose of also occasion self-doubt concerning the feasibility of his scheme for social revolution (see *AF,* XXV:215). He sees his plans imperiled by the multitude of human beings unaware of the necessity for directing the course of change to moral ends or uncomprehendingly opposed to the very idea of change and consequently frustrated without hope of release from frustration. If Steele's synthesis evokes the promise of the heights of man's becoming, of a "plastic" humanity intelligently cooperating to triumph over frustrations that thwart its mental evolution, his descriptive analysis of man's present confusion discloses an abyss of stultified egotisms misguidedly seeking "rigidity" for the species[32] and thereby trying to arrest its development.

The Anatomy thus brings together Wells's diverse concerns as a writer. It does so not simply through its content, through the ambivalent balance between analysis and synthesis, but also in its form. By combining the fictional elements of a life of Steele with the discursive elements of an exposition of his thought, it points to a continuity between Wells's novels and his nonfictional prose. That continuity does not merely subsist in the logical connections Steele's normative social theories have with Wells's early science journalism, and thence with his polemical disquisitions from *Anticipations* (1901) right on through *The Work, Wealth and Happiness of Mankind* (1931). For in its analysis and synthesis, *The Anatomy* defines the complementary aspects of Wells's fundamental and abiding theme: frustration.

III

"Frustration" identifies Wells's theme more precisely and comprehensively than does "unrest and change." As fact and concept, frustration subsumes unrest as one of its symptoms; and in its ambivalence as a stimulus to "plasticity" or rigidification, it includes change as either its result or its cause. Some degree of awareness of the frustrating constrictions of man's present "artificial" environment can provoke an active desire for change—as it does, say, in Mr. Polly. But for the mind oriented towards the past, change itself appears to be the paramount frustration: witness Theodore in *Bulpington.*

Apart from their shared rejection of the present, the "dream worlds" that Polly and Theodore construct are so radically different from one another as to constitute antitheses. Polly's is a "dream" open to new possibilities—and, consequently, to the future. He may be a creature of feeling much more than of intellection, but his impulses take him in the direction the universe is going, towards "things that are altogether new."[33] Theodore's attachment to an aesthetically romanticized past has exactly the opposite effect. He militantly refuses to admit the future into his backward-looking dreamland, which, in contrast to the world from which the angel falls in *The Wonderful Visit* (1895), is in no sense reality.[34] As a result, he becomes increasingly rigid, to the point of schizophrenia.

Theodore represents an extreme of the type of man that, misapprehending the true nature of frustration, tenaciously holds to the moribund and deathly illusions, the specious escapes, that Steele analyzes as the chief sources of frustration. Many of Wells's novels, particularly from the 1920s on, study the variants of this type of mind. He finally concludes, not entirely facetiously, that it is a distinct species of the genus *Homo*. Wilbeck, in *Apropos of Dolores,* calls it *Homo regardant,* "traditional, legal and implacable," as distinguished from the "open-minded and futuristic" *Homo rampant.*[35] In *You Can't Be Too Careful,* Wells renames *Homo regardant Homo Tewler,* a pun he derives eponymously from the surname of Edward Albert Tewler, whom he portrays as the epitome of the "careful" *Homo faber,* uninnovating and mechanically rigid. *Homo Tewler,* he finds, is predominant in the present state of human affairs; but whether he will survive to become *Homo sapiens* is a matter of no less doubt for Wells at the end[36] than at the beginning of his literary career (compare the "prophecy" of human degeneration and extinction with which the Time Traveller traduces the optimistic presumptions of his complacent audience).

Homo Tewler, with his superficial overlay of sublimated habits, is, as Wells's characterization of him suggests, little more than "the culminating ape." Dead set against what *Tewler* refers to as "ideers,"[37] he stands in the way of man's realizing his capabilities as "the highly plastic creature of [cultural] tradition, [moral] suggestion and reasoned thought."[38] The history "of Man," Steele had asserted, "is the story of an excessively pugnacious ape being slowly tamed. . . . In the face of every new necessity he struggles with irrational antagonism to novelty" (*AF,* XII:100). *Homo Tewler,* or *Homo regardant,* personifies that opposition to mental evolution. Essentially, he is man as irrational atavist, the embodiment of apelike impulses and primordial needs. He is the antagonist within, perverting, and finally subverting and destroying, Griffin's dream of transcending the limitations nature imposes (*The Invisible Man* [1897]); and the antagonist without, frustrating the scientist's attempts to control natural evolution and excoriate "the mark of the beast" (*The Island of Dr. Moreau*).[39]

Viewed from a cosmic perspective, *Homo regardant* and *Homo rampant* are compatible intellectual constructs which together explain the dis-ease of a being caught between the backward pull of his evolutionary origins and the impulse forward to self-liberation. Seen close-up, however, on the level of emotional experience, these forces very much conflict.[40] The conjunction of *Homo regardant* and *Homo rampant* is hardly a happy marriage. Certainly Wilbeck in time discovers its dolorous outcome. Though in himself (as his name implies) he uneasily combines tendencies towards "futuristic" self-assertion ("will") with uxorious complaisance ("beck"),[41] still he comes to look upon Dolores—whose unconventionality outdoes convention in its stultifying rigidity—as the apotheosis of all his frustrations.[42]

The conflict in the mind, and interpersonally, between past and future, along with its resultant confusions and frustrations, finds its correlative (as Steele suggests) in societal arrangements which are themselves an unstable compound of the atavistic and the futuristic. Indeed, the unreconstructed social order, which George Ponderevo describes as "commercialised Bladesovery,"[43] is a bad compromise with man's contradictory drives. The restraints it tries to put on the "pugnacious ape" apply equally, if not more, to *Homo sapiens* struggling to emerge. In frustrating both, it gives rise to personal and social disorders, to the former of which the likes of "Tono-Bungay" pretend to minister. But "Tono-Bungay," while it is the brain-child of Edward Ponderevo's legitimate sense of social frustration, is a false panacea, just as its "inventor" is a false prophet. His enterprise offers no true hope for change, except as the trajectory of its progress and decline serves, in the world of the novel, as a parable of the fate of the Bladesover World. It "pseudomorphously" imitates Bladesover in its degenerate expansion, as Crest Hill does London seen as a "tumourous growth-process."[44] The financial empire of Tono-Bungay is similar to the mysterious and inherently amorphous substance "quap," which theoretically holds the promise of (incandescent) light, but in fact does no more than permeate and contaminate everything it comes in contact with, causing decay and destruction. The radioactivity of "quap" is described as *"cancerous"*—"a real disease of matter." The same metaphors apply to Ponderevo's business enterprise: he capitalizes his new investments by selling shares in previous ones, and produces nothing of social utility, merely rottenness and ruin.[45] Nor does Wells allow the collapse of Ponderevo's empire to effect any social upheaval; for it is a parody, rather than the antithesis, of the capitalist economic system.

The only possible way out of a world dominated by frustration, the conclusion of *Tono-Bungay* hints, is through the cosmic vision science affords man the means of achieving. This is the vision George Ponderevo glimpses as he surveys London again—now in its temporal as well as in its spatial dimension—from the deck of his "destroyer" speeding down the Thames. "We are all things that make and pass," he says, "striving upon a hidden mission, out to the open sea" that is the future.[46] In finally seeking the kind of detachment from frustration that precedes a plan for action, he defines himself as the prototype of Steele.

George Ponderevo and William Burroughs Steele are but two examples of the type of mind in quest of values by which man may be able to extricate himself from the frustrating realities of what is basically still a Bladesover World. Both feel the attraction of "futuristic" ideals; neither is oblivious to the countervailing force of those present realities. That Wells himself is likewise, and perpetually, self-divided by his intellectual allegiances to the "empirical present" and the "normative future" is evident in almost all his writings, beginning with *The Time Machine*. *The Anatomy* provides the conceptual means for coming to terms with these "two Wellses," and thus proves to be useful for properly understanding even Wells's "proper novels." The complex relationship—the logical connectedness and actual conflict—between Steele's descriptive analysis and his prescriptive synthesis allows for the unity-in-diversity of Wells's opus. And in "frustration," *The Anatomy* offers the theme by which Wells "revises," in the etymological sense, his past.

Notes

1. See R. D. Mullen, "The Books and Principal Pamphlets of H. G. Wells: A Chronological Survey," *Science-Fiction Studies* 1 (1973): 114–35 (reprinted, revised, and under a slightly different title, in *H. G. Wells and Modern Science Fiction*, ed. Darko Suvin [Lewisburg, Pa.: Bucknell University Press, 1977], 223–68). My own appreciation of the later Wells owes much to Professor Mullen's guidance, through this bibliographical study of his, through his work on Wells generally (some of it still to be published), and through his conversations with me.

2. Ironically enough, the label of "journalist" originated with Wells himself: "I had rather be called a journalist than an artist," he wrote to Henry James (8 July 1915). See *Henry James and H. G. Wells*, ed. Leon Edel and Gordon N. Ray (Urbana: University of Illinois Press, 1958), 264; see also the editors' introduction.

3. See Gordon N. Ray, "The Early Novels of H. G. Wells," reprinted as the introduction to *The History of Mr. Polly* (Boston: Houghton Mifflin, 1960). The phrases quoted come from pp. xlviii–xlix. Ray's essay originally appeared in *Edwardians and Late Victorians*, ed. Richard Ellmann (New York: Columbia University Press, 1959), 106–59, under the title "H. G. Wells Tries to Be a Novelist."

4. See Bernard Bergonzi, *The Early H. G. Wells* (Toronto: University of Toronto Press, 1960), ch. 7.

5. Richard Hauer Costa, *H. G. Wells* (New York: Twayne, 1967), 34. Compare his further discussion, in ch. 11.

6. Extensive summaries of these books can be found in Robert Bloom's *Anatomies of Egotism: A Reading of the Last Novels of H. G. Wells* (Lincoln: University of Nebraska Press, 1977).

7. See the critical commentary by R. M. Philmus and David Y. Hughes in *H. G. Wells: Early Writings in Science and Science Fiction* (Berkeley: University of California Press, 1975), esp. ch. 3. The texts of all of Wells's journalism alluded to or cited in the present article can be found in that volume.

8. Wells adapts "Individual Plasticity" (*Saturday Review* [hereafter designated *SR*] 79 [19 January 1895]: 89–90) as ch. 15 of *Moreau*.

9. Wells recapitulates the argument of "The Man of the Year Million" (*Pall Mall Gazette* 57 [6 November 1893]: 3) in *War of the Worlds*, bk. II, ch. 2. On the "Dorking Controversy," see I. F. Clarke, *The Tales of the Future* (London: Library Association, 1961), 24–59.

10. In ch. 25 of *Lewisham*, Wells gives a satirical version of some of the contents of various essays he wrote for the *Educational Times*.

11. That Wells in his "journalism" articulated a number of ideas which he later transformed into the materials of fiction merely signals the pervasiveness of "journalistic" elements in his other writings. It neither exhausts the catalogue of those elements nor proves that his

journalistic activities influenced the style and structure of his novels and romances. The latter subject, however, is much too lengthy for me to treat here: on the relationship between Wells's literary journalism in *SR,* for example, and his theory and practice of fiction, see the essay by Ray cited in note 3, and also my "H. G. Wells as Literary Critic for the *Saturday Review,*" *Science-Fictions Studies* 4 (1977): 166–75.

12. He uses this phrase in a passage from *The Anatomy* quoted below, in his preface to *World Brain* (1938), and elsewhere.

13. See Philmus and Hughes, ch. 5.

14. "Morals and Civilisation," *Fortnightly Review,* n.s. 61 (February 1897): 268.

15. See *The Atlantic Edition of the Works of H. G. Wells,* 28 vols. (London: T. Fisher Unwin, 1924–27), I, xix–xx: "Reading all these writings over, as this collected edition has at last obliged the writer to do," Wells says, referring to himself in the third person, "he is, he is bound to confess, surprised at his own consistency. There is growth in these writings indeed, but there is continuity." (Internal evidence dates this introduction as having been composed in 1922.)

16. *Works,* I, xvii.

17. I use this term in the Borgesian sense. In "Kafka and His Precursors" (*Other Inquisitions* [New York: Washington Square Press, 1966], 113), Borges propounds the paradox that "Every writer *creates* his precursors"—meaning that he causes the reader to see something in the works of certain of his predecessors which would not be evident had he not written.

18. Anthony West, whose essay is perhaps the origin of the "two Wellses" hypothesis, talks about his father's ambivalence—as a writer and as a human being—in a chapter in *Principles and Persuasions* (New York: Harcourt Brace, 1957), reprinted in *H. G. Wells,* ed. Bernard Bergonzi (Englewood Cliffs, N.J.: Prentice-Hall, 1976), esp. 13–24. See also Darko Suvin, "Wells as the Turning Point of the SF [Science Fiction] Tradition," *Minnesota Review,* n.s., no. 4 (Spring 1975): 112 (reprinted in this volume).

19. Thus speaks George Ponderevo, in *Tono-Bungay,* bk. II, ch. 4, sec. 10; in *Works,* XII, 273—emphasis added. Subsequent citations from *Tono-Bungay* (hereafter referred to as *T-B*) will assume the form (e.g.) II, 4, 10:273, the last number(s) specifying the page(s) in vol. XII of the Atlantic edition on which the quotation is to be found.

20. See, for instance, Wells's lecture before the Royal Institute (1936) on the need for a "world encyclopedia" (*World Brain* [Garden City, N.Y.: Doubleday, Doran, 1938], 3–35).

21. Quotations from *The Anatomy of Frustration (AF)* follow the text of the American edition (New York: Macmillan, 1936). As the pagination there differs from that of the English edition, reference is made to chapter:page(s).

22. "The 'Cyclic' Delusion," *SR* 78 (10 November 1894): 506.

23. Compare Wells's conspectus of the *Outline* in his introduction to *The Science of Life,* 2 vols. (Garden City, N.Y.: Doubleday, Doran, 1931), I, 1: "He dealt with all history as one process. He displayed it—or, rather, it displayed itself . . . —as the appearance of life in space and time, and as an achievement of self-knowledge and a release of will; a story unfolding and developing by a kind of inner necessity, until at last man was revealed, becoming creative, becoming conscious of the possibility of controlling his destiny." See also W. Warren Wagar's discussion of Wells's conception of "the mind of the race," in *H. G. Wells and the World State* (New Haven: Yale University Press, 1961), 98–118.

24. The alternatives Steele mentions here supply the basis for Wells's unqualified pessimism in *Mind at the End of Its Tether* (1945). If Wells's sense of humor finally forsook him, as that fragment perhaps evidences, it did so only in the very last years of his life.

25. "Human Evolution, an Artificial Process," *Fortnightly Review,* n.s. 60 (October 1896): 595.

26. "The Duration of Life," *SR* 79 (23 February 1895): 248.

27. "Death," *SR* 79 (23 March 1895): 377.

28. Surprisingly enough, Marxist critics of Wells, like Christopher Caudwell (*Studies in a Dying Culture* [London: John Lane, 1938]) and A. L. Morton (*The English Utopia* [London:

Lawrence and Wishart, 1952]), seem to have overlooked this particular "contradiction" (which is really a complementarity; see below) in Wells's thought.

29. See *Civilization and Its Discontents*, trans. James Strachey (New York: Norton, 1961), 44, 87. Freud's treatise, published in 1930, was first translated into English in the same year.

30. "My character, my personality, has not kept pace with my wits," Steele declares. "There, I am typical of my time" (*AF,* XIX[c]:192).

31. See "The Scepticism of the Instrument" (a paper delivered to the Oxford Philosophical Society in 1903 and first published in *Mind,* n.s. 13 [July 1904]: 379–93), in *Works,* IX, 348–51, for Wells's discussion of the complementarity of putative antinomies.

32. For the Wellsian meanings of "plastic" and "rigid," see Philmus and Hughes, chs. 1 and 5.

33. See above, note 22.

34. According to the reciprocal inversion of "dream" and "reality" in *The Wonderful Visit,* the angel falls from its reality, which human beings regard as the land of dreams, into their reality, which is the angel's dream world.

It can be inferred that the "reality" to which this peculiarly Wellsian angel belongs is similar to the future Wells foresees in "The Province of Pain" (*Science and Art* 7 [February 1894]: 58–59). There he speculates that the necessity for pain may be no more than "a phase through which life must pass in its evolution from the automatic to the spiritual" (p. 59). If so, the angel's acquiring a susceptibility to pain in the course of its earthly sojourn constitutes a variation on the devolutionary pattern Wells employs in *The Time Machine.*

35. *Apropos of Dolores* (London: Jonathan Cape, 1938), ch. 4, sec. 16, p. 216—hereafter (e.g.) *AD,* 4, 16:216.

36. See *"And After Sapiens?"* bk. V, ch. 5, of *You Can't Be Too Careful;* also bk. V, ch. 3, and above, note 24.

37. For example, in the introduction to *You Can't Be Too Careful.*

38. "Human Evolution . . . ," 594. The phrase "culminating ape" comes from the same place.

39. The quotation appears in ch. 14 of *Moreau* (*Works,* II, 93).

40. The complementarity between *Homo regardant* and *Homo rampant* as concepts resembles that between the "absolute" and "human" standpoints in Wells's writings—on which see Philmus and Hughes, x–xi, 6–7, 51–54.

On the antagonism of the two "sub-species" of man to one another, compare Wilbeck's remark: "First the evolution of the conscious brain gathered *Homo* up into an individual egotism like a clenched fist, and then it (Nature or the Life Force or what you will) seemed to realize it had gone too far and turned upon itself. And so we have our moral conflict" (*AD,* 5, 6:260).

41. Wilbeck's activities as a publisher reveal a similar division of impulse: on the one hand he promotes a *"Way of the World* series" designed to acquaint people with "ideas of a 'world order' " (*AD,* 2, 3:53); but on the other hand, he is also responsible for bringing out books on economics and history that are merely "profitable twaddle" (*AD,* 4, 15:210–11).

42. The significance of Dolores's name, in the abstract and as Wilbeck finally comes to regard her, relates to Wilbeck's quest for happiness and to his questioning of the possibility of humanly attaining it (as in his exchanges with Foxfield on the latter subject). Frustrated, as well as the source of many of her husband's frustrations, Dolores has her prototype in George Ponderevo's Marion.

For an edifying account of what might be called the Darwinian imagery in *AD,* see William J. Scheick's "The Womb of Time: Spengler's Influence on Wells's *Apropos of Dolores,*" *English Literature in Transition* 18 (1975): 217–28.

43. *T-B,* IV, 3, 2:522. The fact that this phrase occurs towards the very end of the novel makes it clear that Bladesover remains George Ponderevo's—and Wells's—paradigm for explaining "the broad slow decay of the great social organism of England" (*T-B,* I, 2, 8:83).

44. Wells defines "pseudomorphous" in *T-B*, I, 1, 3:13; the description of London as a spreading cancer can be found in *T-B*, II, 1, 1:132.

45. On the "cancerous" nature of "quap," see *T-B*, III, 4, 5:446–47. Compare Kenneth B. Newell's analysis of the metaphor of society as an organism in *T-B*, in *Structure in Four Novels by H. G. Wells* (The Hauge: Mouton, 1968), ch. 3, esp. 75–81.

On the usefulness of his uncle's business enterprise, see George Ponderevo's verdict: "He created nothing, he invented nothing, he economised nothing. I cannot claim that a single one of the great businesses we organised added any real value to human life at all" (*T-B*, III, 1, 3:294).

46. *T-B*, IV, 3, 4:530. George identifies the sea with the future when he says, "I and my destroyer tear out to the unknown across a great grey space. We tear into the great spaces of the future" (*T-B*, IV, 3, 2:528). He also speaks of "our mother of change, the Sea!" (*T-B*, IV, 3, 2:526), and thereby equates evolution ("our mother") with "change."

The Man Who Tried to Work Miracles

A. J. P. TAYLOR

H. G. Wells did not expect to last. He did not even want to last, or so he
claimed: "What I write goes now—and will presently die." He was not
interested in being a literary artist, though he had in fact great literary gifts.
He was, he insisted, a journalist, someone who wrote for the day and who
'delivered the goods.' He would be disappointed if the hundredth anniversary
of his birth were marked only by discussions of Wells as a novelist. He would
want to know what had happened to his ideas. Had men listened to his
message? Had they taken what he believed to be the only way to salvation?
The answer would be at first sight even more disappointing for him. His
novels and scientific romances survive as entertainment—widely read in
paperbacks. Hardly anyone bothers about Wells as a thinker, perhaps no one
except a devoted young American, W. Warren Wagar, who has written a
book about *H. G. Wells and the World State* and has produced more recently an
anthology of Wells's prophetic writings.

GIFT FOR SOCIAL COMEDY

Still, I would not dismiss Wells lightly. Going back to his books after not
reading them for many years, I found all sorts of ideas which are running
round the world with little appreciation that Wells started them. Not that
his ideas were as original as he claimed. Wells was more a representative man
than an originator. This does not make him any the less interesting. Of
course his literary gifts are what really count, whatever Wells said in depreciation of them. Taken simply as a writer, Wells had, I think, two qualities, and
these keep him alive. The first was a gift for social comedy. His best book,
The History of Mr. Polly, is a work of irresistible fun. I would say the same,
with some reservations, about *Tono-Bungay* and, with more, about *Kipps.* But
even his least inspired books have occasional flashes of the same spirit. None
of his characters is real—and that goes, to my mind, even for the much-
vaunted *Ann Veronica.* They are caricatures or Humours in the Jonsonian
sense. Mr. Pooter, also a comic figure, is a hundred times more real than Mr.
Polly—you can still meet him in many a suburban street. Do you, does

From the *Listener,* 21 July 1966. Reprinted by permission.

anyone, believe in Mr. Polly, in Uncle Ponderevo, or in Kipps? They are creatures of fantasy to whom comic things happen.

And not only comic things. Each book by Wells begins more or less realistically, usually in rather depressing surroundings, and then the principal character escapes by a miracle. I do not mean merely by an unlikely twist. I mean by something preposterously impossible. Mr. Polly finds an impossible plump middle-aged woman, who owns an impossible riverside inn. Uncle Ponderevo invents an impossible patent medicine and makes an impossible fortune. Kipps comes into an impossible fortune not once but twice. None of Wells's characters gets out of his difficulties by his own strength. The escape comes from outside. It happens to him. The characters who do not escape go off at the end of the book to "think things out," an implication that they will rescue themselves. But if they have not managed to "think things out" during the course of a long book—and they never have—why should they succeed afterwards? Thinking things out only means waiting for a miracle instead of experiencing one.

The need for a miracle even in Wells's apparently realistic novels was of course much greater in his scientific fantasies, was indeed the essence of them. This was Wells's other great gift, one still more unusual—I would venture to say unique. He could pretend and then take the pretence seriously. He would postulate one simple impossible step—a food which produced giants, a man who slept for 200 years, a war of the worlds—and then he would work out calmly, realistically, what would follow. The overwhelming feature of his scientific fantasies is that they are not fantasies, except for the one impossible twist. They are exactly what would happen "if only . . ."

PRISONER OF HIS IMAGINATION

Wells could really live in the imaginary situation which he had created and sometimes, to his dismay, his imagination took him prisoner. He always wanted a glowing future; but the future of his fantasies often turned out to be most unpleasant. At any rate, for good or ill, Wells in these fantasies was "the man who could work miracles"—the title of one of his stories which was later made into a film.

Wells, the thinker and prophet, was the same: he could work miracles, or at any rate wanted to work them. Here again he had the right patter and often the right imagination. He made many inspired guesses about the future developments of machines. For instance he described full-scale battles in the air almost before heavier-than-air machines had got off the ground. He announced more than fifty years ago that men would get to the moon, though he did not foretell correctly what they would find when they got there—but this is hardly surprising, for it seems that they will find precisely nothing. At a time when motor-cars had hardly started, Wells foresaw that the traffic in cities would grind to a halt, as we all know it is doing, and he anticipated other, more sensible forms of transport, such as moving platforms—an idea which is just being aired now. He also foresaw that, thanks to the motor-car, everyone would desert cities for the country and that, in this way, the country would disappear, another gloomy and correct prophecy. He had unbounded faith in the beneficent effects of electricity, a faith which he shared with Lenin, and expected that electrical devices would end the drudgery of housework. And so they have, though only at the price of turning the housewife into their slave. He was sure that one day we should all live on a scientific diet of pills, another prophecy which threatens to come true.

PROPHECIES—OR INSPIRED GUESSES?

These prophecies were wrapped up in scientific jargon. Underneath they were merely inspired guesses and just as likely to be wrong as right. Wells did not really understand what he was talking about. If he wanted something, he assumed that there was a way in which it would happen. For instance, in 1903 he foresaw mechanical monsters fighting each other in a future war, and was later aggrieved when the credit for inventing the tank was denied to him. But he had never faced the technical problems involved in building tanks. He merely described what he wanted and left someone else to work it out. And, though he was right about tanks, he was wrong about the answer to them. Writing in the nineteen-thirties about the next war, he imagined that tanks would be stopped by vast ditches dug across Europe and filled with slime. The more prosaic, successful answer was the anti-tank gun. Wells's inventions for the future brought him much reputation, but of course they were the product of a lively imagination, not the serious work of a disciplined technician. This hardly mattered. They were fun, and the books built round them made good reading.

But the mix-up between what could be and what Wells wanted mattered a good deal more when he came to deal with man. This was Wells's serious concern as a thinker. He was amused to speculate on the ways in which machines could develop. He was passionately resolved on changing man's behaviour, and he believed that this could be done only by changing man himself—changing him in a specifically biological way. Wells claimed that the miracle could be worked by Science, very much with a capital S. Actually it was his own obstinate will: an impatient insistence that the change must happen. The word science was used simply as an incantation. Wells himself claimed to be a scientist. At any rate he had had some elementary training in biology under the great T. H. Huxley. He learnt the doctrine of evolution at its most confident. But he does not seem to have understood what he learnt. If evolution teaches anything, it is that the process of biological change is very slow. It took millions of years to evolve mammals; hundreds of thousands, if not millions, to evolve man. It is surely inconceivable that there should have been any biological evolution in man—any change in his natural make-up—during the few thousand years of civilization, and still more inconceivable that man should have changed during the 150 years or so since the French revolution and the coming of modern industry.

Wells seems to have expected that men would change, you cannot call it evolve, more or less overnight, say in a couple of centuries; and of course men do change their behaviour and even, to some extent, their physical character quite quickly. For instance, the average height of Englishmen has increased markedly in the last fifty years, but such changes have nothing to do with biological evolution. They occur because of what happens to men after they are born, not because of a change in their nature. Englishmen are taller because they, and particularly the lower classes, are better fed than they used to be. Put them back on their old, inferior diet, and the next generation would be back where they started. It is the same with behaviour. Men are warlike or peaceful, brutal or tolerant, religious or atheistic, because that is what they have been taught to be, not because of something in their nature. Wells's appeal to evolution was sales-talk, irrelevant to what really happened. At best it provided him with analogies, and dangerous analogies at that.

The danger was greater still when Wells shifted from man to society and treated even this in biological terms. He regarded society as a sort of animal, subject to the laws of evolution. This is a common trick of historians or, I would prefer to say, of writers who make sweeping generalizations about the past. They talk about old societies, mature societies, even about decaying societies—useful analogies perhaps, but no more. If a man has been around on the earth for a long time, he will really be "old"—his bones will creak, his physical powers will be failing, within a fairly limited time he will die. But there is no reason whatever to suppose that any of this will apply to a society. It may amuse us, it certainly amuses me, to make out that Great Britain is a mature society, wise, experienced, sensible, while the United States is brash, new, blundering, just because our history starts with Boadicea and theirs with George Washington. But we know that it is nonsense, good for a laugh and no more. Wells took the claptrap seriously, as other pontificators about history do. All his thought, if it can be dignified with that word, revolves round the analogy with evolution. Animals adapted themselves to their surroundings, and those who adapted themselves best survived. Men will do the same in their social behaviour. Wells believed that he had only to point out what was wrong in society, and evolution would step in to put it right. Things had been getting better up to now and therefore we were bound to arrive at Utopia.

Wells condemned the contemporary world in every novel and other sort of book that he wrote. The first words uttered by Mr. Polly, as he sat on a stile, can serve as the theme for all Wells's writing: "Hole! *'Ole!* Oh! *Beastly Silly Wheeze of a hole!*" But why was the world a hole? It is easy to understand why Mr. Polly felt so that afternoon. He owned a shop which did not pay, and his wife produced meals which gave him indigestion. These are individual misfortunes which happen to many individuals. Wells insists on generalizing them. He writes solemnly that Mr. Polly was "one of those ill-adjusted units that abound in a society that has failed to develop a collective intelligence and a collective will for order commensurate with its complexities." There is an implication, you see, that in a well-ordered society there will be no inefficient shopkeepers and of course no indigestion.

Wells was not only generalizing from Mr. Polly. He was generalizing from himself. He had been a shop-assistant. He had hated it. He escaped to become a writer. Very considerately, he wanted this to happen to all other shop-assistants—a miracle, in fact; and, though considerate, like so much of Wells's or any other high-minded kindness, very wrong-headed. There are writers, potential or otherwise, who would hate to be shopkeepers. But there are far more shopkeepers who would hate to be writers. Wells had the snobbishness which nearly always goes with intellectual activities. He thought his way of life superior, and he wanted to provide it for others.

This was the "confusion" which he saw in society—too many shopkeepers, not enough devoted thinkers. There was another confusion which bulked large in Wells's novels and which indeed bulked large in his life—the relations between men and women. Somehow they rarely hit if off. Wells seems to have thought that, in a well-ordered society, all would come right of itself, by which he really meant that women would fit in with men's moods. Sometimes they would be satisfied with casual relations; when required, they would settle for something more permanent. But they would never try to hold a man if he wanted to move off. The modern state, as he put it, "must refuse absolutely to recognize or enforce any kind of sexual ownership." This deserves a top prize for Utopia. I suspect Meredith was wiser when he said that woman would be the last thing to be civilized by man.

Wells started before the first world war by wanting to put society right. That war led him into wanting to put the world right as well. And at once he jumped the whole way; there must be a world-state, and that without delay. The final illustration in his *Outline of History* is a map of the world, and scrawled across it in bold letters the words: The United States of the World. He often implied that this would come of itself, according to the supposed laws of evolution. For instance, he says in his *Experiment in Autobiography:*

> A planned world-state . . . is, we perceive, as much a part of the frame in which our lives are set as the roundness and rotation of the earth, as the pressure of the atmosphere or the force of gravitation at the sea level.

And again:

> The modern world-state which was a mere dream in 1900 is today a
> practicable objective; it towers high above the times. The socialist world-state
> has now become a tomorrow as real as today. Thither we go.

But sometimes he had qualms that we were not going there at all. Wells
always bounced easily from optimism to despair. In *Boon,* a book which he
wrote in 1915, he discovered the Mind of the Race, which was working for
salvation. But he concluded also that the Wild Asses of the Devil were
loose—a more likely verdict on the twentieth century.

If the world-state was not coming of itself, what were we to do? Sometimes Wells implied that there was a superior moral force, pulling things the
way in which he wanted them to go—in a phrase borrowed from Matthew
Arnold "that something not ourselves that makes for righteousness." But he
soon confessed that God, in his view, was merely another name for his own
wishes. He wrote:

> My deity was far less like the Heavenly Father of a devout Catholic . . .
> than he was like a personification of, let us say, the Five Year Plan.

Wells admitted, indeed boasted, that he was very near the communist
outlook. Just as the five-year plan was imposed on Russia by Stalin, the
world-state was to be imposed by Wells and a few other enlightened
intellectuals—what he called the Open Conspiracy. In his own words: "If
Russia has done nothing else for mankind, the experiment of the Communist
Party is alone sufficient to justify her revolution." He insisted however that
there was one great difference. Communism was based on class-war and
sought to set up the dictatorship of the proletariat. The Open Conspiracy
would be composed of anyone intelligent enough to accept Wells's ideas, and
principally by the men with real power. Wells thought that the captains of
industry and finance would save the world. William Clissold, one of his
fictional mouthpieces, announces: "I shall travel on the Blue Train to the end
of the chapter." This seems to me another fantasy, more Utopian than the
rest. All experience teaches that, if an élite run affairs, they do so in their
own interests, and this is perhaps truer of business-men than of any other so-
called élite.

Wells became more and more convinced that knowledge would transform the world, if only there were enough of it. In *The Camford Visitation,*
which he wrote in 1937, he imagines a supernatural voice, pointing the way
of salvation:

> There can be no escape for your world, for all mankind, from the ages of
> tragic conflict ahead of you, except so heroic an ordering of knowledge, so

valiant a beating out of opinions, such a refreshment of teaching and such an organization of brains as will constitute a real and living world university, head, eyes and purpose of Man. That is the primary need of your species now. It is your world's primary want. It must come now—if it ever is to come.

In *Babes in the Darkling Wood,* published in 1940, the hero says much the same.

> The Right Thing to Do will be to have a vast, ordered, encyclopedia of fact and thought for its Bible, and a gigantic organization not only of research and record, but of devoted teachers and interpreters. A World Church, a World Brain, and a World Will. . . . We have to find out all that there is to be known and what is afoot in those various movements for documentation, for bibliography, for indexing, for all that micro-photographic recording one hears about distantly and dimly. Make understandings and more understandings. That is the reality of life for every human being.

This is the great contemporary delusion at its wildest: the belief that if only we accumulate enough facts, enough knowledge, the answer will emerge of itself. The facts will provide their own solution. Think of the pundits all over the world who are writing long solemn books about the problem of nuclear warfare and they are no nearer a solution. Yet any child could tell them what to do with nuclear weapons: "Don't have them."

Wells not only demanded ideas; he provided them. He had an unlimited faith in the power of education, and himself wrote books with an educational purpose—an outline of biology, an outline of economics, and, his most successful, an *Outline of History.* This at any rate is not only still read, it is the best general survey of man's history that there is. Wells wrote it to demonstrate that knowledge was superior to art and literature. He remarked slightingly: "An industrious treatment of early nineteenth-century records would make Balzac's *Comédie Humaine* seem flighty stuff"—a view which Karl Marx would not have agreed with. The *Outline of History* was supposed to demonstrate that all recorded history had been moving fumblingly forward towards a planned world-state. It totally fails to demonstrate anything of the kind. It shows that men have always been in conflict and that the rich have always exploited the poor. Sometimes one state or one group in a civilization has come to dominate all the others. This is done by superior force and nothing else. Most people, including Wells, sentimentalize their view of the past. They like to think that the Better Side wins. It doesn't. The Stronger Side wins. The Romans were not more civilized or more enlightened than the Greeks. They merely possessed a more efficient fighting machine. When Europeans established their authority throughout the world in the nineteenth century this was not because they were more civilized. It was because, in Hilaire Belloc's words: "We have the Maxim gun, and they have not." One conqueror, one potential uniter of Europe, perhaps represented a superior cause to the states he conquered. This was Napoleon. No one comes in for rougher treatment in Wells's *Outline of History*.

The *Outline* has a drawing of various national symbols, entitled Tribal Gods for which men would die. This is a true verdict on the history of the last 150 years. More men have died willingly for national loyalty than for any other cause. There is no heroism, and also practically no crime, which they will not perform in its name. If we draw any historical moral from this, it can only be that national states are not likely to vanish, though they may be conquered. Wells repudiated this moral: it did not accord with the world-state. He condemned men for their national loyalties. Though he wrote the *Outline* in order to show that history was going his way, in fact he demanded that men should abandon all their historical habits and behave in exactly the opposite fashion to that in which they had behaved throughout all recorded time. And of course they may. This is why it is so pointless to ask a historian to foretell the future. He can only say what will happen if men go on behaving as they have done in the past. For instance, if the past is any guide, the deterrent will one day fail to deter. There will be nuclear war, and all mankind will be destroyed. If you want the future to be different, the best thing is to forget history, not to try to extract morals from it.

Wells wanted a miracle, that men should change their nature. As he put it in the *Croquet Player:* "Only giants can save the world from complete relapse and so we—we who care for civilization—have to become giants." He was far from becoming a giant himself. Though he condemned the tribal gods of nationalism in theory, no one was a more fervent patriot when it came to war against Germany. In the first world war he wanted to bomb Essen—"a daily service of destruction to Germany." In the second world war he declared that afterwards "a few score thousand [German] criminals need to be shot," and then the world would be all right. Underneath he was too honest to imagine that his Utopia would really work. When he really imagined the future, in his scientific romances, he foresaw that a few clever men would still be exploiting all the rest. When the Sleeper awakes, for instance, 200 years hence, he discovers that the mass of mankind have become slaves, and the Sleeper raises an insurrection in the cause of old-fashioned freedom.

The contradiction was typical of Wells, and rather endearing. He was by nature a radical, a rebel—one of the few Englishmen incidentally who still wrote diatribes against the monarchy. He knew instinctively that dictatorship, ordering people about, would not save them, and yet he could not think of any other way of doing it. In his ideal state, only one set of ideas would be allowed—his own:

> Only one body of philosophy and only one religion, only one statement of men's relation to the universe and the community, can exist in a unified world state.

This is a recipe for stagnation and disaster. Besides, if men turned to the writings of the master for instruction, what would they find? Instead of clear guidance, they would find chaos and confusion. Wells insisted, times without number, on the need for hard precise thinking. He was himself incapable of it. Every attempt at discussion in his books tails off with four dots in a row—a sort of "to be continued in our next." The great prophets of mankind are remembered by a single book, even if they wrote many. Rousseau is remembered by *The Social Contract;* Marx by *Capital;* Darwin by *The Origin of Species.* Wells put himself in their class. Indeed he claimed to be a better thinker than any of them. He wrote more than a hundred books. But when we ask: in which of them is the gospel according to Wells to be found?, his answer is always: in the next book that Wells is going to write.

Actually his last book announced that there was no answer. Men had failed to listen to his teaching. Therefore they were doomed. He wanted his epitaph to be: "God damn you all. I told you so." He had imagined himself as God and was embittered when others did not acknowledge his divinity. But Wells was not God, was not even an inspired prophet. He was a spluttering imaginative little man in a hurry, bouncing from one contradiction to the next. His writings reflected the confusions and delusions of his age. There is not much wisdom in them, but there is a good deal of humanity. Maybe no one reads Wells any more for guidance—there are newer, equally muddled thinkers who provide that. We read Wells now for fun—the fun of the scientific romances, the fun of *Mr. Polly,* even the fun to be found in *The Outline of History.* And fun is a great deal better than worshipping the golden calf of knowledge.

H. G. Wells: Problems
of an Amorous Utopian

JOHN HUNTINGTON

H. G. Wells is probably the most significant utopian voice of the twentieth century. From 1901, with *Anticipations,* to almost the very end of his life, he worked to promote education, science, socialism, the world state, the Declaration of Human Rights, and the open conspiracy of rational and well-intentioned people. And it is the utopianism at the heart of his project that has occasioned some of the most severe criticism of Wells. F. R. Leavis speaks to a broad audience when he uses "Wellsian" as an adjective denoting all that is shallow in scientific culture; for Leavis it is sufficient to call C. P. Snow "Wellsian" to show that he is not a novelist.[1] George Orwell, in "Wells, Hitler, and the World State" (1941), while acknowledging the importance of Wells's liberating intellect early in the century, could denounce his "one-sided imagination" which could treat history simply as "a series of victories won by the scientific man over the romantic man." "Wells," Orwell declares, "is too sane to understand the modern world."[2] For such critics, and they are common, the terms "Wellsian" and "utopian" are synonymous with a thin hyperrationality.

An admirer of Wells has difficulty responding to such criticisms because Wells himself declared that such rationality was the necessary and only salvation of the world. Yet, if Wells is proud of his rationality, we would not be denigrating him or his work if we observed that he is not as purely rational as he believes he is. On the contrary, Wells's work shows signs of a difficult struggle with a deeply selfish and irrational component of himself, and it is for that struggle, rather than for the neat conclusions he champions, that Wells's utopian work may be of greatest interest. To put to somewhat differently, Wells is greater than he himself understood, not because he achieved a pure rationality, but on the contrary, because he describes for us, if we can learn how to read him in this regard, a deep conflict between an ideal rationality and a much less admired, though not therefore contemptible, emotionality which, however, much he will try to smother it, will not be quiet.

Such a reading of Wells, while it clearly opens up dimensions of his

Reprinted with permission from *English Literature in Transition, 1880–1920* 30 (1987).

understanding that he tried to repress, is not entirely antithetical to Wells's own consciousness. In the meditation on Machiavelli which begins *The New Machiavelli,* for instance, he advocates just such a reading of the author of *The Prince.* Wells appreciates the human, even disreputable qualities revealed in Machiavelli's letters. For Wells, "these flaws complete him."[3]

I

Let us begin with the ideal that so offends many humanist critics. Toward the end of *A Modern Utopia* what Wells calls the "Voice" urges clear and bold *will* and *imagination.*

> The new things will be indeed of the substance of the thing that is, but differing just in the measure of the will and imagination that goes to make them. They will be strong and fair as the will is sturdy and organised and the imagination comprehensive and bold; they will be ugly and smeared with wretchedness as the will is fluctuating and the imagination timid and mean.[4]

This is a voice that Wells in 1905 had already practiced for a number of years and which he would continue to perfect for many more. It speaks in bold adjectives of a comfortable, efficient, tolerant, and undemanding world with understood rules. And controlling this world would be the Samurai, who would, in the slightly ironic vision of Marjorie Trafford in *Marriage,*

> lead lives of hard discipline and high effort, under self-imposed rule and restraint. They were to stand a little apart from the excitements and temptations of everyday life, to eat sparingly, drink water, resort greatly to self-criticism and self-examination, and harden their spirits by severe and dangerous exercises.[5]

Our reading of such passages may be affected when we consider that throughout the period when Wells was publicly developing the idea of his harmonious Utopia led by disciplined will and imagination, he was finding the order his wife was so admirably sustaining at Spade House increasingly unsatisfying. The story of Wells's unconventional amatory experiments has been much retold, both by Wells himself and by later writers and biographers.[6] It is not necessary for our purposes to enter into this labyrinth in any detail beyond reminding ourselves that, according to Wells's own version of his life, within a few years of marrying Amy Catherine Robbins, his second wife, he began to have fantasies about relations with other women, and by the middle of the first decade of the century he had begun a continual series of sexual relationships, some frivolous, some serious, which remained the pattern of his life until well after the death of his wife. Wells was in his life revolting against what his own utopian voice calls its "haunting insistence on sacrifice and discipline" (234).

Wells indeed seems to have been proud of his amorous experiments, and in the late 1930s, in *H. G. Wells in Love,* he explains his persistent womanizing as a search for what he calls the Lover-Shadow. This is not a very clear concept. It resembles a Jungian archetype, a sort of *Ewigweibliche* whose proffered but never attained satisfactions are a source of desire and aspiration throughout life. Part of the difficulty Wells has talking about the Lover-Shadow is that, while it is social insofar as it draws one out of pure self-centeredness, at the same time it represents a drive that has no regard for social good. An important difference between *H. G. Wells in Love* and the *Experiment in Autobiography* is that the former depicts a Wells relentlessly intent on his private desires.

In *The New Machiavelli* Wells attempts to focus explicitly on the problem of the disjunction of love and the project to restructure society. Remington's popular phrase, "Love and fine thinking," which he poses as the solution to the political mess, turns out to be a paradox; it points to a union which contains the cause of its own disintegration.[7] The novel is a tale of tragic, toward the end rather operatic, romantic passion. The lovers admit their guilt, and the novel points to the people and causes they betray, but it finally sees them as victims of "the world-wide problem between duty and conscious, passionate love the world has still to solve" (442). Wells acknowledges the conflict, but he poses it as the world's problem, not as a contradiction within his own system of ideals. A better world, so he seems to say, would not have ostracized Remington.

The split between social ideals and personal needs is one that Wells hopes to overcome in his own experience and thought, but, even as he tries to reconcile the two, the split remains embedded in his prose. For instance, in the following passage from *H. G. Wells in Love,* the Lover-Shadow appears as something distinct from the social *persona:*

> The sustaining theme of my *Experiment in Autobiography* has been the development and consolidation of my *persona,* as a devotee, albeit consciously weak and insufficient, to the evocation of a Socialist World-State. If I have not traced the development of my Lover-Shadow, and my search for its realization in responsive flesh and blood, with the same particularity and continuity, I have at least given the broad outline of its essential beginnings.[8]

The phrase "consciously weak and insufficient" might seem to anticipate and apologize for the more narrowly personal desire expressed in the phrase "responsive flesh and blood." Wells does not state that the two aspects of personality are in conflict, but his sense of their unavoidable difference can be seen in such an image as "the *persona* and the Lover-Shadow are, as I see it the hero and heroine of the individual drama most of us make of our lives."[9] The gender antithesis is important here, not because it puts one aspect above the other, but simply because it insists on difference.

In Wells's utopian writings—as opposed to his social novels—the Lover-Shadow is not acknowledged as significant. The usual reading of *A Modern Utopia* finds something like a parody of the Lover-Shadow in the Voice's companion, the botanist, a man apparently determined to make life in Utopia difficult.[10] He can be read as an ironic and finally irrelevant reminder of psychological stances that the utopian future will need to transcend. He comes from and drags with him the world before the Comet, a world of possessive jealousies and amorous fixations. At the end of *A Modern Utopia* a meta-voice opines that the stances represented by the Voice and the botanist are essential and incompatible, one speaking of "a synthetic wider being, the great State, mankind," the other representing "the little lures of the immediate life" (372–73). In this reading, and it seems clearly the one that Wells consciously wanted us to make, the botanist is an embarrassing figure which we have to learn to overcome.

Such a subordination of the desires of the individual to the needs of the whole society or race is one of Wells's favorite themes, and it serves as a rationale for utopian dreams throughout his work. I want to pose a stronger reading of the botanist, however, and hear him as an authentic voice of the Lover-Shadow, a submerged voice that we can hear in one way or another throughout Wells's work, a voice that speaks for aspects of his unconscious that the rational ideals of the utopian world cannot satisfy. If we learn to hear *this* voice as "Wellsian," we shall be in a position to begin to understand some of he central texts of the Wells canon in a new way and to answer the objections of Leavis and Orwell.

II

Behind all the late works in which Wells undertakes to explain as clearly and as forthrightly as he can the amorous dimensions of his life—I am thinking especially of *Experiment in Autobiography,* the recently published *H. G. Wells in Love,* and highly autobiographical fictions such as *Apropos of Dolores* and *Brynhild*—we can point to the long affair with Odette Keun from which Wells had recently disentangled himself. This affair poses an extraordinary puzzle for Wells the rational utopian, one which he can never quite solve: why should a "free" man bind himself voluntarily over a long period of time to a person he finds thoroughly unpleasant? From early in his career as a lover, Wells had complicated his life deeply and, one has to say, compulsively. The relationships with Amber Reeves and Rebecca West are the great instances. Yet these two relationships can be explained because—there is an element of tautology here, but the language is Wells's own—Wells was "in love." But how could the affair with Keun, manifestly a source of considerable discontent, sustained by no social pressures, according to Wells never a "love" affair, continue for eight years? Clearly there is a mystery about the unconscious and about human behavior here that requires psychological explanation and must be taken into account in any rational utopian construction.

In this late period Wells himself was pointing to the importance of the unconscious as a source of unhappiness. In *The Anatomy of Frustration,* another of his attempts to put together a utopian synthesis, the author's fictional voice, William Burroughs Steele, urges that one of the main sources of "frustration" comes from "that dark undertow of unformulated or disguised impulses" which the modern technique of psychoanalysis has revealed.[11] In a loose way Steele is here picking up the theme of Freud's almost contemporaneous *Civilization and Its Discontents,* but there is a radical and significant difference between the ways Freud and Wells understand the unconscious. While Freud might agree with Steele's claim that "the psychoanalysts have opened our eyes to the artificiality of our rationalized conceptions of ourselves and our social relations" (52), he would absolutely disagree with the assertion that "our moral confusion and distress" stem from "our inability to impose any systematic direction of conduct upon the impulses from the subconscious that drive us" (60). For Freud what Wells calls the "release from instinct" (by which he seems to mean *escaping* instinct altogether rather than giving it free rein) and the "restraint upon impulse" are themselves the very sources of "discontent" in civilization. From a very early age one has emotions towards and thoughts about parents and siblings that the social code says are wrong. One has to repress these forbidden feelings and thoughts, thereby creating the guilt that is intrinsic to civilization. The "systematic direction of conduct" that Wells anticipates will, Freud would argue, increase rather than diminish discontent. Freud would warn us that what is repressed will return to plague us in ways that a Wellsian rationality will be unable to control.

For Wells the unconscious is not Freud's repressed but active system of values and desires inspired by guilt and in turn generating further guilt, but the instinctual drives that tend to disrupt the rational and ethical organization of civilization. Perhaps we may see it as something like pure *libido* without the complications created by *ego* and *super-ego.* For Wells the unconscious is simply the "primitive" that in his writings of the 1890s he loved to pit against highly evolved "civilization."[12] It is that irradicable trace of the early animal in the evolved human that must be controlled by education and will. Ultimately, Wells's theory of the unconscious is based, not on Freud, but on Darwin and Huxley.

We see this "evolutionary" conception of the unconscious in *Apropos of Dolores* when Stephen Wilbeck, the novel's narrator and the husband of Dolores, defines Dolores (the Keun figure) as "egotism" and himself (the Wells figure) as "restraint" and argues that the Dolores type must die out in the future. Dolores' egotism, Stephen contends, "is just common humanity unmitigated."[13] He concedes that he and everybody is at the core much the same as Dolores, "but tinted, mercerized . . . , glazed over, trimmed, loaded down," and therefore more advanced, more adapted to the utopian future. For Freud it is the frustration generated by these very overlays that is the source of civilization's discontent. Like Steele's, Wilbeck's analysis, which we have no reason to think of as different from Wells's own, treats the unconscious simply as the evolutionary primitive that must, somehow, be tamed.

Such an "ethical" conception of the unconscious may simplify the utopianist's project, but it makes it extremely difficult for Wells to account for his own behavior in the affair with Keun. In order to allow *Apropos of Dolores* to generate a utopian message rather than a message of despair, Wells must depict Stephen Wilbeck as different from himself in ways that seem minor in the text but are significant given the issues of "egotism" and "restraint." Stephen maintains a strict monogamy. When his first wife has an affair, he promptly divorces her. In his thirteen years of marriage to Dolores he is never unfaithful with another woman. Wells himself, as he makes clear in the *Autobiography, H. G. Wells in Love,* and in his utopian writings, was never committed to monogamy, and in the last years of his affair with Keun he had resumed his passionate relationship with Moura Budberg. The difficult question must arise here: if in the self-justifying fiction of *Apropos of Dolores* he finds it necessary for his moral and social point to make Stephen Wilbeck doggedly and self-sacrificingly "restrained"—and we should note that most of Wells's heroes share these traits of pointed fidelity and rigorous restraint— then what did Wells think of his own comparative "unrestraint"?

From a utopian perspective, Wells's love life poses a double contradiction. It is, first of all, unrestrained. And yet, and this comes out most clearly in the affair with Keun, it is subject to a mysterious restraint that prevents him from breaking off a relationship he claims he detests. Such a contradiction is common enough in human experience. In Wells's case the experience of his distant and disapproving mother, briefly but movingly depicted in the early scenes of *Tono-Bungay,* may in part account for his clinging to a relationship which seems to offer him very little reward.[14] Nevertheless, my aim here is not to perform an analysis of Wells himself, but to show a point of crisis in Wells's utopian vision. A novel like *Apropos of Dolores* is interesting in this context because in its twistings it reveals some of the strain Wells is undergoing in trying to bring into harmony his own life and his utopian ideals. Wells's anger at Keun and his sense of himself as long-suffering seem to have blinded him to the deeper implications of the affair. But such a work can alert us to issues which we can then find Wells working on, more or less consciously, in his earlier writings. An unstated mystery, which his utopian Voice would like to ignore but which his own life repeatedly brings to his attention, is why, in a world in which happiness should be there for the taking, do people make themselves unhappy. Wells addresses this question quite explicitly even when he is writing about a utopia beyond Sirius or an invasion from Mars.

III

We can all agree that the botanist in *A Modern Utopia* serves as an increasingly foolish challenge to the main utopian speculations of the book. But the botanist also expresses the "unrestrained" aspect of Wells himself that we have been looking at, which he cannot acknowledge openly, perhaps even to himself, but which he is unable to deny.

This confused and double quality of the botanist, his paradoxical burden of being mocked by the author for speaking matters that are deeply important to the author, is rendered repeatedly in the text. From the beginning the Voice complains about the botanist in terms that suggest there is more going on here than can be said: "It is strange, but this figure of the botanist will not keep in place. It sprang up between us, dear reader, as a passing illustrative invention. I do not know what put him into my head" (25). This admission of ignorance is casual, but important. It is an acknowledgment that, for the moment at least, the unconscious is dictating. Somewhat later the Voice will again complain that

> when my whole being should be taken up with speculative wonder, this man should be standing by my side, and lugging my attention persistently towards himself, towards his limited futile self. This thing perpetually happens to me, this intrusion of something small and irrelevant and alive, upon my great impressions. (54)

Such a passage, behind its comedy, speaks to deep issues in Wells's own life and work; if we can read it from the proper angle, the passage warns us that the botanist's presence is not trivial: it is recurrent, important, and, most significantly, "alive." It is essential to Wells's honesty even as he strives to develop his Utopia of *will* and *imagination*. The botanist's "paltry egotistical love story" (124; cf. also 69) is, after all, a sketch of the situation Wells will elaborate without comedy in *The Passionate Friends*. "I suppose," the Voice confesses, "I had no power to leave him behind" (179; cf. also 343).

The botanist, then, is an absolutely essential figure for *A Modern Utopia*. Without him, the Voice itself becomes hollow. It might be argued that to attribute so much to such an apparently peripheral figure is to misread the comedy and the repeated trivializations of him in the text. But, as Freud has taught us to see, these very gestures of disregard may be significant; they allow Wells to approach the issues of obsessive and irrational love that the botanist represents and of which Wells himself cannot speak freely and openly.

When the Voice laments, "Is not the suppression of these notes [of amorous sentimentality] my perpetual effort, my undying despair?" (178), he may be acknowledging Wells's own powerful erotic urges in the very act of attempting to exclude them. And the botanist has his own insights into this restrictive aspect of the Voice. At one point, near the end, he complains of the Voice, "You are always talking as though you could kick the past to pieces; as though one could get right out from oneself and begin afresh" (359). This statement is more than just an obstructional balking at utopian energy. In 1904 when he was writing this, Wells may have wished very much that he could "begin afresh" in a number of ways. There are the manifest utopian beginnings, but Wells is also feeling trapped in his marriage. Something here needs to "begin afresh." He is in despair about the power of his amorous impulses, and he dreams of a new, more controlled, utopian self. *A Modern Utopia* can be seen as an attempt to rationalize his frustrations, to keep the botanist in himself, who cannot be entirely denied, at least in his place.

It is a nice irony that a year or two later, when Wells began to meet Amber Reeves at Cambridge, it was the utopian Voice's ideas of group marriage that seem to have, as Wells put it in *H. G. Wells in Love,* "provided all that was necessary for a swift mutual understanding" (75).

IV

I am suggesting that part of the power of Wells's work derives from the repressed recognitions in it of desires which he cannot acknowledge and which are incongruent with his rational, utopian ideals but which he is unable to explain away. To put it another way, it is Wells's hypocrisy as a utopian that makes him an honest artist: as he advocates an order of self-controlled Samurai, "advanced" people who will repress and control their egoistic desires, he himself is exploring ways to escape just such repression and control. His writings depict, however covertly, his emotional desires along with his rational ideals.

This complex surface which renders latent and private meanings in terms of a narrative about public events and policies can be seen in fiction that antedates Wells's explicitly utopian formulations of the first part of the century. *The War of the Worlds,* for instance, while on the surface a tale of imperialist guilt and of civilization restored, is also a more private consideration of the emotional drawbacks of the couple. The main symbol of civilization lost and recovered is the narrator's wife, but the attitudes towards the wife are fraught with unexplained negative emotions. It is remarkable that a figure of such profound symbolic import and of such recurrent obligation should be unnamed and undescribed. She is a counter to be moved, an abstract value to be lost.

We get our first clues to the emotional subtext of the novel in the strangely labored quality of the narrator's self-justifications. When he gets his wife to Leatherhead he gives, over the course of two paragraphs, three different explanations for why he must leave her again: he has his "promise to the innkeeper," he is "feverishly excited," and he admits "in my heart I was not so very sorry that I had to return to Maybury that night."[15] Any one of these excuses would be adequate; the three of them suggest that the real one is being covered up. Much later he finds himself "praying that the Heat-Ray might have suddenly and painlessly struck her out of being" (428). Of course the manifest meaning here is a humane desire that she be spared suffering, but given the general coolness running through the relationship in the novel, we may well hear a more selfish wish-fantasy in these words.

It is telling that anxiety over the narrator's wife is closely connected with the entrance of the curate. That appearance is a strange narrative moment with an almost hallucinatory quality to it:

> It is a curious thing that I felt angry with my wife; I cannot account for it, but my impotent desire to reach Leatherhead worried me excessively.
>
> I do not clearly remember the arrival of the curate, so that probably I dozed. I became aware of him as a seated figure. . . . (360–61)

The claim to be anxious about reaching Leatherhead has all the earmarks of a rationalization to prevent further inquiry into the sources of anger that he has just declared to be unaccountable. At this moment of explicit but inexplicable anger at the narrator's wife, the curate appears.

For the middle part of the novel the curate replaces the wife as the narrator's housemate. Now the "anxiety" for the *absent* companion converts to a declared anger at the *present* one, as can be seen in the subtle movement of the following paragraph:

> My mind was occupied by anxiety for my wife. I figured her at Leatherhead, terrified, in danger, mourning me already as a dead man. I paced the rooms and cried aloud when I thought of how I was cut off from her, of all that might happen to her in my absence. My cousin [at whose house she was] I knew was brave enough for any emergency, but he was not the sort of man to realize danger quickly, to rise promptly. What was needed now was not bravery, but circumspection. My only consolation was to believe that the Martians were moving Londonward and away from her. Such vague anxieties keep the mind sensitive and painful. I grew very weary and irritable with the curate's perpetual ejaculations; tired of the sight of his selfish despair. After some ineffectual remonstrance I kept away from him. . . . (399)

The elision of the two figures of the wife and curate that the prose performs here is carried out in the plot. The narrator and the curate live together, squabbling over household economics, until the narrator, in self-defense, to prevent the curate from revealing their hiding place, clubs him and leaves him to be taken by the Martians. It is a moment of ambiguous responsibilities,[16] not unlike that which terminates Dolores' life in the novel written forty years later.

The expressions of irritation at the curate are echoed in the contemptuous descriptions of Mrs. Elphinstone's yearning for her husband "George," which is, of course, Wells's own name. Mrs. Elphinstone, like the narrator's wife, has become separated from her competent husband, and instead of rising to the occasion (like her sister-in-law), she falls into helpless whinings. She is a completely gratuitous figure as far as the plot of the novel goes, but she is an important presence insofar as she allows the novel to complain about wives without admitting that *the* wife is an object of complaint.

If the curate and Mrs. Elphinstone represent a bitter commentary on the trap of domesticity, the Artillery Man, in his satire on the ordinary man's "little miserable skeddadle through the world" (433) becomes, momentarily, a powerful critic of the domestic ideal: "No proud dreams and no proud lusts; and a man who hasn't one or the other—Lord! what is he but funk and precautions?" "Dreams" here probably means, not utopian ideals, but something like the ambitions of uncle Teddy Ponderevo. Here is a real promise to "begin afresh"! But then the novel takes another twist and renders the vision of amorous liberation as empty boasting. At the same time it treats as impossible the Artillery Man's other dream of an organized underground, a sort of prefiguration of the Open Conspiracy. The amorous and the utopian promises all collapse, and the narrator again leaves home.

The War of the Worlds is an extraordinary work for the way in which it manages to combine creative exuberance and deep pessimism. We can partially account for this combination by observing that the Martians, at one level, offer a fantasy of freedom from the snare of domesticity. Like the Voice in *A Modern Utopia,* they seem to offer an opportunity to "kick the past to pieces" so that the sane man can "begin afresh." The emptiness the narrator feels at the death of the last Martian may be partly caused by his sense that his liberation has been frustrated.[17] And the joy of the final reunion of husband and wife is severely muted. The novel's final words tell, not of promise and renewal, but of the hostile and forbidden thoughts that the novel has lived out: "And strangest of all is it to hold my wife's hand again, and to think that I have counted her, and that she has counted me, among the dead."

V

I do not mean to suggest that Wells was unusual or immoral for having such fantasies. Freud tells us that it is not the fantasies, but the failure to find some outlet for them, that is the cause of "discontent." Wells, of course, went beyond fantasy, not to the point of killing his wife, but certainly to the extent of escaping domesticity. As he became a more active and promiscuous lover, however, he must have had a difficult time reconciling his behavior with his ideals of utopian discipline.

Early in *A Modern Utopia* the Voice, considering for a moment how energetic and charismatic personalities will fit into Utopia, wonders, "What, for instance, will Utopia do with Mr. Roosevelt?" (28) This is, of course, a serious question in itself, but we may be missing the real implications if we do not see that behind it lies an even more difficult, though private, question: "What will Utopia do with H. G. Wells?" In his fiction we can see Wells, obliquely to be sure, but relentlessly too, considering the difficulties his powerful emotions create. Wells is half conscious of these difficulties, but he also, for perfectly understandable reasons, is not likely to be the first person to point to them. After all, his utopian ideal of discipline and restraint was not advanced by the complex and disruptive awarenesses his own life and experience generate. If we are to understand the totality of his enterprise, we need to see past the efficient and persuasive rhetorical surface to the more complex dynamics of each individual Wellsian text. This project does not mean denying the surface meaning, but it does involve inspecting it closely, questioning it, and relating it to Wells's own life.

Notes

1. F. R. Leavis, *Two Cultures? The Significance of C. P. Snow. Being the Richmond Lecture, 1962* (New York: Pantheon Books, 1963).

2. George Orwell, "Wells, Hitler, and the World State," *The Collected Essays, Journalism and Letters of George Orwell,* ed. Sonia Orwell and Ian Angus (New York: Harcourt, Brace, and World, 1968), II:139–45.

3. H. G. Wells, *The New Machiavelli* (New York: Duffield & Co., 1910), 6. All further references to this text are noted in the text in parentheses.

4. H. G. Wells, *A Modern Utopia* (1905; Lincoln: University of Nebraska Press, 1968), 368. All further references to this text are noted in the text in parentheses.

5. H. G. Wells, *Marriage* (1912; London: Hogarth Press, 1986), 222.

6. Wells described his mode of life in somewhat abstract terms in his *Experiment in Autobiography* (1934) and in rather more explicit terms in *H. G. Wells in Love* (published posthumously, 1984). For other angles on this matter, see Norman and Jeanne MacKenzie, *H. G. Wells* (New York: Simon & Schuster, 1973); Anthony West, *H. G. Wells: Aspects of a Life* (New York: Random House, 1984); and David Smith, *H. G. Wells: Desperately Mortal* (New Haven: Yale University Press, 1986).

7. Even as he makes the lovers in the novel out to be "bad" people who injure friends and destroy the promise of utopian reform in England, Wells here, as he will do later in *Apropos of Dolores,* finds it necessary to vary from the reality of his own situation. Remington, though he has engaged in some brief sexual escapades before his marriage, is a faithful husband until after his wife locks him out and he falls passionately "in love" with Isabel Rivers.

8. H. G. Wells, *H. G. Wells in Love: Postscript to an Experiment in Autobiography,* ed. G. P. Wells (Boston: Little, Brown and Co., 1984), 55.

9. Ibid., 55.

10. The botanist has been discussed by Mark Hillegas in his introduction to the Nebraska reprint of *A Modern Utopia* by David Hughes in "The Mood of *A Modern Utopia*," *Extrapolation* 19 (1977): 56–57 (reprinted in this volume), and by myself in *The Logic of Fantasy: H. G. Wells and Science Fiction* (New York: Columbia University Press, 1982), 168.

11. H. G. Wells, *The Anatomy of Frustration: A Modern Synthesis* (New York: Macmillan, 1936), 51.

12. Huntington, *The Logic of Fantasy,* 16–17.

13. H. G. Wells, *Apropos of Dolores* (New York: Scribner's, 1938), 159.

14. See Nancy Steffen-Fluhr, "Paper Tiger: Women and H. G. Wells," *Science-Fiction Studies* 37 (1985): 313 (revised version printed in this volume as "Women and H. G. Wells").

15. H. G. Wells, *The War of the Worlds,* in *Seven Science Fiction Novels of H. G. Wells* (New York: Dover Publications, 1934), 340. All further references to this text are noted in the text in parentheses.

16. Discussed in Huntington, *The Logic of Fantasy,* 75.

17. Ibid., 63, 81.

Women and H. G. Wells

Nancy Steffen-Fluhr

H. G. Wells was a master strategist at several traditional Victorian games of avoidance: using women to avoid women, using sex to avoid intimacy, and using work to avoid anxiety. It is not entirely surprising, then, that Wells's account of his compulsively busy love life in *H. G. Wells in Love*[1] reads a little like the abstract of a chess match, a series of adroit maneuvers designed to evade a mate. (Wells was particularly adept at a maneuver one might call "castling," in which he dodged emotional commitment by periodically exchanging houses and housekeepers.) In this sense at least, the book's title is somewhat misleading. *H. G. Wells In Love* is not primarily a book about being in love; it is a book about being unhappy, a book about permanent, enduring frustration. For Wells, like Alice, it was always "jam tomorrow . . . but never jam today."

G. P. Wells has subtitled this volume *A Postscript to an Experiment in Autobiography,* and so H. G. intended it to be. He left instructions that this account of his many love affairs be joined to his previously published introduction to *The Book of Catherine Wells* and then bound in a single volume with his *Autobiography,* "so all the main masses of my experiences and reactions will fall into proportion" (*Postscript,* 19). Apparently Wells hoped to achieve posthumously, through the magic of bookbinding, the psychic unity that had so eluded him in his life, to suture the story of his body to the story of his brain, a bit of psychosurgery he seems to have learned from Dr. Moreau.

As G. P. Wells has finally arranged it, *Postscript* consists of three principal sections: Well's brief prologue on his wife, Jane, that he wrote in 1928, the year after her death; "On Loves and the Lover-Shadow," in which Wells chronicles his extramarital love affairs from 1901, shortly after the birth of his first son, through 1935; and "The Last Phase," a collection of musings from the "Looseleaf Diary" Wells kept during the late 1930s and early 1940s.

Although familiar, in many ways the brief prologue on Jane is still the most interesting of these pieces. It is certainly the most revealing, replete with that odd admixture of candor and self-deception so typical of Wells's bifurcated personality. Even in Victorian terms, which defined the "companionate marriage" as relatively acceptable, Wells's self-styled *modus vivendi*

A shorter version of this essay appeared as "Paper Tiger: Women and H. G. Wells," *Science-Fiction Studies* 12 (1985).

with his second wife was strange and strained. And yet, it is the one relationship in his life about which he had the fewest conscious regrets. In his philandering fashion, he remained more faithful to the idea of his marriage to Jane than he did to any other idea in his life, even the World State. She, and the succession of houses she maintained for him, were the geographical center of his life around which he moved like a ship at anchor. A great part of the paralyzing anxiety he seems to have experienced in the early 1930s undoubtedly came from the strange sense of being suddenly cut adrift.[2]

Wells met Jane, née Amy Catherine Robbins, in the fall of 1892 when she enrolled in his biology lab section. She was twenty, "a grave little figure . . . dressed in mourning, for her father had been quite recently killed in a railway accident" (*EA*, 6:6:298–99).[3] Wells was twenty-six and a newly-wed, having married his cousin Isabel the previous October. Unfortunately Isabel was sexually frigid as well as hopelessly "book-shy," and soon the hot-blooded Wells turned to "little Miss Robbins" for conversation and consolation. In December 1893, barely a year after they first met, Wells broke with Isabel and ran off with Miss Robbins. They lived together until October 1895, when they were at last free to marry.

Sketched out like this, Wells's relationship with Catherine Robbins sounds quintessentially romantic, a defiant grand passion, rather like D. H. and Frieda Lawrence's. In fact, it was quite the opposite. From beginning to end it was, in Wells's own telling phrase, "an alliance for escape" (*EA*, 7:3:362). This was true for her as well—an escape from family, from penury, from the pressure of "narrow-scope lives," and always foremost, an escape from sexual passion. Appearances to the contrary, Jane was not the suffering heroine of this story, as many commentators have suggested, nor Wells the crude villain. They were fellow victims—of their upbringing, of their culture, and, most of all, of their own decisions to avoid emotional risk-taking.

In the *Autobiography* and again in *Postscript*, Wells presents the story of his first marriage and his elopement with Jane in a series of different versions, as if trying to discover in the act of narration the hidden emotions that motivated his behavior. The first version conforms pretty much to the outline above—the essential incompatibility of the newlyweds, thrown together by mere "proximity and isolation" (*EA*, 5:7:231), the appearance of Destiny in the "fragile figure" of Miss Robbins. Then, a few pages later, in a chapter appropriately entitled "Dissection," Wells suddenly recants: no, it really wasn't like that it all.

Sheer proximity aside, Wells was deeply attracted to Isabel's "withheld femininity" (*EA*, 6:3:259), all the more so, probably, because his mother had exemplified that kind of emotional withholding when he was a child. In wooing his reluctant, somewhat prudish cousin Isabel, he was, in effect, trying to edit the story of his emotionally deprived childhood, to make it come out all right at last. At the same time, he was unconsciously engineering a repetition of those deprivations, unconsciously trying to transform a strange and anxiety-ridden new situation into a familiar and therefore safe old situation. To this end, he gave Isabel what she wanted (a wedding) and then waited to see whether she, in turn, would give him what *he* wanted (which was nothing less than immediate emotional recompense for a quarter century of emotional yearning). When she didn't—couldn't—he immediately distanced himself in a great, frustrated rage. Within a few weeks of his wedding night, he had his first extramarital affair with a "a certain little Miss Kingsmill" (*EA*, 7:2:352). In short, not getting what he wanted with Isabel was exactly what he wanted with Isabel—or at least what he expected. Not surprisingly, his cousin's sheer unresponsiveness continued to obsess Wells for many years. Long after his marriage to Jane, he still fantasized about a dramatic, healing reunion with his abandoned first wife.[4]

His relationship with Amy Catherine Robbins has to be understood in this context. His feeling of camaraderie with her was undoubtedly genuine enough, but he was also probably using her to get a rise out of Isabel, following the premise that an angry reaction is better than no reaction at all. There may have been a more powerful motivation at work as well—Well's covert gynophobia. Wells's dissection of his motives suggests that Isabel's and Jane's sexual fears were matched by certain fears of his own. Although Wells's libido was strong, he was still an apprentice lover and had little experience of prolonged emotional and physical intimacy with a woman. The hidden problem in his relationship with Isabel, and perhaps in his early relationship with Jane as well, seems to have been neither incompatibility or boredom but anxiety (which Wells invariably experienced as claustrophobia).[5]

The whole of Wells's life and art testifies to his ambivalence about irrational states of passion. In his fiction, there is always a bloody fight going on between head and heart, a fight that reflects the tensions within his own personality. A woman, as an occasion for this conflict, as an occasion for uncontrollable desire, was also, therefore, an occasion for uncontrollable fear. Not getting what he wanted was relatively familiar to Wells; it pained him, but it didn't frighten him. Reciprocal desire was quite another matter.

There was nothing unique in Wells's psychological situation with Isabel or with Jane; most new lovers experience some anxiety, some fear of closeness. However, Wells had no models to reassure him of this. His childhood experiences gave him ample precedent for dreading any situation in which he felt helpless, and he seems to have viewed his relationship with Isabel (and later, his relationship with Jane) in terms of this precedent.[6] He wanted intimacy, but he also wanted the kind of willful control that is antithetical to intimacy or passion.

The connection in Wells's mind between sexual passion and suffocation, between intimate touch and life-threatening attack, is evident both in the curious metaphors he uses in *Autobiography* and, even more obviously, in the fight-or-flight imagery that characterizes his science-fiction writing during the crucial period (1891–96) when he was torn between Isabel and Jane. His feelings at this time stimulated some of his best writing, including *The Time Machine* and *The Island of Doctor Moreau*. In a section of *Autobiography* on Isabel entitled "Primary Fixation," he describes his early sexual gropings as "explorations of my emotional tentacles" (7:2:350), a phrase that bridges the gap between the analytical Wells and the mythopoetic Wells of the science-fiction stories. The tentacles of the bloodsucking Martians, the tendrils of the suddenly aggressive "Strange Orchid," the hairy fingers of he carnivorous Morlocks that probe the Time Traveller in his sleep—Well's early work is full of a fear of being touched.

It is also full of hairy, decapitated heads. The most obvious source of these bleeding heads and of the veritable ocean of blood at the end of *The Time Machine* is the series of terrifying tubercular hemorrhages Wells suffered in 1888, and again in 1893 and 1895. However, the bleeding head is also a trite, culturally accessible symbol of the riskiness of desire and of the conse-quent danger of desirable women. In both Europe and England, writers and painters of the 1890s were obsessed by Medusa imagery, especially with the gynophobic image of Salome holding the bleeding head of John the Baptist by its hair—a kind of visual pun whose cautionary moral meaning is "Don't lose your head over a woman."

The sexual implications of Wells's own compulsive Medusa imagery are quite clear. The bleeding head is the female genitalia in its most frightening form; it is a visual representation of the superficially plausible male notion that women are mutilated men and that losing control in the sexual act leaves men vulnerable to similar mutilation. It can also be seen as a type of doppelganger—the estranged female half of the male personality, which returns in ever more distorted and powerful forms to haunt the lives of those who deny its kinship claims.

For instance, in "Our Little Neighbour" (finished just after Wells had eloped with Jane and perhaps written when he was still living with Isabel), a young wife is terrorized by the grinning head of an apelike albino dwarf, who hangs upside down outside the bedroom window of their cosy but claustro-phobically designed house.[7] The husband sprays the "ugly grin" with a garden "syringe," at which the bestial creature falls to its death impaled on its own knife, leaving a red stain on the path to the flower bed.

Or, for example, consider the plot of "Pollock and the Porroh Man," written during the same period and collected in *Thirty Strange Stories*.[8] Pol-lock, a British imperialist of the grimiest sort, is in the act of seducing a native woman when he is attacked by a knife-wielding witch doctor known as the "Porroh man." The Porroh man kills the woman but is then driven off by Pollock, who shoots him in the hand, blowing off three of his fingers. As he flees, he suddenly stops at the doorway, bends his head upside down under his arm, and stares back at Pollock. The Porroh man has put a curse on Pollock, who is haunted in a series of recurring nightmares by the image of "that inverted face" with its ornamental scars and its hair streaming down like a displaced beard, its mouth "grinning at me and showing all his teeth" (425–26). Finally Pollock hires a native assassin, who decapitates the Porroh man and brings his head to Pollock, wrapped in a bloody cloth.

Pollock tries to get rid of the head first by burying it and then by burning it, but it keeps returning, always upside down and grinning. He sails for England and the safety of home, but the head turns up again, pickled in a jar along with some souvenir snakes. Pollock begins to hallucinate; by the time he reaches England, he sees the bleeding head everywhere he goes, an image that Wells now refers to explicitly as a Gorgon (439). He loses three of his fingers in a traffic accident, the same three fingers he had shot from the Porroh man. Now the bleeding head is no longer a merely visual image; he can hear it laugh, and its scars feel real to his touch. In the end, he does the only thing he can. He looks in the mirror and cuts his throat ear to ear, decapitating himself. He becomes the very thing he had sought to flee.

The ending of the story confirms what is hinted at from the very beginning, that the ostensibly civilized Pollock and the ostensibly bestial Porroh man are really doppelgangers, two halves of the same psyche. It is no accident that their names both begin with the letter P; they belong to each other intimately. Their conflict is essentially psychomachical; they are projections of a private war going on inside Wells's own head.

This private war breaks out over and over again in Wells's early fiction, and quite often one of the combatants is defined as a sort of willful Medusa that stubbornly refuses to do what it is told or stay where it is put. For instance, in "The Devotee of Art" (1888; rewritten in 1895 as "The Temptation of Harringay") an artist ignores his dying wife in order to complete a portrait, only to discover that the painted head has acquired a life of its own and a sinister red eye that threatens him. Significantly, the painter's wife is named Isabel.[9]

The most bizarre battle in Wells's internal war occurs in "The Reconciliation" first published in December of 1895.[10] It concerns two men, Temple and Findlay, old school chums who stage a brutal boxing match over a woman. Temple puts a boxing glove on his left hand but surreptitiously slips his right hand into bulla, a whale's ear bone. The bulla, which is said to resemble both a "watch-pocket" and "human brain pan," now becomes a deadly weapon: "[He] thrust the fingers of his right hand into the cavity of the bulla. It took all his fingers, and covered his knuckles and all the back of his hand. And it was so oddly like a thumbless boxing glove!" (212)

Wells's careful phrasing here suggests that the bulla is a metaphorical vagina (The Latin word *vagina* means sheath or pocket). The connection between bleeding heads and bloody women is reinforced by the carefully choreographed fight that follows. Findlay hits Temple with his left hand. Temple hits Findlay with his right, encased in the deadly bulla. The blow lands on Findlay's temple, and his ear begins to bleed—temple connecting with temple and ear with ear, as in a dreamwork pun!

At the sight of blood, Temple loses control of himself. "There remained now only the savage man-animal, the creature that thirsts for blood." He continues to beat at Findlay mechanically until he hears a woman scream: "Then he looked down and saw the thing that had once been the face of Findlay. For an awful minute he remained kneeling agape. Then he staggered to his feet and stood over Findlay's body in the glow of the dying fire, like a man awakening from a nightmare. Suddenly he perceived the bulla on his hand, covered with blood and hair" (214–15).

Metaphorically, all this head bashing is a nightmarish Victorian version of the act of sexual intercourse, of the hymenal and menstrual blood rites that bind men and women in marriage. The conflicts and fears suggested in this scene are Oedipal, psychomachical, and gynophobic all at once. Temple's war with Findlay is a miniature War of the Worlds that, in turn, is a symbolic war of the sexes.

It was from this bloody war and its uncivilized emotions that Wells may have been fleeing when he began to design his relationship with Amy Catherine Robbins. In the *Autobiography,* Wells emphasized that Catherine Robbins was a "symbol" that his "present life [with Isabel] was unendurable" (*EA,* 6:6:300). In this new relationship "the sexual element . . . was very small" (ibid.). He is quite emphatic about this. The letters that passed between him and Catherine Robbins during their courtship "are those of two loving friends and allies, who are not and never had been passionate lovers" (*EA,* 7:2:356). She may have seemed to him, initially at least, a safe place to hide, safe precisely because he felt so little elemental sexual passion for her. Whatever her own feelings in the matter, from the first he defined her as a sister, a confidant, an ego-flattering protégée, a child, a pal. She was to be everything to him but a lover. Wells was always rather proud of this arrangement and how it demonstrated the essential purity of his purpose. In choosing Catherine, he was choosing a life of sublimation in work. Ironically, however, this choice got Wells into more and more trouble in his work as well as in his personal life. His loyalty to his platonic ideal of Jane necessitated an emotional betrayal of himself that left him incomplete and increasingly estranged from his own creative resources. It committed him to a course of public deception and private denial.

In his prologue on Jane, Wells describes his wife as if she were a piece of porcelain representing the Victorian "Angel of the Home": "A little indefatigable smiling figure" (*Postscript,* 28). "Faithful, gentle, wise, and self-forgetful . . . she was a noble wife, a happy mother" (ibid., 44). Most of all, Wells celebrates his wife's absolute honesty: "She never told a lie" (ibid., 35).[11] This is unintentionally ironic. Jane's entire life with him was a lie, at Wells's own insistence. The charades and costume dramas she compulsively staged for her weekend guests at Easton Glebe were not merely entertainments, they were practice sessions for the essential business of her life: play-acting. She always seemed to be exactly what Wells wanted her to be. As she lay slowly dying of cancer, what Wells seems to have feared most was "the dreadful possibility" that her "smiling mask" might at last slip. "Increasing poison in the blood poisons the mind so that it is afflicted with strange fears and unnatural hostilities," he wrote in *Postscript,* "but her mind never lost its integrity" (39). To the bitter end, she accepted without apparent resistance the servant's role Wells cast her in and the simple servant's name that went with it, plain "Jane." She was to be a perfected, good housekeeping version of Wells's own mother, without any of his mother's domination. (This becomes explicit when, after the birth of their first child, Wells begins to address Jane as "little Mummy.")

Unfortunately, this new Mummy managed to dominate Wells's life just as much as the original had and by using many of the same guilt-inducing tactics. Having made the defiant gesture of running off with him, Jane may have felt she was morally stuck with him for life and resolved to bind him to the relationship by whatever passive-aggressive means necessary. Early on she seems to have discovered that, although Wells simply fled in the face of direct pressure and ultimatums, he was susceptible to compliant manipulation. She got what she wanted in the long run by giving in to what he wanted in the short run. For example, when Amber Reeves gave birth to Wells's child, it was Jane who provided the layette.[12] Like so many women of the period, she learned to assert her will by appearing to have none.

Perhaps Wells was oblivious to the aggression latent in Jane's passivity because it was a behavior pattern so very like his own. He had experienced passive aggression with his mother and then slyly turned it against her at crucial moments in his life—getting what he wanted by collapsing and becoming dependent. In any case, as the years went on, the mutual security pact he had negotiated with Jane became a suffocating trap. In an often-quoted passage, heavy with unintentional irony, he praises Jane for having "stuck" to him like flypaper; "She stuck to me so sturdily that in the end I stuck to myself. I do not know what I should have been without her (*Postscript,* 35). The line "I do not know what I should have been without her" is meant to be rhetorical, but, in fact, it contains a hidden program for action. What *would* he have been without her? About 1901, shortly after the birth of his first child, Wells began to look around in earnest for an answer to that question.

The years just before and after the turn of the century were a time of profound crisis and change both in Wells's emotional life and in his writing. In his book, *The Logic of Fantasy,* John Huntington argues persuasively that around 1900 Wells made a crucial, conscious shift in his work from "undirected" to "directed" thought, from fantasizing to forecasting, from "ironic balance toward narrow and dogmatic solutions."[13] Wells's quest for an ultimate solution to the world's problems (crystalized in the idea of the World

State) parallels another simplistic quest in his private life: the search for the perfect woman.

In his fiction before 1900, uses words to paint pictures. He is adept at metaphoric "thinking aside," at creating complex mediating structures that contain and express in very economical terms a whole series of conflicts— gender conflict, intrapsychic conflict, class conflict. Wells literally "thinks in things," in visual, architectonic imagery (a good example is the upstairs-downstairs structure of *The Time Machine*). In this sense, the early Wells is similar to Lévi-Strauss's mythmaking *bricoleurs,* intuitively using the materials at hand to create a new whole out of old parts.

Intrapsychic conflicts don't disappear from Wells's later work or from his later life, but they are expressed discursively rather than visually, in terms of abstract debates between characters who represent simplistically opposed points of view (such as Esau Common and Thomas Smith in "The Loyalty of Esau Common," 1901). Eventually Wells projects his argument with himself onto the world at large, tending to divide humanity (much as St. Augustine did) into two opposing camps: those who support his unifying vision of the World State and those who do not. As he becomes increasingly dogmatic in his thinking, the fantastic mediators, the aliens, the sphinxes, the strange orchids, and crystal eggs all disappear from his fictive world. Quite literally, the color flows out of his art. The emotionally charged red/black oppositions in *The Time Machine* (1895), *The War of the Worlds* (1898), and many of the early stories, such as "The Cone," are replaced by the uniform blue of *When the Sleeper Awakes* (1899) and *The First Men in the Moon* (1901).

Wells's blue period (succeeded by a perpetual gray period) coincided with a time of great stress in his private life. He turned toward "directed thought," with its emphasis on control, order, and stability, just as he seemed to be falling apart both physically and emotionally. From 1897 through 1899 he suffered bouts of illness and "profound melancholia," a depression that recurred in 1903 after Gissing's death and the birth of his second son. David Smith attributes Wells's breakdowns to overwork,[14] but there were probably other forces involved as well, including his increasing dissatisfaction with his life with Jane and the psychological burden of his success as a bourgeois artist.

A little satire entitled "The Wild Asses of the Devil" suggests something of Wells's suppressed anguish during this crucial transitional period. It was published as part of *Boon* in 1915 but was probably written much earlier, perhaps not long after Wells moved to Sandgate in 1899.[15] It concerns "an Author who pursued fame and prosperity in a pleasant villa on the south coast of England. He wrote stories of an acceptable nature and rejoiced in a growing public esteem, carefully offending no one and seeking only to please. He had married under circumstances of qualified and tolerable romance, a lady who wrote occasional but otherwise regular verse" (142). He has a charming little daughter; the rich and famous invite him to dinner. He is careful of his image, not to seem too proud, and self-consciously maintains contact with the lower classes (the better to exploit their quaint mannerisms in his stories). He is getting a bit fat.

This is not precisely a self-portrait (Wells's writing was never so bland or inoffensive), but it contains some fairly sharp self-criticism and suggests, as do many other of his fictional works, how much Wells suffered from what psychologists call an imposter complex, an enduring belief in one's inner unworthiness, which often afflicts people who achieve a sudden, sweeping success that moves them out of the class in which they were raised. The Author in "Wild Asses" is a member of the large "fraternity of frauds that populates Wells's imagination." (Chaffrey is the Master Frater.) He is a phony, a sham whose fame is linked to an ongoing betrayal of the working-class people he has risen above.[16]

He is also an emotional fraud. The facade of his apparently ideal life conceals intense anguish and dissatisfaction. He is suffocated by the security he has worked so hard to achieve. "There were days when this Author had almost to force himself through the wholesome, necessary routines of life" (143). He has difficulty facing himself in the shaving mirror each morning. Secretly, he harbors the feeling that his nice life by the seaside is "about as boring and intolerable a life as any creature with a soul to be damned could possibly pursue" (142).

Appropriately, a proletarian Mephistopheles appears to make manifest the Author's hellish mood. While walking at the seashore during a fierce winter storm, he meets a tattered Lascar stoker, a "poor devil" who turns out literally to be a poor Devil, a lower-class denizen of Hell whose job was to herd the Devil's wild asses. During a momentary lapse of attention (occasioned by a speech on home rule by W. E. Gladstone), he allowed the wild asses to escape to the surface, where they now hide, disguised as people. The poor Devil was condemned perpetually to search the cold, damp Earth to locate the asses and send them back where they belong.

As the Devil tells his story, he bursts into tears. " 'Nobody good to me,' he sobbed . . . and his tears ran down the author's plump little hand—scalding tears." The Author compares him to "an unhappy child." He is "heart-broken," "an exile from a land of great warmth and considerable entertainment" (147). Clearly, he is the Author's (and the author's) very own Devil, a psychomachical double who expresses estranged feelings of deprivation, loneliness, self-pity, and an intense yearning for emotional warmth. At the end of the story, the Author agrees to join the Devil on his mission, his quest. He assumes that he will eventually be able to go back to his safe life by the sea, but he is mistaken; for "whosoever takes unto himself a devil and goes out upon a quest, goes out upon a quest from which there is no returning—Nevermore" (152). Wells's ironic, playful tone distances him from these feelings, but the subtext of the story is a Faustian howl that has personal implications. The Hades the Devil describes is very like Folkstone. And that, of course, is just the point: "*This* is Hell, nor am I out of it."

By 1902 or 1903, Wells was coldly exiling anima from his art, justifying his success by making it serve clear ethical and political goals, while in his private life he was more and more obsessed by a desire to achieve reunion with anima, in the form of an ideal Lover-Shadow. To put the matter more crudely, he began to philander.

Over the next forty years, Wells's compulsive sexual search brought him together with an extraordinary number and variety of women, including a sixteen-year-old girl named May Nisbet; Violet Hunt; Ella D'Arcy; Dorothy Richardson, who "intoned dull clever things" and "was most interestingly hairy on her body", Amber Reeves, whose "fuzz of soft black hair" attracted him and with whom he had a daughter; "Little E," the Grafin von Armin; Rebecca West; Moura Budberg; Odette Keun; and, neither last nor least, a "Coon" prostitute with whom he spent a memorable afternoon in 1906, shortly before having dinner with Teddy Roosevelt at the White House. Sadly, this brief encounter is the only one he describes with much sensual tenderness.

Although Wells's virgin/whore complex was pronounced, it was not the defining characteristic of his love life. He rarely visited prostitutes, not merely out of fastidiousness but because he was looking as much for emotional satisfaction as he was for physical relief. Wells is often at some pains to deny this. Paradoxically, his fear of sexuality moves him to pose as a libertine. ("I wanted, for my own self-respect, to *get* women" (*Postscript*, 60). In both *Postscript* and the *Autobiography*, he insistently denigrates the psychological importance of his sexual restlessness. The World State is the "main theme" of his life; the "sexual system" is secondary (*EA*, 7:1:348). Wells's typical argument is that his philandering is really a testimony to his devotion to the work ethic! "To make love periodically . . . seems to be, for most of us, a necessary condition to efficient working. . . . I resent the necessity at times as I resent the perpetual recurrence of meal-times and sleep" (*Postscript*, 67).

Many reviewers have been inclined to take Wells at his word and to dismiss his antiphonal cry, "It's a mate I have always been after" (*Postscript*, 108), as a sentimental lapse. But it can be argued that it is the cynical Wells, not the romantic Wells, who was something of a fraud. Wells's essential emotional urgency, his sheer love-hunger, comes through clearly in everything he writes. He stayed with Jane and compulsively devoted himself to self-improvement schemes projected on a world scale, but all his repressive efforts never quite succeeded in convincing the stubborn adolescent romantic in him that the whole meaning of life was work.

One of the more alarming, and disarming, qualities of *Postscript* is its sheer adolescent energy. Virtually all of his life, Wells retained his youthful susceptibility and self-absorption. He never stopped looking for his great love; he never stopped getting crushes on women. Indeed, the real purpose of *Postscript* was to allow him to fuss over the last and most disconcerting of his crushes, Moura Budberg.

Wells himself was dimly aware that the way he related to women in general and to Moura in particular had something important to do with the way he related to himself and to his own emotional needs and capabilities. In a crucial chapter of *Postscript,* he tries to understand this connection. It is a rather difficult essay to follow, but it is not, I think, the mere "windy intellectualizing" that many have taken it for. The prose is unfocused because Wells is reaching out for an important psychological insight that lies just beyond his field of vision. It is here that he first refers to the hazy Platonic idea of "the Lover-Shadow":

> I think that in every human mind, possibly from an extremely early age, there exists a continually growing and continually more subtle complex of expectation and hope; . . . reveries of sensuous delights and ecstasies; reveries of understanding and reciprocity; which I will call the Lover-Shadow. . . . No human being, I believe, lives or can live without this vague various protean but very real presence side by side with the *persona,* something which says or says in effect, "Right-O," or "Yes" or "I help" or "My dear." That is what I mean by the Lover-Shadow. It is the inseparable correlative to the *persona,* in the direction of our lives. It may be deprived of all recognition; it may be denied; but it is there. (*Postscript,* 54–55)

Samuel Hynes, in his review of *H. G. Wells In Love* for the *New York Times* (3 March 1985), reads this passage to mean that the "Lover-Shadow" was merely Wells's term for his ideal woman. However, as I have already suggested, one could argue that Wells is really grasping at a much more subtle concept, rather like Jung's notion of anima and animus. He is making the connection between his yearning for intimacy with another person and his more inchoate yearning for intimacy with the estranged parts of his own personality.

Rather, he is almost making that connection. Wells never really embraces his feminine side. The Lover-Shadow remains projective, externalized, more a ghost than a shadow, unconnected to his "unequivocally male" self: "This great Shadow, so largely feminine, stood over me, beside that expansion of myself, my *persona* . . . even while I walked, as I have described, on a Sunday fifty years ago, in my shabby top-hat, with Isabel in Regent's Park. . . . That phantom dwarfed and dominated us . . . [a] dream of inaccessible understanding and reciprocating womanliness . . . (*Postscript,* 56–57). The great phantom that brooded over the whole length of Wells's life was, essentially, a hypostatization of his own estranged yearnings to be nurtured and to be passive and dependent, yearnings that had obviously been unfulfilled in his relationship with his mother. He projected these yearnings onto one woman after another, pursuing his secret shadow-self by pursuing and wooing them.

Because of Wells's misplaced yearnings, these affairs were doomed to failure. Wells was not really interested in the otherness of other people; he was acting out an internal conflict, chasing the shadow cast by his own heart. Paradoxically, he was driven by precisely those feelings that he objected to most in himself, feelings he regarded as fundamentally alien and unmasculine. His characteristic "can't-take-'em, can't-leave-'em-alone" attitude toward women was, thus, correlative to his repeated efforts to abandon what he deemed to be the wretched "womanly" parts of his own personality—his "negative capability."

Nowhere is Wells's paradoxical pursuit of his own shadow more apparent than in his peculiar and relatively enduring affair with Moura Budberg. It is Moura, not Rebecca West, who justifies the title, *H. G. Wells in Love*. She was not really a conquest at all in the usual sense, but rather a mobile red queen with her own strategies for avoiding checkmate.

Wells met Budberg in 1914 during his first trip to Russia. On his second trip in 1920 they met again, and he fell in love with her "more completely and sincerely than I had ever done before" (*Postscript*, 109). Wells's willingness to surrender to his feelings for Budberg may have been aided by the fact that there was so little danger of entanglement: she lived very far away and was, Wells assumed, Maxim Gorky's mistress. He, in turn, had duties toward not one but two families—Jane, Gip, and Frank, and Rebecca West and Anthony.

Significantly, when he finally broke with Rebecca West a few years later (1923), he did not run back to Russia to claim his great love but rather offhandedly set up another parallel household in the south of France with Odette Keun, a woman he vilifies throughout this memoir as a "prostitute-housekeeper" (139). It was only after the death of Jane, an event that suddenly gave Odette seniority status, that Wells began to orient his life around his feelings for Budberg. Of their reunion in Germany in 1929 he writes: "From the moment we met we were lovers, as though there had never been any separation between us" (141). Even then, Wells did not give himself over to his feelings; he remained with Odette in the well-ordered home she maintained for him (Lou Pidou) until 1933.

Wells himself is somewhat at a loss to explain this "long-period of shilly-shally" (141). Ironically, his avoidance and evasion are an inverse measure of the depth of his feeling for Budberg. He was simply terrified of getting what he wanted. In the end, as he had with Isabel, he arranged the scenario so that he would *not* get what he wanted, so that his grim expectations would be confirmed. It was a choice of deep depression over high anxiety, and it set a seal of sorts on Wells's inner life.[17]

This hidden need to prove Moura too good to be true explains Wells's explosive reaction to "a few unguarded remarks at a party in Moscow in July 1934" (16). He learned then that Moura had gone several times to visit Gorky in Russia without telling him—"She did lie; she did cheat" (183). For Wells, this was the end of everything: "So in an evening my splendid Moura was smashed to atoms. . . . I never slept for the rest of my time in Russia. I was wounded excessively in my pride and hope. I was wounded as I had never been wounded by any human being before. It was unbelievable. I lay in bed and wept like a disappointed child" (*Postscript,* 176). This is a repetition of a scene Wells had acted out some thirty-six years earlier with Isabel, which, in turn, reflected the whole sad pattern of his childhood. In 1898, three years after his divorce and remarriage, Wells rode his bicycle out to the farm where his ex-wife lived:

> We used our old intimate names for each other. Suddenly I found myself overcome by the sense of our separation. I wanted fantastically to recover her. I implored her for the last time in vain. . . . "But how can things be like that now?" she asked. I gave way to a wild storm of weeping. I wept in her arms like a disappointed child . . . unable to understand the peculiar keenness of my unhappiness. I felt like an automaton, I felt as though all purpose had been drained out of me and nothing remained worth while. The world was dead and I was dead and I had only just discovered it. (*EA,* 7:2:359)

Wells did not in fact break with Moura as he had broken with Isabel. Moura remained his companion and his mistress to the end of his life, but on an altered basis. As far as Wells was concerned, their *modus vivendi* had changed. The dream of reunion with the Lover-Shadow was dead, and, once again, Wells "felt like an automaton."

After July 1934, Wells entered into a period of depression that lasted essentially until his death. His emotional atrophy is painfully obvious in the bleak work he produced during this period, including *The Anatomy of Frustration, The Croquet Player,* and his odd, almost psychotic film script for *Things to Come.* Well below the waterline of this suffocating depression, there seems to have been a great reservoir of unresolved sexual fear and quasi-Oedipal jealousy. Over and over again, Wells refers to his anxieties about Moura's love for him as "a sore," "a canker" on his mind (*Postscript,* 180). He often seems obsessed by her real or imagined uncleanliness, her messiness (a complaint he had also made about Isabel).[19] For Wells, Moura seems to have been a fragment of ancient myth come to life, an avatar of the large-bodied goddesses who haunted his adolescent wet dreams (*EA,* 2:5:56), a Medusa whose steady gaze paralyzed him so that he could neither move away nor move toward her. The Medusa connection is particularly evident in Wells's account of "a disagreeable dream" he had in 1934 during the height of his crisis with Moura:

I dreamt I was wandering late at night in a certain vague strange evil slum—grotesque and yet familiar, which has been a sort of dream background in my mind for years—and I began to think of her, as I have thought of her so often in so many places, with longing, with a sort of heart-ache hope for her. Then suddenly, she was before me, my Moura, carrying that voluminous bag of hers.

"What's in that bag of yours?" said I and seized upon it before she could resist.

And then, after the incoherent fashion of dreams, the bag having vanished, there appeared her stays wrapped in newspaper. In this slum!

"Who have you been with?" I cried, and forthwith I was beating her furiously. I was weeping and beating at her. She fell to pieces, not like a human being but like a lay figure [sic], with hollow pasteboard limbs, and her head was a plaster thing that rolled away from me. I pounced on it and it was hollow and had no brains in it. . . .

I woke up in a state of pale and dreadful anger and hate. (*Postscript*, 184–85)

From the very beginning to the very end of his sexual life, Wells's imagination was haunted by the twin image of the brainless body and the bodiless brain—each a synechdoche for the uncontrollability of passion. It is Wells' *images*, not his vaunted ideas, that provide the real unity in his life's work. In 1934, Moura was the focus of that imagery because she was the most uncontrollable force in his life. As the dream itself suggests, she was a woman who did pretty much what she wanted to and was not much inclined either to self-sacrifice or to intellectualization of her emotions: he quotes her as saying, "Darling. Why do you always *reason* about love?" (*Postscript*, 210). Wells finally coped with her by turning down the volume on his emotional receiving set, but the life that remained to him was muted thereby.

If Moura Budberg was Wells's Lover-Shadow, his missing "other half," who, then, was Rebecca West? *Postscript* raises more questions than it answers on this titillating topic. In particular, it raises questions about the interpretation of the Wells-West affair given in Gordon N. Ray's less than unbiased book, *H. G. Wells and Rebecca West*. In 1970, at the inception of his project, Ray apparently obtained West's permission for access to her correspondence, which was subsequently closed to other scholars until the death of her son, Anthony (it is housed at Yale).[21] This access gave him a privileged view of her life but also subtly compromised the use he made of the material. His preface, full of deference to his "collaborator," Dame Rebecca, reads a little like a segment of *The Aspern Papers*.[22] It would be disingenuous, however, not to admit to being grateful for Ray's book. In his eagerness to ensure her cooperation, he gave West something that few people ever get, the right to edit her own life; it is interesting to guess how she used her "final cut" to reshape her experience in retrospect.[23]

The most important bit of reshaping is apparent in the opening line of

Ray's introduction. In this telling of the tale, Rebecca West is to be regarded as "*the* woman" in H. G. Wells's life (rather like Irene Adler and Sherlock Holmes). As I have already suggested, Wells himself did not share this view, at least by the time he got around to writing his memoirs in 1934. In *Postscript* (60), he names three women he has "really loved," and Rebecca West is not among them. She is a footnote of sorts: "I do not know if I loved Rebecca West, though I was certainly in love with her towards the latter part of our liaison" (60–61). Wells is not being cleverly evasive here, I think, although he is certainly capable of that maneuver. It is simply that it is difficult to summon up emotions of love one no longer feels. In 1934, Wells was utterly obsessed with Moura Budberg. His relationship with West had ended more than a decade earlier. Moreover, even at the height of his involvement with West, he seems to have been deeply ambivalent about her. It is probably more accurate to regard West, not as *the* woman, but as one of a sequence of women whom Wells auditioned for the same role, apprentice Lover-Shadows.

West's desire to portray herself as the only Dark Lady in Wells's life is understandable. After all, she was stuck with the popular conception that he was *the* man in her life. Although she was a talented and original writer in her own right and although she lived a long and varied life, nothing she ever wrote or did was quite as interesting to most people as the fact that she had once had an affair with H. G. Wells and had borne his illegitimate child. Social shame and sexual guilt aside, how it must irked her to know that her life had been so significantly determined, not by the power of her formidable brain or the force of her formidable will, but by a little accident that happened to her when she was barely twenty years old.

The precise nature of this little accident is still a hot controversy nearly three-quarters of a century after the fact. Ray's account of the early stages of the affair and Rebecca West's pregnancy differs significantly from Wells's own account. Ray writes, "In an angry moment, when he feared that Rebecca might leave him, Wells intentionally omitted his usual precautions in the hope that pregnancy might bind her to him" (Ray, 32). The attribution of motive implicit in the word *intentionally* can only come from Dame Rebecca herself, and here, at least, her candor may be something less than absolute. It is understandable that she eventually came to *feel* "bound" to Wells against her will and best interests, but that this was Wells's initial intent seems unlikely. He is quite clear about this in *Postscript*: "She came to see me at my flat in St. James's Court one afternoon when we were in danger of being interrupted by a valet; it was our second encounter and she became pregnant. It was entirely unpremeditated. Nothing of the sort was in our intention. She wanted to write. It should not have happened, and since I was the experienced person, the blame is wholly mine" (96).

Of the two accounts, Wells's seems more plausible, at least at first glance. West had worked so hard to get Wells, had declared her yearning for him so openly, that it seems unlikely that he would have been afraid of losing her on only their second tryst.[24] Moreover, Wells was not really that keen on children; he seems to have regarded his sons with Jane not only as impediments to his freedom but also as rivals for her affection. Yet who is to say? Accidents often express hidden wishes and fears. Throughout his life, Wells had demonstrated a sure instinct for painting himself into corners; he fled in horror from possessiveness in others yet was incapable of distinguishing between loving and controling when his own feelings were at stake. He certainly must have sensed that, for all her youth and insecurity, West would not be as tractable as Jane. Perhaps he did want to tether her to some convenient locale. On so many other psychological issues in their relationship, West's intuition is more reliable than Wells's labored analysis. Perhaps she was right after all. (Which, of course, doesn't excuse Ray for having presented West's version as if it were fact.)

The only event that is undisputed among the principals is that in August of 1914, West gave birth to a son, Anthony.[25] She and Wells gave him the odd middle name of Panther, and therein lies a tale. Panther (or Panfer, in babytalk) was Well's pet name for Rebecca West; he was Jaguar. Together they were an androgynous beast called the Panguar. In discussing this jungle love imagery, Ray writes that these names "stood for the whole attitude toward life evolved by Rebecca and Wells. . . . They emphasized the ruthless withdrawal from society that the relationship entailed, the fact that Rebecca and Wells were not part of the pack and did not acknowledge its law. . . . The names implied the free recognition by Rebecca and Wells of the animal side of their love" (Ray, 35–38). This is a clear and persuasive analysis, as far as it goes, but then Ray muddies the waters by insisting that the Panther/Jaguar imagery belonged primarily to West's creative imagination (36).

In fact, Wells was also fond of cats, and his letters to other women, both before and after West, often use feline imagery, with special emphasis on fur.[26] Like many Victorian men, Wells had a hair fetish.[27] The threatening coils of serpentine hair that flow from the heads of women in so many *fin de siècle* paintings also appear with obsessive regularity in the visual imagery of Wells's early science fiction, but in estranged form: the idealized women of the pre-Raphaelites have been transmuted into hairy, inhuman beasts (the brainless Morlocks) or hostile, Medusa-like aliens (the bloodsucking Martians). Flowing female hair becomes literally serpentine—tendrils or tentacles that entangle and suffocate and kill. The bleeding Beast People in *The Island of Dr. Moreau* are, among other things, metaphorical women, at once both victims and predators. Moreau's experiment, too, is metaphorical, projective, and implicitly sexual: he seeks to control the beast within himself by "taming" the hairy little beasts around him. Appropriately, Moreau is finally killed by a female, feline Beast Person, the puma.[28]

Although Gordon Ray surely knows Wells's work as well as anyone, he largely ignores the connection between the Panfer/Jaguar baby talk and the powerful gynophobic imagery in Wells's early fiction (it is clearly Dame Rebecca and her work that fascinate Ray). Consequently, his interpretation of the Wells/West affair focuses too much on practical matters and misses much of the psychological nuance. In particular, Ray misses the significance of the androgynous term Panguar that Wells and West coined to describe themselves à deux. In a sense, the Beast People in The Island of Dr. Moreau are "panguars" manqué, an early, failed experiment in androgyny.[29] They are metaphorical mediators who literally fall apart at the seams. The need for such mediators, the need to create a unified whole out of the disparate, warring forces in his own psyche, drove Wells all his life, both in his art and in his serial love affairs. In his relationship with West, at least in the first few years, he seems to have found a paradigm for a new self-definition. She was a sort of Beast Person he had never seen before: a brain and a body.

Although West was literally young enough to have been Wells's daughter, it was she, I sense, who provided Wells with a role model as a lover during these years. He must have seen himself in her, in her very youth—a sort of Ghost of Christmas Past. That is conveyed strongly in the jungle imagery in Wells's letters and, even more poignantly, in the little "picshuas" that accompany them. It wasn't merely that he metaphorized her as a great cat, but that he imaged himself in the same furry, feline terms. She seems to have brought out the woman in him.

Perhaps that is what worried Wells about West; perhaps that is why he arranged to hold her pinioned at a distance. In trying to keep both Rebecca and Jane, separately, in ferrying himself back and forth between them, Wells was merely acting out in real life the kind of psychomachy that he had previously used to structure his science fiction. Wells represented ego. Jane and Rebecca played the parts of superego and id respectively.

This tidy arrangement must have served the needs of all three of them fairly well, for it endured for a decade. If it had been in Wells's power to manage it, it might have endured much longer. His account in Postscript supports Ray's contention that West finally ended the affair, just as it had been she who initiated it. "I was more hurt to lose her than she to be quit of me. . . . I still wanted to go on with the liaison. . . . Rebecca had become for me the symbol of the Lover-Shadow and . . . I was unable to conceive of it in any other form than hers—or exist without it" (Postscript, 102–3, 110).

H. G. Wells's unfinished quest for his Lover-Shadow comes full circle in Anthony West's quest for his elusive Father-Shadow in the poignant but problematic H. G. Wells: Aspects of a Life (1984). Aspects of a Life is not likely to rival the Mackenzies' volume or Smith's Desperately Mortal as the definitive biography of Wells, but it is seeded with little pearls of analysis. West's long apprenticeship with his mother made him especially adept at spotting the hidden motives behind apparently innocuous behavior. For example, his portrait of Jane Wells, although rather brutal, exposes far better than most standard biographies the aggressive underside of her extreme passivity. (See *Aspects,* 37–39.)

West's long account of Jane's death is a good corrective to the self-serving version of the same event Wells himself gives in *Postscript,* with its luminous vision of the gallant old couple facing death hand in hand. Wells was obviously terrified of Jane's dying, as well as mightily inconvenienced by it, and reacted to his fears first by denying the seriousness of her illness (a tactic that left his youngest son to bear the burden alone) and then by evading any intimacy with her pain by keeping the house full of distracting guests. Ten days after the funeral, he was back "home" with Odette (113–21).

West also offers an especially acute analysis of Wells's status as a rebellious mama's boy and the ways he internalized the conflict of wills between his parents. He recognizes the defensiveness in Wells's critique of Freud's Oedipus complex in the *Autobiography,* and demonstrates quite plausibly how Wells repeated his parents' behavior in his marriages to Isabel and Jane. He sees the element of sibling rivalry in Wells's reaction to the birth of his two sons by Jane (178–82; 200–2; 257–60). Most perceptive of all is his analysis (299) of a pair of extraordinary photographs (to my knowledge not previously published) that Wells took himself. They are close-ups of his mother's implacable face as she lay embalmed in her coffin.

In the end, Wells's efforts to understand and define himself were no more successful than his rather pathetic attempts to capture his dead mother's secret power within a frozen photographic frame. It is not surprising that his would-be biographers have fared even less well. By instinctive design, his motile personality was difficult to catch and harder to pin down. Even now, forty-one years after his death—121 years after his birth—his work still generates more heat than light, not because of the difficulty of his ideas, but because of the ingratiating perversity of the man himself.

More than virtually any other comparable writer, Wells *was* his work. Everything he touched he transmuted into self-expression. Even the other people in his life served him as avatars of qualities in himself. In the end, like all solipsists, he seems to have regretted having only himself for company; in the end, like all workaholics, he seems to have experienced the emptiness of mere goal-getting. A putative success, he judged himself a secret fraud, an imposter. A self-styled proponent of world unity, he remained a dramatically divided Brain, at ostensible war with itself and with the mere body to which it remained stubbornly attached.

In both the *Autobiography* and *Postscript,* Wells describes himself as a Brain as if "brain" were a simple synonym for the word "mind." But, of course, it is not. It is a visual image manqué, a reliquary "talking head" retrieved from Wells's store of science-fiction props, a shadow Martian. Moreover, like the Martians, the "talking brain" is a paradox, an oxymoron—an image of disembodied, almost godlike intellectual power and, simultaneously, of terrible, skinless vulnerability. What is more helpless than a "mere brain"? An "invisible man," perhaps.

Despite his Faustian efforts at transcendence and because of them, Wells remained an Invisible Man to the very end—angry, self-defeating, ultimately naked and alone in the snow—but never compromising, always secretly whole, secretly fierce. Even in despair, Wells's urge to express himself was absolute and consuming. In this sense and in many others, he was the very thing he most denied being: an artist for art's own sake. His voice may drone on and on, but it is *his* voice, not an imitation of somebody's else's. It speaks still, this voice, this Talking Brain, as if the grave itself were mere inconvenience.

Notes

1. *H. G. Wells in Love: Postscript to an Experiment in Autobiography*, ed. G. P. Wells (Boston: Little, Brown, 1984).

2. See the prelude to H. G. Wells, *Experiment in Autobiography: Discoveries and Conclusions of a Very Ordinary Brain* (New York: Macmillan, 1934).

3. Anthony West, in *H. G. Wells: Aspects of a Life* (New York: Random House, 1984), suggests that Catherine Robbins's father's death was a suicide, brought on by business failures. In either case, it is reasonable to assume that in 1892 she was in an extremely insecure state, both economically and emotionally, and that she may have been looking for a surrogate father in Wells (instead of the surrogate son she in fact got).

4. The separation and reunion of lovers is a recurring theme in Wells's fiction, see *The Dream* (1924), especially chs. 5–7.

5. For a discussion of the claustrophobic aspect of Wells's early fiction, see Robert P. Weeks, "Disentanglement as a Theme in H. G. Wells' Fiction," *Papers of the Michigan Academy of Science, Arts and Letters* 39 (1954): 439–44.

6. Wells himself raises this interpretation in a series of artfully evasive rhetorical questions in which he characteristically expresses his emotions by projecting them onto mankind in general (see *EA*, 7:2:354).

7. The couple's "peculiar little house" is built into a hillside on the north and east; there is a garden in the front and also a garden in the back, virtually above the house ("an attic garden"). On the exposed side is a brick wall covered with ivy. The gargoyle-like dwarf (called a "bogle") climbs up this ivy to the bedroom. The young wife is also said to "cling," as ivy, or tentacles, might. J. R. Hammond, ed., *The Man with a Nose, and Other Uncollected Short Stories of H. G. Wells* (London: Athlone, 1984), 117–25.

8. H. G. Wells, *Thirty Strange Stories* (1898; reprinted, New York: Causeway Books, 1974), 416–31.

9. "The Devotee of Art," *The Man with a Nose*, 50–60.

10. *Thirty Strange Stories*, 205–15.

11. *The Book of Catherine Wells* (London: Chatto & Windus, 1928) suggests that Jane had a more intense inner life than Wells wished to know. Her stories are rather more accomplished and less sentimental than one might expect—atmospheric and rich in psychological nuance. Like the early H. G., Jane "thinks in things;" physical objects (houses, gardens) are charged with the emotions which the characters themselves often seem to lack. There is a great deal of suppressed love-hunger; there is also a surprising amount of sadism and violence and a

preoccupation with death and suicide. Like Jane herself, many of her characters lose their chance for passion by being unwilling to take a risk: "I can't run any risks," says one unhappily married woman, refusing a potential lover. "All this life I have led so long has come to fit me like my skin. If it was torn off me, I should bleed to death." ("May Afternoon," 121.) The most interesting story concerns requited love between two women. Mary Hastings, a thirty-five-year-old painter, is content with her virginity, in large measure because she has a satisfying relationship with a young girl, Sylvia. They live together in an exquisite little cottage called "Love O'Women." Nothing more explicit than a little intense hand-kissing goes on, but the homoerotic content of the relationship is clear: "In a hundred ways then Mary knew what it might be to have a lover." ("The Beautiful House," 82.)

12. West, *Aspects of a Life*, 34.

13. John Huntington, *The Logic of Fantasy* (New York: Columbia University Press, 1982), 114.

14. David Smith, *H. G. Wells: Desperately Mortal* (New Haven: Yale University Press, 1986), 59.

15. H. G. Wells, *Boon, The Mind of the Race . . .* (New York: George H. Doran, 1915), 229–57. For the story and its history, see *The Man with a Nose*, vii, 142–52.

16. For a discussion of the fraud figure in Wells's early fictions, see Huntington, *Logic of Fantasy*, 88, 111–14.

17. In *Aspects of a Life* (144–46) West argues that Budberg was a spy attached to Wells by the Soviet government and that this knowledge is what shattered H. G. David Smith concludes she was, at most, a courier (*Desperately Mortal*, 426). Wells's own account (*Postscript*, 178, 181) emphasizes his sexual jealousy. His extreme possessiveness and his deep-seated fear of being loved are in evidence in many places in *Postscript* but especially in this passage in which he recounts how a well-meaning friend tried to convince him to relax a little about Moura. ("Why doubt that a woman has a heart until you have torn it out?"): "But I cared too deeply for Moura to keep things at that superficial level. I wanted her, skin and bones, nerves and dreams—or it seemed to me that I did not want her at all. I could not be happy about the things below her masks. I wanted truth and love there. I could not give her the benefit of the doubt" (*Postscript*, 183–84).

18. In *Things to Come* (1936) the tone of hysterical high-mindedness is almost unrelieved. Only Theotocopulus, an effete artist, mounts any objection to the compulsive joylessness of Cabal's "great white world." He incites the mob to attack the "space gun . . . a symbol of all that drives us." But the rebellion is brief and ineffectual. The space gun shoots, sending Cabal's daughter and her lover off to seed the stars. At the end Wells has Cabal speak directly to Theotocopulus's rather pertinent question, "Is man never to rest?": "Rest enough for the individual man . . . ," says Cabal, "but for Man no rest and no ending. He must go on, conquest after conquest." "But we're such little creatures, so fragile, so weak, little animals," his colleague objects. "If we are no more than little animals, we must snatch each scrap of happiness and live and suffer and pass, mattering no more than all the other animals do or have done. Is it *this* or *that*," rolling his eyes toward the heavens. "All the universe or nothing. Which shall it be? Which shall it be?"

Artistically, this is pretty sad stuff; but it conveys, perhaps more clearly than the better work, how much Wells's idea-factory was powered by his existential fears—his horror of helplessness. The extreme helplessness he apparently experienced as a child seems to have marked him for life, to have made him even more intolerant than most of us are of the contingent, uncontrollable nature of existence. Any form of passivity, even normal tranquil contemplation, seems to have been extremely anxiety-provoking for Wells.

19. Significantly, Wells praises Jane for her extreme tidiness. Even as a corpse she was "clean."

20. Smith (*Desperately Mortal*, 425) suggests she remained stubbornly in love with her second husband.

21. Ibid., 364.

22. "Dame Rebecca read the successive drafts of my story with the most scrupulous care. She corrected errors of fact, filled in the inevitable omissions of a narrative based on fragmentary materials, and set down with her accustomed force and wit how she herself regarded this part of her life. This collaboration continued, indeed, until my typescript went to the printer. Her candor was absolute." Gordon Ray, *H. G. Wells and Rebecca West* (New Haven: Yale University Press, 1974), xii.

23. Ray's initial plan, to reconstruct the Wells-West relationship from their correspondence, was complicated by the fact that, although there were more than 800 letters from Wells to West, only five of her letters to him had apparently survived, Wells having allegedly burned the others en masse and she having kept no copies. In *Aspects of a Life* Anthony West implies that copies of the letters that she wrote to Wells do indeed exist: "The originals of the letters that she wrote to my father before their affair had properly begun have not survived, but the copies of them that she rather remarkably made and kept leave no room for doubt [that she initiated the affair]" (5). West neither cites his sources nor offers any further comment on this crucial matter, so it remains unclear how many letters he is talking about and whether he has direct evidence of their existence. Perhaps the Ray book itself is his source, and he is merely referring to the five surviving letters of hers which appear there. Later West makes another reference to the missing letters: "How my mother answered [Wells] isn't altogether clear, since her side of this prolonged exchange isn't for the time being available" (91–92). Here he is presumably referring to the restricted materials in the Beinecke Library's archive of Rebecca West's papers. Anthony West's coyness whenever he writes about his mother's letters reflects his belief that she was an inveterate liar and that she retroactively fabricated letters and other documents in order to manipulate her biographers, including Ray (57–58).

24. In an early letters to Wells, one of the five Ray says survived, West pours out her love for him and threatens suicide: "You have done for me utterly. . . . I would give my whole life to feel your arms around me again. . . . Don't leave me utterly alone" (Ray, *Wells and West*, 22–23). Part of the poignancy of this letter now is that it reminds one so much of Wells's own lovelorn obsessions with Isabel and Moura. Wells and West both seem to have been wounded children, each looking for a missing parent in the other.

25. There *is* dispute about the exact day of Anthony West's birth. Wells gives it as 4 August, "the day of the British declaration of war against Germany" (*Postscript*, 96), and most authorities, including Ray, have used this date. However, West himself insists that he was really born "in the first few minutes of August 5" (*Aspects of a Life*, 3).

26. For example, he equates the "tamed" version of Moura with a "great black cat" he owned at Lou Pidou (*Postscript*, 209).

27. For an incisive discussion of the Victorian male's obsession with hair, see Elizabeth G. Glitter, "The Power of Woman's Hair in the Victorian Imagination," *PMLA* 99 (1984): 936–54.

28. See *The Island of Dr. Moreau* (1896; reprint, New York: Berkley, 1964), 95. Moreau's fate is not unique. Even in Wells's later novels, when his visual imagination had all but dimmed, jungle imagery recurs obsessively, and his heroes are often attacked by big cats. For instance, Trafford is wounded by a lynx in *Marriage* (1912), a novel written *before* Wells met West. Bentham in *The Research Magnificent* is an intellectual driven by a phobia about wild animals, especially tigers. For a thorough account of Wells's jungle and cat imagery, see John R. Reed, *The Natural History of H. G. Wells* (Athens: Ohio University Press, 1982), 35–40, passim.

29. The great progenitor of the nineteenth-century movement toward androgyny in the visual arts was the French symbolist painter Gustave Moreau, particularly in his odd, anxiety-filled renderings of Oedipus and the Sphinx. Thus it is a lovely coincidence (if, indeed, it is a coincidence) that Wells gave the name *Moreau* to the one figure in his work whose explicit function is to create "Sphinxes" (beast + human = beastman = sphinx). Doctor Moreau's

amorality, his bloody, mutilating methodology, express Wells's conservative fear of androgyny (conceived as a loss of masculinity), but the sinuous forms of the cat-people express his fascination with it.

It is unlikely that Wells saw any of Moreau's most famous works themselves, but he may well have seen prints, and surely he knew of Moreau indirectly through J. K. Huysmans, Oscar Wilde, and other sources—for instance, an article published in the *Dial* in 1893 in which Charles Ricketts describes in detail a number of Moreau's Medusan paintings. Interestingly enough, Wells begins *The Island of Dr. Moreau* by referring obliquely to another famous painting, "The Raft of the Medusa."

Wells's Common Readers

ROBERT CROSSLEY

In the summer of 1918 H. G. Wells received a letter from a soldier in France, Eric Williams, who told how he had "built up from your writings a sort of unseen parent stirring me to a better & finer way of living, & teaching me an altogether new & splendid conception of life." Many such letters came to Wells during the Great War and, as he often did, he invited Williams to visit him at Easton Glebe. The opportunity never arose, but 21 years later Wells came home from his 1939 lecture tour to Australia to discover a letter from the same Eric Williams. He had heard Wells speak in Sydney but, unable to meet him, he wrote enclosing a snapshot of himself along with the letter Wells had sent to him in the trenches in 1918. This is what Eric Williams said:

> For every one of your followers who could be classified as "distinguished" there are many thousands of ordinary people who look to you as the World Leader in clarified thinking. . . . When I was a youth—the discovery of your writings marked a complete revolution in my thinking. The continued reading of your books made me, in actual fact, "a new man." The confused ideas lodged in my mind were swept away, permanently, by the logic of your reasoning & your lucid presentation of facts. For this I owe you a personal debt of gratitude which is quite beyond the range of adequate expression.[1]

Unlike some correspondents, Eric Williams was not asking for something (a gift of money, influence in getting a manuscript published, or assistance in being freed from a mental asylum—to name the three most common requests made of Wells in his fan mail). But Williams's two letters typify the responses of the ordinary, undistinguished readers who wrote letters of thanks to Wells throughout his career. The private and public observations of celebrities have become part of the gospel about Wells: how Conrad exclaimed over *The Invisible Man,* what Bennett made of Wells as a doctrinaire reformist, Zamyatin's enthusiasm for the romances, and James's disappointments with the discussion novels. But the finely turned phrases of reviewers and fellow writers may not offer the most useful insights into

From *H. G. Wells under Revision,* ed. Patrick Parrinder and Christopher Rolfe (Selinsgrove, Pa.: Susquehanna University Press, 1990). Reprinted with permission.

Wells the populist utopian—a writer who wanted to be an educational force in the world, who wanted to stimulate the moral imagination and critical awareness of the widest possible range of readers, who wanted especially to improve the quality of ordinary people's lives. Studying some of the letters from unknown readers in the Wells Archive at Illinois deepens one's appreciation for the *difference* Wells made in the lives of a great variety of people. Let me itemize a few of them: the Anglican priest for whom *Kipps* had been "an event in my life" and who found in Wells's wartime writing about religion a mirror of his own doubts and faith; the sailor from Glasgow who borrowed a copy of *The Work, Wealth and Happiness of Mankind* from the library of the Seafarer's Education Service and finished it exclaiming, "Now I have read a real history"; the New York bricklayer who told Wells that his "dayly [*sic*] efforts to keep the misery of Boots at a minimum" were relieved by the two authors he most cherished, "Victor Hugo and Yourself, dear Sir"; a French boy for whom *Mr. Polly* "was the first thing I read that showed me that many things in life were stupid and irrational and should be changed"; a self-described "obscure American schoolmaster" from Missouri whose reading of *An Experiment in Autobiography* made him "estimate what the development of your brain has meant to the development of mine"; an Irish apprentice in a shipyard inspired by *The New Machiavelli* to work for a B.Sc. in his spare time; a British civil servant in Calcutta, recalling *The Passionate Friends* as the "bright star" in his reading and thanking Wells "for the effect of your literary work on my existence."[2] Such a roll call could be extended, and even an indiscriminate miscellany of Wellsian common readers would be instructive, but the chief themes of Wells's correspondents can be seen to best advantage in a selection of responses grouped according to three overlapping phases of Wells's authorship: the scientific romancer, the sociological novelist, and the utopian propagandist.

Wells the scientific romancer can be treated most briefly. The Wells archive contains relatively few letters prompted by the early romances, the most delightful of which came from the proprietor of a gentleman's bootshop, offering Wells a "quantity of *Bones,* apparently of the Neolithic period" in gratitude for *A Story of the Stone Age.*[3] But, remarkably, most readers say little about the art or adventure of Wells's scientific romances and instead lavishly admire them as vehicles for social and scientific ideas. Unaffected by the consensus of literary critics of the past sixty years, these readers see no falling-off in Wells's desertion of romances for sociological fiction and polemical essays. Wells's eagerness to apply his ingenuity as a fabulator to a commitment to educate the citizens of a new world met with a corresponding eagerness on the part of his readers. They liked Wells because he stretched their minds, and they therefore felt no strain between art and ideas or between the earlier and later work. An American student started reading *The Food of the Gods,* moved on to others of what he called Wells's "fabulous yarns," and as a result, he told Wells, "I have really started a new life. I know now what I'm doing and I am leaving my stuffy Arts course where you learn about life for a Science course where you handle life and become part of it. . . . You have taught me a hundred times more than all the prosy little professors and now that I am launched on a great quest I know that I get more out of their poetry (or rather the poetry they handle) than they and all their classes put together."[4] A young French reader asked Wells in 1910 for a new romance that would make socialism attractive to the masses: "People want to be shown realities in the light of dreams, & it is your special capacity to do it. *People are thirsty for idealism and imagination*."[5] One correspondent who would have to be classified as an *uncommon* reader when he wrote to Wells in 1932 called up a memory of himself as an ordinary adolescent reader 34 years earlier: "In 1898 I read your 'War of the Worlds.' I was sixteen years old, and the new viewpoints of scientific applications, as well as the compelling realism of the thing, made a deep impression. The spell was complete about a year afterward, and I decided that what might conservatively be called 'high altitude research' was the most fascinating problem in existence." That teenager became a pioneer of twentieth-century rocketry, the physicist R. H. Goddard, but in 1932 Goddard recalled the scientific romances only to emphasize his "greatest admiration" for Wells's later work, whose optimism he found "inspiring" and which he considered, as he believed Wells must, "much more important than your writings of the nineties."[6] Readers who communicated with Wells about his scientific romances were likely not to value them exclusively but to see them as a prologue to his life's work of educating world-citizens.

Wells received some of his most impressive letters in response to his novels about society in transition. Most Western literary critics assume that Henry James "won" the dispute with Wells over the nature and purpose of fiction.[7] But a jury of common readers might reach a different verdict. Mabel Dearmer, the wife of a parson, wrote Wells after *Ann Veronica* was denounced in the *Spectator* to insist that such attacks were the product of male discomfort because the book told "the truth about women absolutely clearly. Of course women are not free (I don't mean a mere vote)—they are always at the mercy of some man or another. Ann Veronica was never free—there was always some man waiting to devour her." Women readers, Mrs. Dearmer told Wells, do not condemn the book as immoral or as artless because they understand the immorality of women's social condition and because they know the book offers a portrait of things as they are.[8] Mrs. Dearmer may have been wrong to assume that gender, rather than social station or aesthetic temperament, was the decisive factor in judgments of Wells's discussion novels. Virginia Woolf, we may remember, scorned *Joan and Peter* because it lacked the cool detachments of the modernist aesthetic, because it sinned by telling too much and moralizing too earnestly, because it was allegorical rather than symbolic, because its ideas had priority over its form, because, as the final sentence of

Woolf's review transparently reveals, Wells was and aimed to be a *popular* writer.[9] But place Woolf's debunking next to this analysis by an utterly unknown reader from Surrey:

> I don't see how you can write a book like 'Joan and Peter' and escape pestering letters. This is one of them. I have just closed it with a bang & an indrawn breath. . . . You have turned our minds up towards the sun & made things grow. You have made us infinitely indebted to you. But, in the heat of reading, you seem to have done more than that. It seems to me a mental history of these days—a picture of our unrest, confusion, outreaching & aspiration. I found it wholesome, stirring & inspiring. It set me tingling with desire to be a worker in the new world. This is no bit of photography. It's deep sea sounding. . . . It is the public who read & they have opinions. Mine is that everyone who feels as I do ought to write & tell you how tremendously big it seems, how vastly important & how grateful to you it makes him feel. And having written he should not expect you to spend your time replying to his outburst. That's how I feel.[10]

While talk of wholesome and inspiring novels might have occasioned amusement in Bloomsbury, some themes in this letter from F. J. Paradise recur in many other letters written about Wells's sociological fiction: the acknowledgment of a permanent debt for a way of thinking and for the prospect of a more satisfying life; a conviction that Wells speaks for them on contemporary issues and that he teaches them the words and forms for naming their own aspirations;[11] the energizing effect of wanting to work to implement Wells's social ideas; Wells's canonization as a chronicler of the modern era rather than a high priest of modernism; and finally, the touching wish simultaneously to tell Wells the practical and immediate good he has done and to protect him from any sense of obligation to those he has helped.

Of all Wells's novels the one that produced the greatest outpouring of mail was *Mr. Britling Sees It Through.* In recent years patronized as an unwieldy literary souvenir of the Great War, *Mr. Britling* remains a fascinating hybrid of the kind of self-referential sociological novel Wells favored before the war and the utopian propaganda which is the outstanding achievement of his final decades. It may also be one of the most perfect expressions of Wells the populist educator; Mr. Britling himself prefigures the "sample brain" that narrates the *Experiment in Autobiography,* an impersonation designed to represent the group mind of an age, making articulate the doubts, frustrations, and longings of the ordinary citizen.[12] In the draft of his open letter to Germany which concludes the novel, Mr. Britling writes that "the common man here is in a state of political perplexity from the cradle to the grave."[13] As Mr. Britling becomes the spokesman for those perplexities, shaping them into a political and ethical agenda for the future, so too Wells wanted to name and thereby to tame the anxieties of an age in order to release his readers to think and act more productively. Through the medium of an ambiguously patriotic fiction he disclosed a larger vision for the future, finding in the catastrophic mistakes and horrors of the Great War the signposts for a great utopian reconstruction.

That *Mr. Britling Sees It Through* did not—and could not—fully satisfy such ambitions is less important than the obvious impact it had on how people thought about the war. A German woman from a Junker family wrote to Wells from New York:

> I wonder whether a thousand victories on either side could accomplish what Mr. Britling will accomplish—and I know that they cannot destroy the good it will do. While I was reading I caught myself wishing that the author were one of my countrymen . . . , but that only showed that I had not yet learnt the book's lesson. I will understand better as time goes on, and help others to understand here and in my own country. We are all so hypnotized into certain beliefs that even as I write I have moments of doubt as to whether in doing so I am not disloyal. But if loyalty means denying the truth or leaving it unspoken, I will choose to be disloyal. I am holding out my hand to you across the ocean. Will you shake?[14]

Civilian readers told Wells that *Mr. Britling* appeared at the crucial psychological moment when uncertainty about the aims of the war—and more importantly about what would come after the war—was growing in intensity among ordinary citizens. The question preoccupying Mr. Britling—"What is all this for?"—was increasingly in the minds if not on the lips of a great many people on the home front.[15]

The book altered the lives of people who did not think of themselves as intellectuals or even as readers. Many soldiers received *Mr. Britling* as a Christmas gift in 1916,[16] and a Red Cross nurse described to Wells the reactions of one wounded infantryman she was caring for: "He asked me where he was, & I told him *Essex,* at which he sat up & said in a muted voice, to my intense astonishment—'Oh! I'm fine & glad I'm in Essex. That's H. G. Wells Country.' I thought he must have been some servant of yours, but he told me, no—only, *the only book he'd ever read was "Mr. Britling"*—he knew it almost by heart—& launched at once into Letty's View of the War."[17] In addition to soldiers Wells also heard from bereaved parents. Two letters are particularly striking. William Farren wrote in 1917 thanking Wells for "the one book written during this war that brings comfort to the stricken—most surely you have touched all our hearts and given consolation and hope and what more can any great writer hope for?"[18] Like many letter writers he took Hugh Britling as the exemplar for many young soldiers and he assumed that Wells might have lost his own son in the war. The other letter worth special attention is from Florence Collins, who had written many years earlier about *Love and Mr. Lewisham* and had received a kind reply. In early 1917 she read *Mr. Britling* with an uncomfortable sense that the fictional parent's struggle to deal with the loss of his son in the war might be prophetic. Shortly afterwards, she heard that her son's ship had struck a mine and that he had died at sea. In her grief she wrote to Wells: "I find it quite impossible to take any comfort from the usual sources. . . . One craves for the human touch and grasp of his big hand; and a remote heaven leaves me cold. I want my son as he *was,* the splendid big funny boy. . . . I am like poor Mr. Britling, incessantly tormented by 'if only'—and the thousand little memories of trivial lovely things, which made my boy so adorable. Now there is nothing but the pride in his sacrifice, and a black wall in front of me which shuts out all my happiness. Can you help me?"[19]

To resurrect Florence Collins's *cri de coeur* 70 years later is, I hope, not a ghoulish act but a demonstration of the extraordinary empathy Wells had with readers who were, in effect, anonymous to him. He was their voice, their intellectual leader, their champion, their substitute-parent, their comrade-in-arms, their vocational counselor, their psychotherapist, their neighbor across counties and oceans. Wells the busy world traveller hobnobbing with the political, scientific, and literary figures of his day is so familiar an image that it is worth emphasizing the bond he also felt with the ordinary citizen, the common reader. There is no doubt that Wells had very mixed feelings about that mythological being named "the common man." W. Warren Wagar has demonstrated how paternalistic Wells's view of the common person was, and Patrick Parrinder has made a careful analysis of the slipperiness of Wells's concept of the "common man" as both an idealized vision of possibility and a rhetorical figment invented to accommodate Wellsianism to a mass audience.[20] From the devastating caricature of newspaper-readers at their breakfast table in *The War of the Worlds* to the gloomy assessment forty years later in *The Fate of Man* of the difficulty of increasing the ordinary man or woman's level of critical reading, there is a measure of impatience and dismay in Wells's account of the common reader. He knew from his own painful self-education some of the common person's limitations, and unlike Samuel Johnson he did not "rejoice to concur" with the common reader's judgments. Wells wanted to exhort, surprise, intrigue, admonish, and push readers; he wanted to show the way, not trust them to follow their instincts. At the same time he could identify himself powerfully with the interests of ordinary readers, as in his famous letter scolding James Joyce over *Finnegans Wake* and *Ulysses:* "You have turned your back on common men—on their elementary needs and their restricted time and intelligence, and you have elaborated. What is the result? Vast riddles. Your last two works have been more amusing and exciting to write than they will ever be to read. Take me as a typical common reader. Do I get much pleasure from this work? No. . . . So I ask! Who the hell is this Joyce who demands so many waking hours of the few thousands I have still to live for a proper appreciation of his quirks and fancies and flashes of rendering?"[21]

Was Wells disingenuous to ask Joyce to take him as a "typical common reader"? As with his persona of a "sample brain" in the *Autobiography,* there may be as much truth as calculation in Wells's pose as a typical reader. His correspondents repeatedly testify that his books remained alive to the issues that mattered to people. An American woman, watching the last of her children grow up, recited a list of the formative books of her own youth from *Tono-Bungay* to *Joan and Peter* and recalled how she "first began to find some answers in your books to questions which parents and school did not or could not answer. I have only just begun to realize how important this influence has been to me at different stages of my development." Wells taught her, she said, that no one "could remain indifferent to the meaning of world events and their relationship to our personal lives, nor fail to make an attempt to find light and hope in the muddled darkness of men's stupidity."[22] An Englishwoman also wrote retrospectively of a lifetime's reading of Wells: "When you were young you interpreted us to ourselves. . . . We grow old but you seem perennially young, with a mind open to fresh ideas."[23]

As befits a writer whose utopian perspective was global, Wells had readers responding to him from every part of the earth. He must have been pleased when he heard from J. B. S. Haldane that Charlotte Haldane, visiting China in 1938, found many women soldiers in Mao's army reading *The Shape of Things to Come*.[24] But one extravagant letter from a foreign reader may reveal more about Wells's power to reach all the potential citizens of a new world. The letter came late in Wells's life and proposed that his works on human rights were greater "than any other book that this world has," including the Bible. As a moral force who "told the truth about the treatment of a common man by this world," Wells had, according to his correspondent, only one rival and that was Jesus Christ.[25] When Wells replied to Lance-Corporal Aaron Hlope, he began with a gruff dismissal of the most hyperbolic of the letter's comparisons: "What you write about Jesus Christ and me is the most utter nonsense." Instead, he insisted that he was a representative voice, a sample brain rather than a lone prophet: "I happen to be a speculative writer who has made one or two good guesses at the problem of tomorrow, but what I think, a lot of other people are coming to think, and you mustn't compare one single man with the whole movement of liberal thought in the world."[26] Wells, who could be devastating when he suspected shamming or stupidity, nevertheless wrote affectionately to Aaron Hlope; indeed Hlope's letter inspired both a speech and a newspaper article from Wells in the following months.[27] The reason for Wells's thoughtful response is not hard to find. In his concluding page Hlope apologizes for his shaky command of English, reveals his race and nationality, and connects Wells's "world of ideas & ideals" to his own most recent experience as a Zulu in the Middle East Forces in Cairo in the summer of 1942:

What has shocked every black man from South Africa is the behavior of your British Tommies. Their character is wonderful & to explain it, can need many pages. They shake hands with us, they talk to us, they sit next to us in cinemas, they drink beer with us, they smoke cigarettes with us. Even when one goes to the British hospital, he gets the same food with them, he lines into one line with them, he is given a bed in the ward same to other beds & blankets, he is sent to the ward according to the nature of his sickness. They have offered us more kindness than God has done. It is the first time in life that we have seen people of that kind.

In Aaron Hlope's mind Wells stood as both teacher and prototype of those British Tommies, and what the Christian Bible had not accomplished among white South Africans he hoped the utopian vision of H. G. Wells might yet supply. Half a century has elapsed since Hlope and Wells exchanged letters, and the official Anglo-American response to the oppression of black South Africans might seem reason enough to be depressed by the world's recalcitrance to Wells's utopian vision. Nevertheless—and that is the word that reading the letters sent to Wells by people like Aaron Hlope, Mabel Dearmer, Florence Collins, and F. J. Paradise seems always to demand—just as the British Tommies in Egypt exemplified a higher standard of common humanity than the world figures who had brought them to war, so our hope for a future may be strengthened in the conviction that Wells's words remain potent enough to continue to educate readers to a more generous global vision than that provided by Reaganism and Thatcherism. It was just such an invigorating, inquiring, activist hope that seems to have been the essential appeal of Wells to the ordinary reader.

Notes

1. The two letters of Eric Williams to Wells are dated 18 July 1918 and 17 March 1939. Like all other letters cited, unless otherwise noted, they are deposited in the Wells Archive at the University of Illinois Library. I gratefully acknowledge the energetic assistance of the curator, Gene Rinkel, and the Rare Book Room staff, particularly Louise Fitton.

2. Letter from John A. Leng to Wells, 10 May 1917; letter signed "SGD" to the Seafarer's Education Service, 20 April 1936, enclosed in a letter from the Organising Secretary of the Service to Wells, 23 April 1936; letter of Emil Eriksen to Wells, 10 December 1922; letter of Henri Jullien to Wells, 16 February, year not given; letter of Blandford Jennings to Wells, 22 September 1936; letter of Richard Lee to Wells, 6 August 1926; letter of Godfrey T. B. Harvey to Wells, 30 January 1917.

3. Letter of Sydney Hook to Wells, 7 December 1903.

4. Letter of Harry C. Elliott to Wells, 13 June 1926,

5. Letter of E. J. Coulomb to Wells, 31 December 1910.

6. Letter of R. H. Goddard to Wells, 20 April 1932.

7. Although some doubts have been registered in recent years, by far most Anglo-American literary historians have championed the Jamesian virtues of formal delicacy and theoretical rigor and have gleefully declared Wells the loser for his unseemly didacticism, his preference for saturation over selection, and his disdain for modernist canons of art. But Dr. Karpal Singh of the National University of Singapore argues that Asian readers are never embarrassed by the notion of the writer as sage and teacher and they assume that Wells

properly repudiated James's stingy and inhumane aesthetic. Singh presented his alternative view in "H. G. Wells and Social Change: An Asian Perspective," an address given to the International Symposium of the H. G. Wells Society in London, 27 July 1986.

8. Letter of Mabel Dearmer to Wells, 11 December 1909. She told Wells that during a supper party at the vicarage a man launched into a diatribe on the "infamy" of *Ann Veronica* and every woman at the table, "decent conventional women, turned on him."

9. Virginia Woolf's unsigned review appeared in the *Times Literary Supplement*, 19 September 1918, 439, and is reprinted in *H. G. Wells: The Critical Heritage*, ed. Patrick Parrinder (London: Routledge & Kegan Paul, 1972), 244–47. Woolf concludes her review with a dismissal of what she takes to be Wells's indifference to anything but the needs of the present moment: "But if he is one of those writers who snap their fingers in the face of the future, the roar of genuine applause which salutes every new work of his more than makes up, we are sure, for the dubious silence, and possibly the unconcealed boredom, of posterity."

10. Letter of F. J. Paradise to Wells, 31 October 1918.

11. Cf. two similar observations: Rosalind Scott Dunkin's acknowledgment in a letter of 24 July 1925, "Two big things I get from reading your writings—I am stimulated to think and I find you crystalize for me thoughts that have been groping around in my mind unable to find adequate expression," and Sir William Rothstein's metaphors sprung from the Great War, in a letter to Wells of 16 June 1918, "It is your particular privilege to be able to express in strong & trenchant form the beliefs most people hold in a shadowy & timid one. You give them courage & body & coax their halting minds to peep over the top. Barbed wire keeps men's imagination in as well as the enemy out & the world is too much sandbagged, there are too many & too deep saps in which men's instincts & generosity take shelter: you bring back open warfare."

12. Note, for instance, Wells's reference to Mr. Britling's brain as a "specimen" of the "multitude of other brains" in Europe in 1914; his description of Britling as "a sample Englishman"; and Mr. Britling's inclination to see his own son Hugh as "a fair sample of his generation." *Mr. Britling Sees It Through* (London: Hogarth, 1985), 132–33, 205, 317.

13. *Mr. Britling Sees It Through*, 425.

14. Letter of Irmgart Hutcheson to Wells, 24 June 1917.

15. Besides Irmgart Hutcheson's letter, the other most revealing civilian letter is from J. Melbourne Shortliffe, 1 January 1917 [misdated 1916], which claims that *Mr. Britling* embodies his own evolving reactions to the war: "Moreover the thoughts I had already about the war and about war in general and about the underlying causes of all wars prepared the way for my appreciation of Mr. Britling's repeated query—what is it all about?"

16. R. L. Henderson wrote Wells on 15 January 1917 while on sick leave at a Swiss Red Cross hospital with 14 other officers, nearly all of them, he said, had just received a copy of *Mr. Britling*.

17. Letter of Mrs. M. Calverley to Wells, 25 August [1918?].

18. Letter of William Farren to Wells, 23 January 1917.

19. Letter of Florence Collins to Wells, 3 August 1917.

20. See W. W. Wagar, *H. G. Wells and the World State* (New Haven: Yale University Press, 1961), 172, and Patrick Parrinder, *H. G. Wells* (New York: Putnam's, 1970), 100–2. A dramatic instance of Wells's dismay at the sentimentality and recidivist patriotism of the average Briton is his reaction to the street celebrations at the end of the Great War: " 'And this,' thought I, 'is the reality of democracy; this is the proletariat of dear old Marx in being. This is the real people. This seething multitude of vague kindly uncritical brains is the stuff that old dogmatist counted upon for his dictatorship of the proletariat, to direct the novel and complex organization of a better world!' " H. G. Wells, *Experiment in Autobiography: Discoveries and Conclusions of a Very Ordinary Brain (since 1866)* (New York: Macmillan, 1934), 594.

21. Letter of H. G. Wells to James Joyce, 23 November 1928, as printed in *H. G.*

Wells's Literary Criticism, ed. Patrick Parrinder and Robert Philmus (Totowa, N.J.: Barnes & Noble, 1980), 177.

22. Letter of Virginia E. Bray to Wells, 7 May 1941.

23. Letter of Esther Grierson to Wells, 31 March 1932.

24. Letter from J. B. S. Haldane to Wells, 26 October 1938.

25. Letter of Aaron Hlope to Wells, 6 August 1942. Startling as these comparisons must seem, they were not quite unique in Wells's fan mail. The Chicago clubwoman Rosalind Scott Dunkin used to tell her associates that the foundation of any good library was "The Bible, Shakespeare and H. G. Wells" (24 July 1925), and the Anglican priest John Leng, while insisting that "I could not for a moment look to you as I look to Jesus of Nazareth," came close to idolatry in saying about Wells's performance in *God the Invisible King:* "I have come to regard you as one who is really bearing the sins of the world."

26. Letter of H. G. Wells to Aaron Hlope, 24 November 1942.

27. The article prompted by Hlope's letter, "What a Zulu Thinks of the English," was a prophecy of "the inevitable adjustment" and "convulsion" that must lie in the future if "the petty white tyranny" in South Africa continued to resist "the breath of freedom" blowing through Africa as through the rest of the world. It appeared in the *Evening Standard,* 16 March 1943, p. 6, and was expanded as part of *'42 to '44: A Contemporary Memoir* (London: Secker & Warburg, 1944). Aaron Hlope appeared again in a speech called "On Putting the Common Man Back Where He Belongs," delivered to the Roadfarer's Club early in 1944. An excerpt from the speech, focusing of the anecdote about Hlope, was printed in the *New Leader* as "Back to the Old Round?—No Fear," 11 March 1944. The typescript of the complete speech is in the Wells Archive at the University of Illinois Library.

Index

◆

For purposes of this index, Wells's works have been organized according to the classifications in J. R. Hammond, *Herbert George Wells: An Annotated Bibliography of His Works* (New York & London: Garland, 1977).